THE OMEGA WATCHERS

"As it was in the Days of Noah"

Jane E. Woodlee Hedrick

The Omega Watchers
"As it was in the Days of Noah"
by Jane E. Woodlee Hedrick

Printed in the United States of America

ISBN 9781498418393

www.xulonpress.com

ACKNOWLEDGMENTS

First I want to thank my husband, Russell, who so patiently gave me the time and seclusion I needed for creative writing. His continual encouragement and faith in me gave the confidence to push forward. If ever there was a soul-mate, he truly is mine.

In the early stages of writing my first book I had several friends that would read a few chapters and give me feedback that helped me to find a path towards creating pictures, emotions, scenery and empathy with mere words. These special friends all played a part in getting me on the path towards feeling like a true author.

My daughter-in-law, Dreama Hedrick, was with me every step of the way from the very first drafts that continually changed until I truly knew my characters, their personalities and the story began to unfold. Thank you for the endless hours of editing, suggesting and critiquing. Then (when we thought we were finished) suggestions on what to delete when there were too many "words" and yet again for final edits. Words cannot express my deep gratitude!

Thank you to my dear friend, Richard Everts, who also edited and was a tremendous help in the technical dialogue. He is a brilliant man and his knowledge was invaluable. He also stayed with me on what seemed an endless journey to completion.

To Cornelia Stone, who read the book after completion with eyes that were not confused by the endless drafts and changes thank you for your honest review. It meant more than you will ever know.

Thank you to all who are reading this book now. Countless hours of research, prayer and study surrounded every chapter and my heart's desire is "blinded eyes will be open" to the great deception that is about to come upon the earth.

Jane E. Woodlee Hedrick

"As it was in the days of Noah, so it will be at the coming of the Son of Man." *Matthew 24:37*

We all have preconceived ideas of what the preceding scripture means. "The Omega Watchers" will challenge your paradigm and, hopefully, open your eyes to deeper truths of the days of Noah. I challenge each reader to research and (above all) pray the truth of God's Word enlightens your mind and births understanding in your spirit.

Although this book is a fictional writing and based on fictional characters, it portrays the essence of demonic deception that will take many forms and grow even stronger as the day approaches when the Anti-Christ will be revealed. As the human soul longs for supernatural truth, many 'gods' (deceiving spirits) are offering themselves to those that are without spiritual knowledge. Their intent is to counterfeit the One True Holy God.

A great deception is coming to the inhabitants of this earth. If this book saves one soul from being caught in this satanic trap my labor has not been in vain.

"For false Christs and false prophets will appear and perform great signs and miracles to deceive even the elect— if that were possible." Matthew 24:24

Chapter 1

The cave grew darker and darker until sunlight could no longer filter through the hot, desert opening above them. Only the lights the four team members carried directed their paths. Gabriella's heart was racing and her crystal blue eyes widened in anticipation as she felt an unseen force pulling them deeper and deeper into the lava cave.

A voice deep within was warning her to turn around. "Go back!" But she knew in spite of the danger she was on the precipice of ancient truths. She could feel it in her archaeological bones.

She followed close behind Caleb as he led the team over fallen rocks and through openings barely large enough to squeeze through as they searched each nook and cranny of the lava tunnels. He knew exactly what he was doing and without a spoken word they pushed deeper into the darkness, each team member sensing this cave was different from any they had previously explored.

The warning inside Gabriella became a resounding echo exploding in her soul. "Turn back now! Turn back now...turn back now..."

Her stubborn determination pushed her forward as she battled the inner feelings of impending danger. She thought about her father, remembering their explorations together as she was growing up. There was never a moment she feared in the myriads of caves they journeyed through. "If only he were here. He would know what to do," she whispered beneath her breath. She refocused on Caleb's strong shoulders and determined countenance. He looked back at her with a wink and she stepped closer to him drawing from his strength.

"I won't be afraid!" She silently reassured herself. To get her mind off the impending danger, she allowed her thoughts to be drawn back in time to the month of September after her high school graduation. She remembered well the kind face of the funeral director as he led her in to view her father's closed casket. "This was his wish, Gabriella. He wanted you to remember him as he was. Not as he is now."

"I know." She whispered. "But I want to see him one more time...just one more time." She would never feel more alone than she did at that moment. She had no other family, no close friends. He was everything to her.

Everything in her life changed over night. There would be no more explorations with her father...no more digging in remote locations searching for ancient truths and...no more exploring for mythical gods drawn millenniums ago on cave walls. Her life spent in the underground side by side with him was gone forever. Saying goodbye to him was the hardest thing she had ever done.

She had always known her childhood was far from the normality of others but after her mother passed away when she was only five years old nothing was normal again. They left their home in North Carolina and her father rotated year by year as an Acting Temporary Professor in universities across several continents. This gave them the rare opportunity to spend her growing up years exploring ancient civilizations searching for secrets hidden in the archives of time.

Tears stung her cheeks and she quickly wiped them away and tried to focus back on the cave. "How deep are we, Caleb?"

Caleb was an expert when it came to the underground world of rock formations and she knew he would never compromise their safety. She just needed to hear his reassuring voice. "We're good, Gabi. Not to worry." His German accent was more pronounced than normal which indicated to the team Caleb sensed something very different in this exploration.

"I don't know about this." Faith interjected cautiously, pushing her dark rimmed glasses higher on her nose. "Something doesn't feel right."

Gabriella stopped and turned her light towards Faith's face which displayed obvious fear. Gabriella wanted to sooth her best friend's concerns even though she, too, was feeling the same haunting warnings. "We're on to something, Faith! I just know it! We can't turn back now." Faith could hear a slight quiver in Gabriella's normally confident voice.

"Maybe we should have listened to the Bedouins." Faith whispered struggling to compose herself.

"Come on, Faith! Really? Do you really believe these lava caves are homes to the Jinn spirits?" Gabriella tried to lighten the atmosphere. She felt something ominous but spirits of the dead were not something she feared nor did she even remotely believe in. "That's just Bedouin folklore!"

Faith was not pacified. "Something just isn't right, Gabi. I think you know it, too. The Bedouins tried to warn us. We should have listened to them!"

Gabriella tried to convince her best friend that it was only local legends and such were common to all civilizations. Sharing her personal knowledge drawn from childhood explorations helped Gabriella to relieve her own fears. "Faith, all cultures have mythical spirits similar to the Jinn but called by different names. The Hindu call them 'asura'. The Ancient Assyrians refer to them as 'genies'. The Greek know them as 'demigods'. The list goes on of civilizations with mythical stories that have been passed from generation to generation. The names may be different but the legends are about the same. All cultures describe their gods as coming from the heavens with supernatural powers, intermarrying with human woman and producing children that became the powerful gods they worshiped."

Faith was not to be deterred with a lecture on mythical gods. "The Bedouins were very serious, Gabi! They really believe entering these caves will release spirits that have been held captive for millenniums. It's very real to them!"

Gabriella just shook her head with her long, blonde ponytail bouncing against her face. "I know they believe it! And they also believe whoever releases them will be cursed. Surely you don't believe that, too?" Gabriella's voice was patronizing.

Caleb's voice interrupted their conversation. He had stopped to survey more closely the rock formations as the women had their battle of words. "Come here! Look!"

They gathered closer in with their lights shining on a lava tube descending from the cave floor. It was barely large enough to squeeze through but the penetration of Caleb's light showed it opened to a larger cavern below.

"We've come too far to turn back now." Gabriella spoke with uncertain determination, trying to sound confident.

"Are you sure it's safe, Caleb?" Faith tried to suppress her growing apprehension as they hooked the rappelling equipment for Caleb to start the tandem descent.

"If it isn't safe you'll be the first to know," he said jokingly as he rappelled down the tube. The rope went deeper and deeper. Then they heard the chamber below echo with Caleb's voice. "I'm coming back up!" They all held their breath in anticipation.

When he reached the top his face told them everything. He rechecked the rope for the team's safety and grabbed his gear. "Let's go, team!"

They descended one by one through the small passage way to the rock floor below. No one spoke as they moved their lights around the cave walls. It was an eerie silence that surrounded them. One lone horizontal lava tube came into view lined with molten rock jutting at the entrance, giving the impression of hands reaching to grab anyone that came near and daring them to pass.

Faith turned her light to get a full view of Aaron's face. His eyes never lied. He was the most conservative of the team members in every way, a man of few words and completely blunt in his communications. He had not spoken the entire time since entering the deeper recesses of the cave.

Faith peered into his dark eyes as best the light would allow. "Aaron, you were talking with one of the locals as we left the hotel this morning. It sounded to me like he was giving some kind of warning. You never told us what he said." Aaron knew the Arabic language well and communicated on the team's behalf. They only knew what he translated back to them.

Faith stared him in the eyes waiting for his reply. "What was it the Bedouin told you when we were leaving the hotel this morning, Aaron? He said something you haven't told us."

Aaron hesitated, obviously not wanting to repeat it. Gabriella and Caleb both turned their lights toward him, too. They waited for his answer and Aaron knew it could not be avoided any longer.

Aaron took a deep breath. "He asked what the supplies were for I was loading in the jeep. I told him we were going to the Al-Sulb plateau where the virgin lava caves had recently been found." Aaron hesitated once again trying to remember the man's exact words. "The Bedouin said we were going to the area known in Arabic as Abu al-Hol. That translates to 'Father of Fear.'" Aaron could not disguise the concern in his voice as he continued. "When I was leaving he warned me somewhere in this area is the entrance to Tartarus, the place of the fallen stars."

Aaron's dark eyes narrowed which meant he was very serious. He ran his fingers through his short, black hair and then finished the desert dweller's warning. "The Bedouin said to stay away. He hurried away from me but then stopped. He turned and muttered Abbadon is imprisoned there. Then he ran away." Faith's countenance changed dramatically from concern to outright fear.

They could not see Caleb's face but heard him laughing as he turned to continue through the passageway. "Don't let the local legends scare you, guys. There's no truth to them. The Arabians are a strange sort. I've been in hundreds of caves and not met any spirits yet." He laughed again as he resumed their exploration.

Gabriella agreed with Caleb but Aaron and Faith weren't convinced. As Jews they had been taught the ancient writings that told of fallen angels imprisoned in the abyss. Where? No one knew for sure but the prophets wrote they were held in chambers of darkness to be released at the end of days.

"Maybe, just maybe, the desert dwellers know something we don't." Faith muttered under her breath as she unwillingly followed the track Caleb led.

As they entered a small lava tunnel Caleb instructed them in a strong and confident voice that cautiously put the team at ease. "Stay close. There's nothing to be afraid of. These tunnels are as secure as concrete. Can't help but wonder how many thousands of years ago a volcano exploded and created this majestic underworld. All indications say this one has never been explored."

Slowly and cautiously they maneuvered through the narrow passageway. Within minutes they exited the end entering a room about thirty feet deep and a football field wide displaying numerous adjacent chambers. In total silence they moved from chamber to chamber finding majestic displays of stalactites and stalagmites. There were breathtaking mineral formations that twisted and turned in different directions like stars dancing in the moonlight.

With all the magnificence and splendor of these hidden masterpieces time had sculpted in the underworld beauty, Gabriella knew she had entered into a mystical place never before beheld with human eyes. She was drawn in by its quiet, stealth seduction and her soul was being captured by its very essence.

"I have never seen anything so beautiful!" Gabriella was the first to break the silence and it seemed her words were unwelcome as they echoed through the mysterious chamber. Its majestic aura was demanding complete reverence in this splendiferous tomb of time.

No other words were spoken as their eyes turned upward to the hanging stalactites. Below them suspended "cave pearls" that are only created in perfect conditions of small drops of water coating over and over with crystalline calcite until they become perfectly round. The beauty was transcendental and seemed to vibrate with spirituality too sacred for words.

As Gabriella's eyes came back to the floor she could see the iridescent reflection of water puddles from the light that swayed back and forth in Aaron's hand as he surveyed the walls. The sound of the drops cascading from the pastel colored hanging pearls was hypnotizing to the senses. The single splashes serenely echoed in the cave creating an atmosphere that captured the imagination. Their appearance was like diamonds falling from the skies as they were unexpectedly caught by the intrusive light. These spectacular formations that had been created over thousands of years seemed to seductively beckon the team to enter the deeper chambers.

Slowly moving and searching, Gabriella's light fell on an alcove with walls of ivory hues. The mystifying colors reflected millenniums of time that had formed this fantasy world beneath the hot, dry desert sands above. What had begun with such arcane beauty quickly took a sinister turn.

As Gabriella was drawn deeper into the cave she could feel the rush of warm air brushing against her face. The very strength of it suggested a huge chamber hidden behind a sealed wall. A single lava rock was blocking an entrance barely large enough to crawl through.

"This is strange." Caleb mused as he closely inspected the sealed entrance. "It looks like this was placed here but that's impossible." He moved his hand around the edges. "I can feel heat coming out."

"Could there be active lava behind it?" Aaron asked.

"Maybe. I think we can pry it loose. It's worth a try." Caleb pulled tools from his back pack and Aaron joined him as they chiseled at the edges.

Gabriella and Faith found a rock to sit on as they watched the men in their determined efforts.

With a few moments to reflect, Gabriella's mind drifted back over the past decade and the reason they were here. The team was following a trail of recently discovered caves in this remote desert area of northern Arabia near the oil fields of Iraq. This was the cradle of the world...where life began. And clues to the past were hidden in caves and written on their walls by ancient civilizations. Maybe, just maybe, today their mission would be complete.

She looked over at her best friend who was rubbing her hands together. "Are you alright, Faith?"

"Yeah, I'm ok." Her words were not at all convincing. "It's just this cave is different. Something feels really strange."

They were silent for a few minutes as they watched Caleb and Aaron continue their efforts to break through.

"I want more than anything to find what the Professor needs." Faith again pushed her dark rimmed glasses up further on her nose as if refocusing on their purpose for being there. "This project has consumed him for years."

"Me, too," Gabriella assured her. "He's a determined man, that's for sure. And I admire him for it. In fact the work has consumed all of us since we first joined the research project."

"I know, but do you think it's realistic? Is it possible we could find antediluvian written messages hidden in a cave somewhere?" Faith needed reassurance their work was not in vain.

"You never know what secrets are concealed in caves, Faith. It was the Dead Sea Scrolls found in the caves of Qumran that started all this. Working on their translations became the Professor's obsession...and as a result we're all obsessed along with him."

Faith totally agreed with Gabriella. "Dr. Brotman is a brilliant linguist and what an honor for him to have been part of the elite team that translated the scrolls. I feel privileged to be working with him."

Gabriella nodded in agreement. "He reminds me so much of my father. He was brilliant, too. The years of explorations with my father proved to me there was a highly intelligent civilization that existed before the great flood. We found all kinds of artifacts, cave drawings and such when we explored. Those were the best times of my life."

"I know you still miss him, Gabi."

Gabi quickly changed the subject. The pain was still too deep even though it had been twelve years. "In all my exploring I have just become more confused about ancient gods. I want to know what truths these myths and legends were built on. I have no doubt there's reality in there somewhere but it's all become muddled through time. Hard to believe the stories of gods that were half men and half animal, or half angel and half human. And yet we found them drawn all over cave walls on all the different continents. Something had to inspire the ancient artists and I think it was more than a wild imagination."

"Well, you know what I believe." Faith said emphatically.

"Yes, Jew girl. I know exactly what you believe. You've told me plenty of times. There is only one true God and his name is Yahweh. Got that long ago!" Gabi pushed her playfully.

Faith leaned against Gabriella and they both laughed. They had this conversation many times through the years. "Some day you'll see, Gabi. You'll see."

Gabriella swung her long, curly ponytail back across her shoulder in a playful act of indignation. "Show me, Faith. I'm a scientist and I have to see to believe."

They were interrupted by Caleb's excited voice. "We've almost got it!" He motioned for them to come closer.

"Sure took long enough," Gabriella teased him. She watched his strong arms tug at the lava rock that Aaron was prying loose. After several efforts Caleb stopped to take a deep breath and push his blond hair out of his eyes.

"One more time, Aaron!" Aaron pushed the metal bar deep between the rock and the cave wall and pulled forward as Caleb grabbed the lava rock and groaned with everything in him. The rock finally gave way and the dark entry opened with a rush of hot, pressurized winds swirling around them.

"I'll go first," Caleb said. "Don't come through until I give the word." They watched him push his way through, cautiously moving his light from side to side. After a few minutes he motioned for them to follow.

They entered another huge volcanic chamber. Was the swirling air pressure built up from active lava or was it something more? Gabriella sensed something extremely sinister. It felt as though an imprisoned, evil force was waiting for a day of escape.

"Stay close," Caleb told the others as they moved their lights around the walls. The esoteric colors from the enchanting chamber quickly changed to just black lava when they squeezed through the forced opening.

Gabriella could hear the muted sounds of Caleb warning her to stay closer to him. But in the distance was a sound of moaning drawing her. Cold chills crept up her arms in spite of the immense heat. An overwhelming smell of sulfur penetrated the air. Faint voices from behind were calling for her to stop. But she was being pulled deeper and deeper into the cave by a force she couldn't see or touch.

Caleb rushed to catch up with her. "Stop, Gabi! *Stop!*"

His strong arms wrapped around her. "Didn't you hear me? We're going too deep! We won't have enough oxygen."

As he released her his spotlight swept across the molten cave wall and then she saw it! She cautiously moved closer holding her light next to the wall. Catching her breath she motioned for the others to come closer.

She forgot to breathe as the etchings on the cave wall came into full focus. There was a nefarious feeling overshadowing her as she felt another presence with them. She turned quickly shining her light in every direction. But only shadows swirled around them.

Her light stopped on a large hole in the cave floor directly in front of them. A rush of hot air was pushing out the repugnant smell of sulfur. A few more feet and she would have fallen in. She quickly stepped backwards realizing what would have happened if Caleb had not stopped her.

Caleb picked up a piece of molten rock and tossed it in the hole to try to determine the depth. There was no sound...none at all.

Faith's quivering voice could be heard. "The Bedouin warned us that these caves have bottomless holes that reach into the prisons of the Jinn."

Gabriella caught a glimpse of Caleb's face. She had never seen that expression before. It was deep concern mixed with grave uncertainty. Caleb was always in total control. Unadulterated fear gripped her.

"These aren't Jinn, team. This is active lava! We've come too deep. We need to turn back."

Instead Gabriella motioned for them to come closer to the wall. "Caleb, hold your light so Aaron can get a good look at this." Caleb moved next to the wall and stood between her and the bottomless pit. He stretched out his long, strong arms both to hold the light and protect her. They watched as Aaron surveyed each inch of the etching on the cave wall.

"Heaven help us!" Aaron spoke with a voice filled with amazement. "I think we've found something!"

"What, Aaron?" She asked. "What do you think we've found?"

Aaron surveyed the wall again and with his vast knowledge of ancient languages he stated as a matter of fact: "These etchings are very similar to the tablets of writings that Dr. Brotman has in his possession!

"Are you sure, Aaron?" Gabriella remembered well the clay fragments that the Professor had shown the team when they first joined his research project. They were etched in a language linguists had never seen before.

"I'm almost positive! But what's really odd is there are scratches through the words as though someone or something has tried to destroy it!" The words were barely out of Aaron's mouth when a cold wind encircled Gabriella. She turned quickly, shining her light in every direction, but again only shadows encircled her.

Shooting through Gabriella's mind was the warnings of the Bedouin. She found herself questioning, "Am I standing in the middle of the place where no man should tread? Could this be the place that mythical legends blend into reality?"

The entire team knew something wasn't right. Caleb gave stern instructions. "Let's get the pictures we need and get out of here!"

They hurriedly got to work, took the pictures and samples they needed, and quickly retraced their path out of the inner recesses of the lava tubes. They all sensed a dark mystery in their discovery. They had no idea this was a day their lives would change forever.

As they exited the cave Gabriella could not shake the eerie feeling that someone, or some "thing"....was watching.

Chapter 2

The team took their last looks at the mystical beauty of the cave as they returned to the desert above them. The entire time they were exiting, Gabriella felt a strange sensation of a force trying to pull her back in to the cave. Caleb held her hand and pulled her behind him as though he discerned the mysterious drawing. Ascending back to reality made the whole experience feel like a dream with ominous dark shadows that continued to lurk in the corners of her mind.

One by one they climbed back up through the lava tunnel and into the light. The sun was starting to go down and the air was cooling. After loading their jeep Caleb marked their location with his GPS.

He motioned for them to get in the vehicle. "I've got the cave entrance marked. You know these desert locations never look the same after winds blow through and shift the sands."

It was a several hour drive back to Ma'aqala, a small town north of Riyadh, Saudi Arabia. The team was mostly silent from exhaustion and reflection of the discovery of the day. Thoughts both exhilarating and tormenting infiltrated their minds. Gabriella watched the western sky as the sun went down over the Rub'al-Khaili desert which is one of the largest continuous bodies of sand in the world. It was no wonder the Bedouin desert dwellers had warned them about exploring alone.

Caleb had not been at all hesitant about the exploration. He was an accomplished speleologist and had every detail well planned and documented. Gabriella realized how truly amazing he was on so many levels. She glanced at him as he was driving and he turned briefly to look at her.

"Quite a day, Gabi Girl," he said with a wink.

"Dr. Brotman will be ecstatic." She was trying to make conversation and forget the eerie presence she felt in the cave. "This will be a dream come true for him."

Caleb took another long look at Gabriella and knew something wasn't quite right. "Guess you're exhausted?"

She nodded and leaned her head back to watch the western sky. The clouds began to thicken darkening the beautiful sunset. She could hear the sound of thunder in the distance.

"That's rare," Aaron observed as he peered out the window. The dark clouds moved closer and the raindrops started to fall hard and heavy.

It was ironic to Gabriella how the dark storm seemed to reflect the feelings that had haunted her inside the cave.

The intensity of the winds escalated creating a sandstorm. Caleb slowed the vehicle, kept both hands on the wheel and stayed totally focused on the road that had almost disappeared. No one said a word. The rain was beating against the window and the thunder was growing louder. She could hear Aaron muttering one of his Jewish prayers and somehow it brought a sense of peace. Amazingly within a few minutes the storm passed over and the moon began to rise casting a beam of light across the red sand dunes.

"Was that some kind of omen?" Caleb laughed knowing the danger had passed.

Again she heard Aaron and Faith both say at the same time, "Thank you, Yahweh, for your protecting hand."

Gabriella wasn't one to pray but she was thankful the storm had passed and she could see the relief on Caleb's face. He caught her watching him and reassured her with his pronounced German accent that was his way of lightening the atmosphere. "A little rough there for a bit but all is well." He took her hand for a minute then put both hands back on the wheel. "We're only about half hour from the hotel."

"Great, I'm starving." Aaron replied. He made no observation about the uncanny storm but his voice was edged with uneasiness.

They finished the few miles to the hotel and pulled to the front door. Dim oil lights were reflecting on the mud-brick walls that accented each side of the entryway. They climbed out of the vehicle, unloaded their gear and made their way inside. There were two huge red clay pots on each side of the door with large cyperus plants gracing the entrance. The long green blades of the plant made an umbrella shape and at the base sprung little green cascades of flowers only found in desert regions.

The hotel owner came from his apartment in back and greeted them in broken English as they entered the small time worn lobby. No matter what time of day or night Abdul always looked the same wearing his floor length white linen thobe and the traditional white gutra on his head held in place by a red and white taiga. His beard covered most of his face that always had a smile for them.

Abdul knew their routine of coming in late in the evening, going to their rooms to clean up and returning for a late dinner. Aaron confirmed their menu in Arabic and Abdul nodded his head rushing off to begin preparations.

When they returned for dinner, the evening breezes were moving through the open windows and the room was lit only by oil lamps. It was a serene and peaceful atmosphere, the perfect place to unwind and discuss the events of the day.

They settled into the deeply padded chairs covered in deep red tapestry slightly frayed on the edges. Beneath their table was a plush rug of deep shades of indigo blue that accented the bright colored mosaic tile table. Dark wood walls were built between the table areas defining each as separate and secluded. The Ottoman décor had been perfectly blended with Persian accents for comfort and a relaxing atmosphere which they badly needed.

"I love this room." Gabriella said looking at the colorful surroundings she had enjoyed during their stay there.

"I can't believe we've been here for six months. I feel like we've been through every cave in Arabia." Faith mused. "I'm so ready to go home." Her words reflected the feelings of the entire team. "I really want to be with my family during the High Holy Days."

Gabriella wasn't concerned about any traditional, religious holidays but she was definitely ready to get away from what had haunted her in the cave. She tried not to dwell on it. "I'm with you, Faith. So ready to go home!"

Aaron was making notes and preparing to email their discovery to Dr. Brotman. "I'm about ready to send the Professor some pictures."

"Aaron, are you sure the writing we found today was antediluvian?" Faith asked knowing his expertise in ancient writings.

Aaron nodded with certainty. "No doubt in my mind. It has some markings of Ge'ez that the Professor used in translating the Dead Sea Scrolls but must be a much earlier form. It's nothing like I've ever seen."

"I took various pictures of the cave walls and formations as we went through for better evaluation when we get home." Caleb inserted. "But I have no doubt this volcanic cave is pre-flood."

"Explain that to the people that don't even believe in Noah's flood and the antediluvian period." Aaron retorted straight to the point as usual.

Gabriella and her father had studied numerous cultural stories of a great flood and her father often noted evidences of such in their explorations.

"Beliefs in a devastating, earth changing flood are common to most all cultures, especially in the Mesopotamian area. Not just Noah's flood." Gabriella said as she shared some of her childhood experiences with the team. "Stories of a great flood also appear in Greek, German, and Irish mythology, and in the legends of the Mayans, the Hindu, the Chinese, along with the lore of Central and South America. I won't bore you with the exhaustive list. But Noah's flood, which is referred to as the Antediluvian Age, is the most common among Israelis and anyone that believes in the Bible."

Their conversation was interrupted when Abdul served their dinner. Small talk about the project continued as they ate and anxiously awaited a response from Dr. Brotman.

"Do you suppose we'll find out why the project has been so secretive if we've found what the Professor needs?" Faith asked curiously. "How many times have we asked and he just tells us when the time's right."

"I'm sure he has his reasons." Gabriella replied. "How many times have we ventured guesses? Sure would be nice to finally know."

"We all agree on that." Aaron commented while checking his email one more time for any word from the Professor.

During the entire dinner no one referred to the ominous feeling in the cave. As the evening waned Gabriella was convincing herself it was all in her mind. The lack of oxygen in the cave, the smell of sulfur and the overwhelming heat had affected her senses. "That has to be it," she thought as she rested her head on the high-back, cushioned chair and tried to categorize the events in her mind.

Since their arrival at this quaint hotel they had finished each dinner with the traditional Arabic gawa coffee specially blended with mocha and cardamom. It was a pleasant discovery in this remote desert area and offered a relaxing end to the strenuous days of exploring. During their coffee conversation the email came and Aaron's face told them what they all wanted to hear.

"We're going home?" Faith jumped up from the table.

Aaron nodded his head. "On the first flight out we can get!"

The girls could not wait to start packing and headed upstairs to their room. Aaron searched for flights and booked their seats for the next afternoon. He emailed the Professor telling him of their arrival time. A long journey was about to come to a climax.

Faith was chattering away about her excitement of finally going home and being back with her family. There was a sting in Gabriella's heart knowing she had no family to go home to.

Faith looked over at Gabriella. "I'm so sorry. I know it's hard for you going home to an empty apartment."

She tried to make light of it and smiled at Faith. "After six months of rooming with you, Jew girl, it will be a pleasant relief to have some alone time."

Faith giggled remembering when they met. "I remember when you walked into Archeology 101 on our first day of class as freshman students, Gabi. You looked like a woman on a mission, full of confidence and ready for anything. I really admired you right away. I was glad when you sat down next to me."

"One of the best days of my life." Gabriella admitted. "It was a blessing from the gods, whoever they are, that we met. Since I was home schooled structured classes were a new experience for me and I wasn't nearly as confident as I pretended to be. I had no idea what to expect."

Faith looked straight at her, pulled her glasses off and raised her eyebrows. Gabi laughed patronizingly knowing Faith did not like her comment about the gods. "I know, Faith, there is only one true God and his name is Yahweh."

"You'll see someday, Gabi. You'll see." Faith prayed with all of her heart that Gabriella would find the truth.

Gabriella tried to concentrate on packing but other thoughts kept creeping back in her mind and she continued to battle the eerie feeling that attached to her in the cave. She wasn't one to over react or to dramatize. She convinced herself with a good night's rest it would all feel different.

Faith was already in her bed and asleep when Gabriella finally turned out the light and slid between the white cotton sheets. The bed was old but comfortable and she had no trouble sleeping the entire time of their stay. Not until tonight.

She tossed and turned pulling the cotton sheets back and forth. She continually plumped her feather pillow moving her head from side to side. She would doze and then be wide- awake. Knowing she was fighting a losing battle, she rolled out of her tumbled bed and moved silently around the room so she would not awaken Faith.

She silently moved to the window and stared out watching for any signs of movement. The storm had left behind water puddles lining the street below. The only movement was the flicker of the gaslights reflecting in the rain waters. Nothing seemed amiss.

"Snap out of it, Gabi." She said to herself.

She moved quietly back to her bed. As she passed the dresser mirror she could have sworn she saw the reflection of someone watching her from behind. She swirled around ready to scream but the room was still.

"This is ridiculous." She muttered as she slid back into bed hoping to finally go to sleep.

The foreboding feelings that overshadowed her were like a cloak of darkness that she could not shed. Her mission here had been articulately planned, like everything else in her life, and now it was complete and time to report back home. She should be feeling a huge sense of satisfaction instead of battling feelings of ominous trepidation.

It was after four in the morning when she finally drifted into a restless sleep. Dark dreams tormented her. When she would doze she had the sensation of falling into a bottomless pit. As she screamed for help an unseen hand would catch her and lift her to safety. She would awaken sweating and her heart racing. When she would doze again the dream repeated.

"I'm in control! It's only exhaustion. Everything is fine!" She tried to reassure herself. But in the shadows of her mind she knew something changed on this fateful day.

Chapter 3

The sunlight peeped between the soft cotton curtains that gently swayed in the cool morning breeze. As Gabriella tried to force her eyes open she immediately felt the tormenting thoughts of the night come rushing into her clouded mind. She kept repeating over and over the events of the previous day. Her mind twisted and turned through each detail separating reality from the horrible dreams.

Faith was already up, packed and apparently left for the lobby. Gabriella quickly dressed in her shorts, t-shirt and sandals ready for the hot trip back to the airport. She washed her face noting the black circles from lack of sleep. She barely brushed her long, curly hair then pulled it into a ponytail. Since make-up was not part of her daily routine she was ready to roll. She decided long ago all that girly stuff took too much time from the important things in life.

Pulling her over-stuffed luggage to the lobby, she realized she was way behind the rest. Aaron and Faith had already gone ahead to get all of their gear checked in at the Riyadh Airport. The second jeep was waiting to transport Gabriella and Caleb. Caleb quickly took her luggage and helped her inside.

"Good morning, Gabi Girl. I was just getting ready to come and awaken sleeping beauty." Caleb said with a teasing smile. "Guess you're rested and ready to start the next phase of this magnificent journey?" Gabriella was not about to admit what a tormenting night she had.

"Morning," she muttered back in a sound more like a kitten moaning. Caleb could read her like a book and knew something was bothering her but he would wait until she was ready to talk.

The driver was patiently waiting for them to settle in for the transport. But then the Bedouins were never in a hurry. They were not like the Westerners that never took time to enjoy life and savor the moment. This had been Gabriella for as long as she could remember. As soon as she achieved the goal she was working so hard for, her mind was already planning the tactics needed for her next challenge.

As Caleb practically picked her up and set her in the back seat she wondered who the man was in the front seat. At that moment the driver turned and asked in his broken English if they were all ready. The front passenger nodded but said nothing. With a jerk they were on their way.

Her mind was racing knowing she had to codify her research information into a suitable format to present to Dr. Brotman as soon as they returned to Haifa. She decided she would make her notes on the plane minus the wind and the swirling desert sands. She leaned her head back to relax.

Unwillingly, she kept glancing towards the front seat trying to get a better view of the unknown passenger. Once he turned to the driver and said something in Arabic that she didn't understand. It allowed her to get a glimpse of the high cheekbones, the dark complexion, and the dark eyes that were accented by his shoulder length jet black hair. The wind picked up with the speed of the jeep and the sunlight caught on the locks of the stranger's ebony hair blowing in the wind, seemingly dancing to the music that he began to hum. It was melodic, almost hypnotizing.

Gabriella closed her eyes and tried to refocus on the tasks at hand but she could not drown out that melancholy sound and the beautiful tone of his voice. She finally opened her eyes to see if she could get another glimpse of that perfectly formed face. Her thoughts were of this mysterious man now and not the forbidden cave. She convinced herself she deserved a mental break. What was the harm?

About that time the jeep hit a dip in the road and Gabriella fell against the window. The alluring man turned to her. His face now was in perfect view.

"Are you alright?" His voice was deep and captivating. This time he spoke in perfect English. Her breath caught and she felt her face flush. She could barely whisper when she tried to respond. She decided immediately that he was the most beautiful man she had ever seen.

Her mouth twisted in an attempt to smile and she nodded as his piercing eyes seemed to penetrate into her soul. She quickly looked the other way. She could feel his stare even after their eye contact ceased. She suddenly became aware of how she must look to him. Then she scolded herself for even thinking about it at all.

The stranger in the front seat seemed to read her thoughts. He twisted in his seat to get a full view of her. With one side of his mouth slightly upturned in what was a questionable smile, but could have been sarcasm, he asked her: "And for what reason is a beautiful American woman in this hot Arabian Desert?" Caleb had been dozing but came to full attention when he heard the stranger address Gabriella as beautiful. Caleb looked at Gabriella and saw her face flushed and immediately decided he would answer the stranger's question for her. He did not want anything said that might open a conversation about their project.

"We're cave explorers and always looking for a new adventure." Caleb answered the stranger. Gabriella was glad he had taken control of the conversation. Her mind was spinning and she felt dizzy. She had not taken time to eat before they left and mixed with the hot winds blowing in her face she felt slightly ill.

The stranger did not look at Caleb when he answered. He kept his eyes focused on Gabriella. She could feel her cheeks burning and hoped he would notnotice. Caleb did not like the way he was looking at her and tried to divert his attention.

"And why are you in the middle of the desert?" Caleb asked.

The stranger shot him a quick stare that clearly showed his agitation but then smoothly replied. "I used to live here." That was all he said and then his eyes went straight back to Gabriella as she was struggling for composure.

His eyes lingered on her for what Caleb thought was an inappropriate amount of time. The stranger twisted back around in the front passenger seat and seemed to focus only on the sandy road ahead. He made a couple of more comments to the driver in what sounded like the Arabic dialect of the region. Having lived here that would be normal.

She tried to make light conversation with the stranger so she would not appear to be an absolute idiot. "What kind of work do you do?" She realized as she said the words he would be turning to look at her again and could already feel her face flushing.

He turned back to her smiling. He seemed pleased that she was trying to keep a conversation going. "I guess you would call me a tour guide."

"You guess?" Caleb inserted himself back in the conversation with a slight sarcasm that demanded explanation. He did not like the man staring at Gabriella. Something just did not feel right.

The stranger turned around and looked Caleb directly in the eyes and asked, "Are you two married?"

Caleb stared him down and simply stated, "No, not yet." Gabriella shot Caleb a look of shock. Why would he indicate they were going to ever be married? What was Caleb thinking? Then she realized he did not trust this man. He was a quick judge of character and she never had known him to be wrong.

Gabriella tried to sooth the harshness of Caleb's tone with another question to the stranger. "What sort of tours do you do?"

"I offer private tours to some of the most beautiful places imaginable. Perhaps sometime you would want to join me." He said with a beguiling smile.

Caleb made a face at Gabriella the stranger could not see. He mouthed the words silently, "Not if I have any say about it." It was obvious Caleb wanted the conversation over.

The stranger's eyes lingered on Gabriella and then shot one more glaring look at Caleb. From that point no more words were spoken. Within the hour they would be at the airport and soon boarding the plane for Israel.

Gabriella reminded herself she would never see this man again. It was time to focus on her mental notes.

The stranger continued humming the hypnotic melody and she struggled to block out the sound. A few minutes later she gave up and laid her head back engulfed in the beauty of his voice. It was the first moment of true serenity she had since entering the lava cave.

The humming stopped and she opened her eyes. "Where are we?"

She glanced over at Caleb's strong and handsome face. His blonde hair that became streaked with platinum in the desert sun fell across his eyes as he rested. The bleached strands beautifully accented his tan face and high cheek bones.

Without opening his eyes he asked her, "Are you staring at me?" His mouth twisted upwards in a mischievous smile.

He had struggled to get his long legs comfortable in the back of the vehicle and had stretched them out next to Gabriella. She could feel them brushing against the skin of her calf. She always felt safe when he was near. That was what best friends were for. She could not help but smile as she thought of him protecting her from the tempting stranger.

"Only because you're taking up the entire back seat!" She giggled and playfully pushed his legs away from her which he promptly put across her lap and closed his eyes pretending to sleep.

Okay, you win." She loved the comforting feeling of having him close but would not dare admit it to him, but he knew. No words were necessary.

Gabriella tried not to watch the stranger but her eyes were constantly drawn to him. She remembered how she looked as she caught a glimpse of her self in the mirror when leaving the hotel. No man would find that look attractive.

Caleb was almost asleep and totally unaware that Gabriella for the first time wanted to be beautiful. But if he had known he would have told her she was the most beautiful woman he had ever known, both inside and out.

Chapter 4

Gabriella had fallen asleep shortly before they reached the King Khalid International Airport north of Riyadh. The noise of the airport traffic awakened her and the first thought that struck her mind was not the caves, nor the exhilarating discoveries but the man sitting in the front passenger seat.

She opened her eyes to enjoy the beauty of the Persian influenced architecture of the Royal Terminal as they approached the entry to passenger check-in. The terminal was built especially for the Royal family and the beautiful Royal Pavilion awaited any VIPs that would be flying into Riyadh. The sun illuminated the magnificent glass walls as travelers approached the main gates.

The stranger asked them if they had flown into Riyadh before. Caleb immediately took control of the conversation. "Only when we arrived," he answered bluntly making it obvious he wanted no further conversation.

The stranger ignored him and became a wealth of information giving them a lesson in the airport's architecture.

He pointed to the right of the Royal Terminal. "The Masjid Mosque you see in the distance stands over forty feet high directly in the middle of the airport complex. The massive golden dome at the top is a spiritual sign for all travelers to see as their flights approach. The mosque is the focal point of the entire complex silently stating to every traveler the importance of their Islamic faith. It accommodates over 5000 worshipers inside and another 5000 in the plaza outside."

"That's a lot of worshipers." Caleb said dryly. Gabriella shot him a look that silently said shut-up.

The stranger was not deterred. "The Muslims are extremely dedicated to their faith and pray many times a day. The mosque allows travelers a place to worship and pray." As they drove past the opulent structure Gabriella was once again reminded of the many diverse religions worldwide and questioned if any of them were real. Apparently the Saudis thought so.

Gabriella was captured by the deep tone of his voice and amazed at his perfect English as he continued: "There are eight huge air bridges surrounding the airport and it has the highest control tower in the world. The land mass of the King Kahlid Airport is also the largest in the world."

As they drove across one of the connecting air bridges and down towards the last stretch before arriving at the departure terminal, Gabriella gasped at the beauty of the landscaping. When they had flown in to the airport six months before it was already dark and she had totally missed these awe-inspiring views.

"Isn't it beautiful?" The stranger turned to see the expression on her face. "The extravagant landscaping is filled with tropical plants and foliage that require little water and can sustain the desert heat. Over a quarter of a million trees and plants line the streets and surround the massive area."

Gabriella had to admit they were breathtaking and thought the opulence appropriate since Saudi Arabia was the richest nation on the earth due to their massive oil exportation.

Gabriella's eyes were focused on the magnificent beauty of the Persian architecture but her mind was focused on the enchanting stranger. She wanted to ask his name but she did not dare. She knew what Caleb's reaction to that would be. She felt she needed to say something to break the uncomfortable silence.

"Are you a religious man?" She asked the stranger. She did not want to right out ask if he was of the Muslim faith.

He did not hesitate to answer and stated emphatically: "I believe in a supreme being if that is what you mean. I know there are great powers in the universe."

"How can you be so sure?" She asked with a desire to truly know. She could see Caleb out of the corner of her eye watching her.

"When you see, you believe," he said as the jeep came to a quick stop at Terminal Three. They were arriving late so Caleb jumped out to grab their bags. Normally he would open the door and help her out but they were pushing against the clock.

Gabriella reached for the handle to open the door when it suddenly opened and a hand was reaching to help her out of her seat. She knew without looking up who it was and she suddenly could not breathe. She looked fully into his eyes as she could feel the strength of his arms lift her from her seat. Yes, he was beautiful but there was something very discomforting in his stare. She felt drawn to him but at the same time wanted to escape. It was the same sensation she experienced in the cave. Her scientific mind could not explain these conflicting emotions.

In a breathless voice that could barely be heard she whispered, "Thank you". Quickly she moved towards Caleb to help with the bags. If she could just get to Caleb's side she would forget all of this nonsense. Plus, they had to hurry or they would miss their plane.

Gabriella never looked back. She wondered if he was watching her, she felt he was. She tried to blot out the vision of the mesmerizing dark eyes that could penetrate through to her soul and the ebony hair that danced in the wind. She tried to convince herself she would not ever think of him again. But she was absolutely sure he was watching as they were rushing through security and to their departure gate.

Gabriella could see Faith motioning for them and could hear her voice calling. "We were afraid you weren't gonna make it! The plane is boarding now. Hurry!"

They were the last four to board the Lufthansa flight to Haifa. Gabriella was out of breath as she dropped into her seat. Caleb sat down next to her as Faith and Aaron sat down in the seats just across the aisle. They were all thankful for the first class accommodations and to have room to relax and begin compiling their individual notes to present to the Professor.

As they prepared for take-off Aaron was looking at the digital pictures on his camera. Caleb was making notes of the physical properties and structure of the discovered cave. Faith was researching already explored lava caves. Gabriella was wondering if she would ever see the stranger again. Part of her so wanted to and another part sickened at the thought. As the plane taxied to the runway each of the team was lost in their individual thoughts.

After arriving at the Haifa International Airport they shared a taxi to their apartments in Haifa Bay that stretched along the beautiful

Mediterranean coast of Northern Israel. Gabriella loved the atmosphere of the old town community being close to coffee shops, interesting people and within walking distance of museums, beautiful gardens and the sea.

Living close to her team made it simple for study and research. They would usually gather at her apartment which had a panoramic view of the bay with the backdrop of the majestic Mt. Carmel slopes. The balcony was the perfect size for the four to enjoy the sea breezes and talk for hours as they watched the sailboats come and go from the Kishon Marina. The soft, blue cushion chairs and white cast iron table had been the setting for many planning sessions and deep discussions through the years.

They planned to meet there the next morning for a brain storming session before meeting with Dr. Brotman in the afternoon. Gabriella was convinced a good night's sleep was all she needed to be ready to come back to reality, forget the stranger, the eerie cave and focus on their research project.

She decided a hot bubble bath would relax her and be just the medicine to get her re- focused. So many thoughts were tangled in her mind. She had to sort out the silly attraction from the real truths they had discovered. As she undressed and slipped into the tub she again had that uncanny feeling of an unexplainable presence. She convinced herself that the months of exploration was playing tricks on her mind. Being back in her safe surroundings and sleeping in her own bed would pull her back to normality.

She settled in her bed shortly before midnight and waited for the phone to ring. Caleb always called the last thing at night to make sure all was well and tell her goodnight. As expected the call came.

She was so sure it was him she did not even glance at the caller identification. "Hi, Caleb", she said in a drowsy voice. There was no sound on the other end.

"Caleb, stop teasing me," she said getting irritated. "I'm too tired for joking tonight." Still there was no sound. She knew Caleb wouldn't ignore her if she was truly upset so she quickly disconnected the call and checked the caller ID. It showed "blocked call".

Immediately she called Caleb. He answered in his teasing voice. "A little ESP going on, Gabi. I was just getting ready to call you."

"I'm going to bed now. Just wanted to let you know all is well. Night, Caleb."

His teasing voice quickly vanished and was replaced with concern. "You sure you're okay?"

"Just tired. I'll see you in the morning." She disconnected the call with Caleb convincing herself the blocked call was just a wrong number.

She settled in her comfortable bed pulling the fluffy white comforter around her shoulders and trying to fight the uneasy feeling of the unknown caller. "It must have been a wrong number." She turned out the light and closed her eyes.

She was entering the transition of muted reality and deep sleep when she felt a presence in the room. She was not sure if she was awake or asleep when she realized someone was standing by the window. She shot straight up in the bed. Her heart was racing and she was reaching for the phone to call Caleb when he stepped from the shadows. It was her stranger smiling down on her.

"Who are you?" she whispered. The fear had dispelled and it did not cross her mind to wonder how he knew where she lived or had access into her apartment. He did not say a word but he was humming the same melodic sound she remembered so well. She could see from moonlight streaming through the terrace window his tall frame and gleaming black hair. She felt her eyes grow heavy and when she opened them again sunlight was shining in where the stranger had stood.

She sat straight up in the bed looking for the stranger. "I must have been dreaming! It felt so real."

She forced herself out of the bed to enter what should be one of the most exciting days of her life. The thought of another piece of the project puzzle falling into place was exhilarating. She was sure her dream would fade to the background in light of today's meeting with Dr. Brotman.

A morning walk would clear her head, she thought, and decided to make her personal notes at the Old Town Coffee Corner that she frequented on Masada Street. She had plenty of time before the team would meet.

It was a beautiful late summer day and the air was fresh and energizing. The cool breezes from the sea were rustling through the trees. It was an exhilarating change from the hot desert sands.

Gabriella walked the few blocks to the café enjoying the beauty of the old buildings and the Ottoman architecture. A group of orthodox Jewish teens passed her on their way to their Hebrew school. Haifa being the largest city in northern Israel was home to a diverse culture. The largest population was Jewish and a quarter of those were immigrants from Russia just as Faith's family was. She enjoyed every aspect of it.

She loved everything about the area in spite of the constant threat of attacks from radical Muslim groups using Lebanon to the north as their training ground. There had been numerous bombings in the twelve years she had lived here but it never crossed her mind to leave. Israel was her home.

She arrived at the café, ordered her coffee and starting making notes. As she relived the exploration into the lava cave every detail came flooding back to her. In all the caves and all the years of exploring she never before felt the ominous feelings she experienced in that cave. Yes, it was beautiful beyond belief but it was a very seductive beauty that seemed to pull one deeper and deeper to a place that wanted to embrace and hold you forever. She was thankful Caleb had been there to keep her sanity balanced.

While she was deep in contemplation, she felt someone standing beside her. Turning her head slightly she caught a glimpse of an old Jewish man that seemed to be waiting for a chance to speak to her.

"Can I help you?" she asked. She turned sideways in her chair to get a full view of him. A Hasidic Jew with his long, mostly gray beard, traditional brimmed black hat and black jacket stood beside her. He wore tinted dark glasses that prevented her from seeing his eyes.

He spoke to her in English with a heavy Hebrew accent. His voice was low as though he wanted no one else to hear. "Can I please have a moment of your time?" He asked. She motioned for him to take a seat at her table. He sat down quickly, obviously in a great hurry. She could not imagine what this Jewish man could possibly want from her.

The old man got straight to the point and spoke with certainty. "I know you are working with Dr. Brotman and I know the nature of the research. I cannot tell you how I know, but I know. I have knowledge of things that are about to happen in Israel and your research could be very important to these events. I have information that, when added to your discoveries, will reveal ancient secrets. There are powerful people that do not want this revealed. But it must be for those that have ears to hear. Secrets are about to be revealed to you and I am warning you to be very careful. Beware of time and untime!"

Gabriella was not sure whether to laugh or cry. This man was either absolutely insane or was on the inside of the group funding their project. Her team was not allowed to know who they were "for their safety" they were told. She thought to herself, "then how could this man know about the project unless he was an insider and, in that case, he must be taken seriously."

"Why are you telling me this? What kind of danger am I in and what do I need to do?" Her gaze did not waiver as she waited for his reply.

"I cannot tell you now but I will visit you again soon with information you'll need in this quest for truth. It's not by accident that you desire this knowledge and you've been chosen to help reveal these ancient secrets. You will be greatly tested and must stand true to your search. There will soon be a great deception in our land and the time has come for the ancient truths to start unfolding. May Yahweh, the Lord of Spirits, guide and protect you." With this statement the old man hurried away.

She sat frozen in shock. When she regained her mental clarity she tried to find him outside the café but he was nowhere to be seen. What could he possibly mean by beware of time and un-time? She was chosen? What kind of danger was she in? He said he would visit her again. When? Where? The feeling that overshadowed her in the depth of the cave seemed to be tightening its grip.

Chapter 5

It was almost time for her team to meet. Gabriella rushed back to her apartment with her head spinning in both fear and confusion. With each step she tried to shake the feeling someone was following her. She had enough to sort out from the cave exploration and now this? It was overwhelming! She did not like the feeling of losing control...not at all.

When she approached the lobby of her apartment building, Caleb was standing at the elevator. She stopped and looked behind her trying to catch a glimpse of any unwanted follower.

"Hey, Gabi Girl, what's up? Something wrong?" For the first time since he had met her she actually looked vulnerable and fragile. The elevator opened and she motioned for him to get inside. On the ride to the top floor she did not say a word. She just reached for Caleb's hand and held it tightly. Caleb knew there was definitely something wrong.

As they entered her apartment, she shut the door behind them and wrapped her arms around his waist needing the assurance of his protection.

"Please, just hold me a minute." She said with a pleading voice. Caleb wrapped his arms of safety around her. "What is it, Gabi?" She relaxed against him resting in his strong, protective arms.

Caleb could sense she was regaining control and reluctantly released his embrace. A closer look told him she was extremely agitated.

"Ok, Gabi, tell me what's going on". He asked with his eyes reflecting deep concern.

The fear was easing and she was so thankful for her dear friend. "Okay," she whispered in a quivering voice.

She knew she had to get control of her emotions before she tried to talk. She took Caleb's hand and led him out on the balcony overlooking the tranquil bay. The peace she would normally draw from this panoramic view escaped her as she battled to gain emotional control. They sat down and she took a deep breath carefully forming her words.

"I'll try to explain." She was about to begin when Faith and Aaron arrived. She waited for them realizing if this old man knew about the research project then Aaron and Faith needed to know, too.

The team settled in their usual seats on the balcony and she began to recount the events of the morning. She tried to tell them word for word what he had said.

They knew Gabriella well enough to know that she did not fantasize or embellish anything. When she spoke it was emphatic, with no drama at all. With that in mind they listened and wondered as detail by detail they relived her morning with her.

After she finished she looked out towards the sea with the morning sunlight kissing the waves and wondered how things could be so serene around her and so tumultuous inside her soul. She waited for their response.

"Gabi, you gotta tell Dr. Brotman." Faith's eyes were filled with consternation. "He's the only one that can tell us if this man is connected to the project." Without saying it they all knew if he was not connected in any way they had an even bigger problem. Someone outside the inner circle knew.

The team left for the university with a feeling of foreboding. Gabriella stared out the window of Caleb's car. She was thinking about the two polar events of the last twelve hours...a mystical dream and a dire warning both involving complete strangers. She usually shared everything with Caleb but she could not bring herself to tell him she was dreaming of the man in the transport they shared back to the airport. He would probably be very aggravated knowing she dreamt of another man, especially that particular man.

It was only about a twenty-minute drive from her apartment to their meeting with Dr. Brotman. Gabriella watched as they approached the university. She never tired of the beauty of the campus that spread along one of the long, sloped ridges of the Carmel Mountain Range surrounded by the enchanting Carmel National Park.

She always enjoyed the walk across the stone paths that were lined with beautiful shrubs and seasonal flowers. All of the campus' natural beauty was crowned with the majestic mountain backdrop. This morning, however, her thoughts were captured by the old man and her mind replayed his words over and over.

The setting for the International Studies Building was serene and picturesque. How fortunate she felt to have been a student in this beautiful setting. Her graduation was immediately followed with the opportunity to join Dr. Brotman's research team as she continued studying towards her Master's Degree. School and work had been the focus of her life since her father's death.

Gabriella's thoughts were reflected in her next words. "Every time we come back from exploration I realize even more how beautiful Israel is. There's no place on earth like it." The team agreed as they entered the building and walked the long hallway of faculty offices. At the end they entered the door displaying a bronze plate with the name 'Dr. Manny Brotman'.

They were greeted by the smiling face of Sandee, Dr. Brotman's Administrative Assistant, and the disembodied voice of the professor calling from his inner office, "Welcome home, my team!"

He came hurriedly through his office door to Gabriella first with a fatherly hug and then another for the rest of the team. "You sure have been missed around here. Come on in." He pushed the door back and made way for them to pass. "Sandee, hold all my calls."

"Yes, sir," she said with a salute. They laughed at her knowing she really was the one that ran his office but allowed him to think he did.

"I'm so glad you're home and just in time for the High Holy Days!" The Professor could not contain his excitement as the most sacred holidays on the Jewish calendar were just days away. "We will all celebrate together."

He led them into his office and closed the door behind them for total privacy. "Sandee just brought in some fresh coffee and tea." He motioned towards the black, metal coffee cart filled with various flavors to choose from. "Sorry we don't have any of that strange Arabian tea you told me about." He laughed at his own humor and sat down at the head of the table.

They knew the Professor was anxious to get started. Gabriella settled into the comfortable brown chair next to Dr. Brotman as the rest of the team quickly got their drinks and joined them at the conference table. She ran her hand down the familiar arm- rest feeling the soft leather worn from the years they had spent brainstorming, planning and researching.

She loved the intellectual décor of the room. It reminded her so much of her father's offices when she was growing up. The walls were filled with hundreds of books. She was sure the Professor had every book written on ancient languages and had studied each one thoroughly. The smell of the old leather and the aromatic fragrance of the Professor's pipe saturated the air. It was the same cherry flavor her father smoked when she was growing up.

They were so much alike. Both were tall with thick, black hair and dark brown eyes. The Professor's hair was only slightly streaked with gray even though he was in his early seventies, the same age her father would have been. He was strong willed and yet kind and gentle, a mixture of traits that made him so endearing. Their main difference was the Professor was a religious man and her father never was. Her father believed only what he could see and prove through science and she was proud to be just like him, but she always respected the beliefs of Dr. Brotman.

After only a few moments of pleasantries he was ready to begin. "I was able to enlarge the size of the pictures Aaron sent and I contacted the founders last night to inform them of what you'd found. Of course, I'll be giving them a complete update after our meeting."

"Will we ever know who the founders are?" Gabriella threw her hands up in a gesture of frustration. "We've been working all these years for people we haven't even met and don't know their names."

"I really wish I could tell you, Gabi. More than you know. But for the team's safety as well as safety of the founders that just isn't possible for now."

The team waited expectantly as Dr. Brotman pushed his glasses up closer to his eyes and laid his pipe in a glass tray. The smoke from the pipe circled around him creating an enigmatic atmosphere as he pulled the pictures from his briefcase. With his magnifying glass he began to move it slowly across each one inspecting every inch of the ancient writings one more time before he spoke. He carefully laid the magnifying glass back on the table and leaned back in his chair. "It's the same. This is what we've been searching for." A smile spread from ear to ear across his face deepening the wrinkles around his eyes. His excitement was unmistakable.

"I knew it!" Aaron jumped up from his seat as his olive skin flushed in a display of emotion rare for him. "I was sure it was the same!" He went to the end of the table and joined the professor as they compared the writings.

As Aaron detailed comparisons the Professor looked up at the team. "I believe it's an earlier form of the ancient Ge'ez language from which most forensic linguists agree all Middle Eastern Semitic languages were derived. Over thousands of years the original language evolved into numerous languages and dialects."

He picked up his pipe, took another puff and briefly stared out the window. "Most rabbinical scholars even believe, in its original form, it is the language of God that was given to man at creation." The last few words were spoken with reverence.

Gabriella asked almost in a whisper. "Could this be the original form?" The others waited breathlessly for his answer.

The Professor looked at Gabriella as if together they had conquered the world. "I believe it very well could be." He leaned back not yet willing to go too far out on the linguistic limb. "What can you tell me about the cave?"

Faith gave her report from her view as an anthropologist. "We know lava tunnels in the desert's volcanic caves were used for thousands of years as underground homes or tunnels for travel out of the hot sun. In these particular lava tunnels we found no signs anywhere they had been traveled through or inhabited in any way."

"In fact," Caleb added, "I would bet my speleology degree on the fact it was a virgin tunnel, except for the writing we found on the wall. Someone had to have been there at some time but there were no other signs of ancient life."

"*And*," Aaron added solemnly, "There were scratches through the writing as though someone was trying to destroy it. If it was a virgin cave how was that possible?" Aaron pointed to the pictures where the scratches were visible.

The Professor made no reply to Aaron's comment but instead changed the subject. "Caleb, what's your professional view on the age of the volcano tunnels? Before or after the great flood?"

"Definitely before." Caleb confirmed. "And from all indications the writing is also antediluvian."

The Professor leaned back in his chair to allow the information to process in his mind. With all the excitement over their discovery they knew there was a 'but' still to come. They did not have to wait long.

"But, we've still a lot of work to do." The Professor continued. "Our research has now gone to another level. Team, we've raised the bar. It's a major discovery just in the language itself. Now we must translate the writing and hope and pray it's the information we need." Aaron also being a linguistic scientist especially understood the challenge ahead.

The team was not sure exactly what messages the professor was looking for but it did not dampen their excitement. They began an animated discussion outlining the next steps needed to move the project forward... except for Gabriella whose mind was obviously elsewhere.

The Professor interrupted their discussion and turned to her. "Ok, Gabi. Let's have it. What's bothering you?"

She had been waiting for the right opportunity. "I'm sorry, Professor. Something very concerning happened this morning."

She had his full attention. Gabriella was never frightened by anything and the Professor knew anyone that could crawl into the deepest, darkest caves known to archeologists had nerves of steel.

She proceeded to give vivid details of the morning's encounter. She ended with, "You've told us the only people that know about our project are the founders. How could this man know and what did he mean?"

She could not read his reaction to her news. He just picked up his pipe and leaned back in his chair. His voice grew deeper with emotion as he spoke: "I've tried to keep you four on the safe side of the Omega Watchers Project. And I've been able to for over a decade but we've crossed a threshold now. It's time you know."

The Professor got up from his chair and walked to the window and looked out at the panoramic view of the Carmel Mountains. It seemed to help him collect his thoughts when there was something difficult to explain. The team looked at each other not knowing what to expect.

He turned and faced them and suddenly the words started rolling, recounting the series of events that brought them to this place. The result had a profound affect on his young team.

"You're all aware the first Dead Sea Scrolls were discovered in Israel's West Bank Qumran caves in 1947. Three shepherds found them when one accidently fell into a cave. I will never forget his name Muhammed

Edh-Dhib. One simple shepherd's mishap became a discovery that would impact the world. Always amazes me how Yahweh uses people often considered insignificant to accomplish His purposes."

"Over a period of the next several years numerous scrolls and bronze fragments were found, a total of 972. The texts proved to be of great historical, religious, prophetic and linguistic significance. They included some of the earliest known surviving manuscripts many of which are included in both the Old and New Testaments of the Bible. There were also numerous scrolls found that are deuterocanonical, meaning inspired writings not included in the Old Testament. These preserved valuable information of the history of Israel and mankind's future not found in the Bible we have today. The manuscripts found can be dated as late as 318 CE. The scrolls written after the late first century were post New Testament and gave us personal accounts of the persecution of the Jews as the Roman Catholic Church became the dominating religion of the known world."

The Professor took a puff from his pipe allowing himself time for mental recollection then continued his verbal journey into the past. "I was asked to join the small group of forensic linguists in 1983. Progress had already been made but there was still much laborious work ahead. The scrolls were mainly written in Hebrew, Aramaic, Greek and Nabataean, all languages in which I had a great deal of proficiency along with the others on the translating team. Where my expertise was most needed was the translation of the ancient scrolls that were written in Ge'ez. I am one of the few men left in the world that can still read and translate this rare language."

The Professor took a long puff from his pipe and again the room was saturated with the wonderful aroma of the cherry tobacco. Then he continued: "It was believed the oldest scrolls were hidden in these particular caves starting some 2500 years ago because they had the perfect temperature conditions for preservation over a long period of time. The priests were hiding them in an effort to protect the sacred writings from destruction as the Babylonians were invading Israel. This invasion had been prophesied by the prophet Isaiah over a hundred years prior and by the prophet Jeremiah who lived at the time of the conquering. Both prophets warned Israel if they didn't repent of their rebellion against

Yahweh, Babylon would conquer their nation and destroy their temple. They refused and the prophecies became a reality in 586 BC.

"I personally deciphered crucial timelines as I was translating the scrolls. They have never been released to the public or even beyond the group that financed the translations. I was told the timelines could not be proven and most likely were in error. Further, I was instructed to never make them known through publication, lecture or discussion. Not even with the group of linguists I worked with in the translations. When I'm employed to do a job I do exactly as my employers tell me."

He paced back and forth on the dark mahogany floor puffing on his pipe as he continued to unfold the mystery. "I endured inner struggle like nothing I've ever experienced to keep this information to myself."

The Professor had their full attention as he continued to unfold the conundrum layer by layer. "What I translated from the oldest of the ancient scrolls was a prophecy given before the flood to Enoch, the great grandfather of Noah, describing the events in the history of mankind from Enoch's day to the end of days.

Dr. Brotman stopped pacing the floor and sat back down at the table. "In addition to the scrolls hidden before the destruction of the first temple, many more scrolls were hidden around 70 AD when the second Jewish Temple was destroyed. Both were destroyed on the 9th of Av which is another story for later. Again the scrolls were hidden for the same reasons...to protect the sacred writings. Carbon dating allowed us to determine their age." Dr. Brotman knew his team completely understood that process and continued his précis.

"The scrolls I personally translated were from the first temple destruction. They were written in Ge'ez. I believe those scrolls had been translated from earlier forms of writings, perhaps even the language you found in the cave."

Aaron was especially curious. "Can I ask why you thought that?"

The Professor proceeded to answer his question. "Some of the letters strayed from the Ge'ez and could not be translated. I could determine most of the message but it was as though the language was in a transitional stage when it was written so I wasn't able to translate the complete message."

He took a puff on his pipe and exhaled a fresh fragrance of cherry tobacco into the air that was already saturated with mystery. "Most of the

Dead Sea Scrolls we deciphered still exist and are commonly available in present day languages. Discovering these scrolls was verification of the authenticity of the ancient writings that some have tried to dilute over time. However, there were additional ancient writings that had been lost to the modern world. I believe Yahweh had them hidden to be revealed at the end of days."

The Professor leaned forward towards his team with his voice slightly quivering. "As I stated, I always do what my employers ask me. I told no one of my discovery. I began to do my own personal research about events that Enoch and other prophets foretold would happen at the end of days. The timelines begin to connect but there were still pieces missing. It was in the summer of 2000, the year before the four of you began your fall semester here at the university, I was becoming very discouraged. I had run out of physical resources. I couldn't discuss the research with my linguistic peers. I was at a stalemate. It was at that time an unknown man with the appearance of a Hasidic Jew came to my office.

He gazed out the window and allowed his mind to relive the encounter. "I can remember it like it was yesterday. Sandee came to my door and told me there was a man in her office that wanted a few minutes of my time. I told her to show him in. He came through the door and walked to my desk without saying a word. He handed me two clay tablets. Each was about twelve inches by twelve inches.

Gabriella suddenly wondered if the Jewish man that visited Dr. Brotman could possibly be the same man that visited her that very morning. The description certainly was the same. But, she did not dare interrupt him.

The Professor continued: "He was a man of very few words. He simply handed me the fragments and stated, 'As it was in the days of Noah it will be again at the end of days.' Then he left my office. He was quoting from the prophecy of Yeshua in the Book of Matthew, Chapter 24, and I knew immediately it was a sign I was to continue my research. I've wondered many times why he came to me. Or even why I was chosen to translate the prophecies from the Dead Sea Scrolls. I've never seen him again but he gave me information that encouraged me to continue my research at a time when I was ready to give it all up."

The Professor was silent for a few minutes. Gabriella knew he was reflecting on the encounter with the old man and the profound affect it had on his life. She was almost certain he was the same man that had visited her at the cafe.

"After that timely encounter I always referred to him as the Prophet. Seemed appropriate." The Professor spoke in a solemn voice as he looked at each team member allowing the information to sink in before he continued.

"Some bible scholars and forensic linguistics have tried to discount many of the Dead Sea Scrolls to be a pseudepigraphical work, meaning they believe someone wrote the scrolls many years later than they are dated and assumed the name of the ancient prophets. I don't believe so. Everything points to authenticity. The scroll manuscripts bring a greater prophetic understanding to what is written in the Holy Scriptures. I am convinced I have found the timelines given for the end of days" His voice changed dramatically as he added, "The prophesied end of days are those in which we now live, my young friends."

"What do you mean, Professor, the end of days?" Gabriella could barely get the words out. She looked at Caleb and he seemed as confused as she was.

"Gabriella," he answered, "it can't be explained in a simple statement. And that is why this mission is so important. Aaron and Faith have been taught the Torah and the writings of the prophets. They are among the very few who understand the ancient prophecies that tell of events that will come on the earth when time as we know it is reaching its end. If you continue with the project you'll understand."

Gabriella did not know what he meant about "if" she continued but she kept silent as the Professor explained. "As I said, the Prophet gave me two tablets. One was written in Ge'ez and the other was in a language I had never seen before. There was a map etched at the bottom of the second tablet. The founders and I tried to determine the exact location indicated on the ancient map but there were not enough reference points to do so. That led to the many explorations you were sent on which all turned out to be a wild goose chase."

"Then last year something very significant was discovered that led to your last exploration." The Professor knew this would hold their full attention. "There was an ancient Agade map found in Iraq marking specific locations in northern Saudi Arabia. In biblical times that area was part of Babylon, known today as Iraq, which is considered to be the cradle of the world. When I surveyed the Agade map I realized it was exactly the same location that was etched on the clay tablet. This gave me the approximate geographical location. Thus, your exploration in northeast Saudi Arabia began."

After another short puff on his pipe the Professor continued. "Apparently the Dead Sea Scroll I was told to not discuss and the information on the tablets connect in some way and the Prophet was telling me to continue the search. The founders of the project believed there were still truths to be found or the Prophet wouldn't have appeared."

Dr. Brotman's voice lowered as he spoke the next words: "I've told you we didn't want you to know who the founders and financial backers of the project are for their protection and for yours. There's a group of very powerful people that want the prophetic timelines silenced. They have an agenda for a new world order and will allow nothing to interfere. They are fully aware these prophecies and timelines could actually expose what they plan to do. This puts us all in very grave danger."

The team looked at each other and then stared at the Professor wondering what could be so dangerous to them. They were just researchers and explorers. No threat to anyone. What they were about to hear was beyond what any of them could have imagined.

Chapter 6

The Professor stood staring at the Carmel Mountain range with majestic Mt. Hermon looming in the background. When he took time to collect his thoughts, as he was doing now, they knew something profound would soon be spoken. He turned to them with a look of consternation.

Finally, he spoke: "Until now you've only been researching and exploring for artifacts or cave writings that might produce a connection to the project. I couldn't divulge the reasons behind the research. The time has come, my friends, for you to know."

His expression was grave as he continued: "No one wants to hear that time as we know it is about to come to an end. They especially don't want to hear a great deception is getting ready to take place that will involve everyone on the face of the earth. Can you imagine the reaction if that was on the nightly news?" The Professor chuckled to himself at the thought.

"But, we are at the point in The Omega Watcher Project where you must know everything and the possible dangers. Then you can decide what you want to do. If you decide to bow out I will understand."

The team could not imagine the Professor telling them anything that would change their minds about being part of the project. They all sat silently waiting for his next words.

"All you've known to this point is I was researching the civilization before Noah's flood in an effort to understand what the culture was like in the antediluvian era and, of course, trying to find any writings that matched the clay tablets. I realize not revealing the founders and financial backers or the reason for the research kept the entire project a mystery, but it was necessary at the time." It was obvious he was struggling with what he was about to share.

"It goes much, much deeper than that. There are ancient writings that tell why Yahweh, the Creator of all things, sent a great flood upon all the earth. Anyone that studies the Jewish Torah, which is the first five books of the biblical Old Testament, will find that after the creation of mankind people became increasingly wicked. It came to the point that Yahweh repented that He had even made man; however, it wasn't just man being evil it was much deeper and perverse."

He picked up his copy of the bible which was always with him and began to read from Genesis Chapter Six: *"When human beings began to increase in number on the earth and daughters were born to them, the sons of God saw that the daughters of humans were beautiful and they married any of them they chose.*

The nephilim were on the earth in those days—and also afterward—when the sons of God went into the daughters of humans and had children by them. These were the giants of old, men of renown.

The LORD saw how great the wickedness of the human race had become on the earth, and that every inclination of the thoughts of the human heart was only evil all the time. The LORD regretted that he had made human beings on the earth and his heart was deeply troubled. So the LORD said, "I will wipe from the face of the earth the human race I have created—and with them the animals, the birds and the creatures that move along the ground—for I regret that I have made them." But Noah found favor in the eyes of the LORD."

The professor crossed the wooden floor and stood by the rustic stone fireplace behind his desk. He leaned against the mantel with his pipe in hand and the team knew he was struggling to continue. "I'm coming to the most important part of our mission. The founders firmly believe that Yahweh created the heavens and the earth. Our Torah, which we believe is the divine Word of the one true God, tells us this. He first created the heavens and His heavenly angels. Then He created earth and man. He assigned a group of His angels as 'Watchers' who would be guardians of mankind. The Torah identifies these Watchers as 'Sons of God.'"

"Ancient writings from the Prophet Enoch tell us there were two hundred of these Watchers that met at the summit of Mt. Hermon. The apex of the mountain was their supernatural gateway between the natural and the supernatural worlds. Einstein actually gave a name to those supernatural gateways. He called them wormholes. He theorized it was scientifically possible to 'shortcut' through time and space and from dimension to dimension via these wormholes. Whatever you call it, these portals do exist!"

The professor went back to the window and pointed toward Mt. Carmel. "Just beyond the Carmel Mountains you can see the mountain top I'm talking about. Yes, it's the same Mt. Hermon that we can see in the distance on any clear day from Haifa."

Anyone who lived in Israel was familiar with Mt. Hermon. It was the highest point on the Golan Heights reaching over 9000 feet above sea level. It was the safety buffer zone for Israel from the constant threats of attacks from both Lebanon and Syria.

Dr. Brotman turned back around to face the team. "It was on Mt. Hermon the Watchers swore an oath together to defy God and willfully sin. They made the choice to leave their heavenly estate and take the beautiful daughters of man as wives, knowing this would eternally separate them from their Creator. They were fully aware there would be no redemption for their rebellion."

Glancing back towards the mountains, the Professor verified his belief with another biblical scripture, this time from the New Testament. "The Book of Jude verifies the writings of Moses and Enoch. '*He has also held in eternal chains those angels who did not keep their own position but abandoned their assigned place. They are held in deepest darkness for judgment on the great day.*'"

Dr. Brotman took his seat back at the head of the conference table and laid his pipe down before he continued. He knew the ancient truths were not stories one wanted to hear. "This interbreeding of God's human creation and the fallen angels produced a hybrid race of half human/half spirit beings. The bible refers to them as 'giants'. In Hebrew it means 'nephilim'. They were extremely large in stature, very powerful, possessed supernatural knowledge and became very evil. The evil got worse with each generation and over a period of about 2000 years every being on earth had this hybrid DNA with the exception of Noah's family."

The Professor paused, picked up his pipe and then laid it back in the cradle without even taking a puff. It was as though he did not want to even go to the next level of vileness that had come upon the earth.

Then he cautiously continued. "The evil went to the extent that the fallen angels started procreating with animals, producing powerful, supernatural beings that were half human and half beast. You can see these hybrid creatures in numerous ancient drawings. Yahweh regretted ever making man and wiped the earth clean with the flood and began again."

Gabriella did not respond verbally but her first thought was how ridiculous this all sounded. Could anyone really believe such nonsense? Silence penetrated the air until finally Aaron spoke.

Aaron sarcastically chuckled. "Man messed it all up again. Like you just read, Professor, there were nephilim on the earth before the flood and also afterwards. Giants were the reason Israel was afraid to go into the land Yahweh promised them. David killed a giant. The list goes on. They found a way to come back after the flood."

Faith entered the conversation. "From the time I was a child I was taught these stories. But no one ever explained where the giants came from or who they were from a biblical point. Explorers know that skeletons of giant humans have been discovered all over the world. The scientific community is quick to dismiss any artifacts or fossil records that dispute their presupposed interpretation of the period and what they can't explain scientifically they hide from the general public, oftentimes with the help of governments."

Gabriella was not sarcastic in her next words but spoke with knowledge of many years of study. "Professor, you know the Genesis story sounds a lot like many other ancient stories of the mythical gods. There's a long list of hybrid 'gods' that were half human and half animal. The Great Sphinx of Giza in Egypt is known around the world and it has the body of a lion with a human head. It's probably the more famous one but there are hundreds of mythical gods that were hybrids."

"You say 'mythical', Gabi." Dr. Brotman answered her. "What if they weren't a myth? What if they were in fact descendents of the fallen angels? There were many names for these hybrid offsprings. They were known by the proper names of Rephaim, Emim, Anakim, and Zamzummim. Maybe, Gabi, it's not all myth. People just prefer to skip over the parts of the Bible they don't understand and as a result they have a diluted truth."

Gabriella got up from the table and walked to the window tracing the steps Dr. Brotman had taken. Mt. Hermon loomed in the horizon. "How could something so beautiful be a portal for evil?" She spoke without turning. "Professor, how can you be so certain the biblical stories are not just another mythical account warped from someone's fantasy and developed over time?"

Dr. Brotman went to the window and put his arm around her shoulder. "How do I know? It's plain and simple...prophecy."

She looked at him with an expression of total confusion. "Prophecy?"

"Gabi, if someone tells you something is going to happen and it does, would you trust them? And if they repeatedly gave you more and more information and it all happened just as they said it would, would you believe what they were saying?"

"Yes, I suppose I would." She admitted.

"That is a definition of biblical prophecy. These are God's warnings delivered through His prophets as He would tell in advance of future events to prepare His people Israel. God also promised he would do nothing until he first told his prophets. This was divine proof to a human world that He knew everything past, present and future.

Dr. Brotman led her back to the conference table. "That is why Enoch's prophecy along with many biblical prophecies written thousands of years ago is both a warning and a timeline for the end of days."

The team looked at each other as Dr. Brotman's words were sinking in. He laid his glasses on the table next to his pipe and in a voice filled with consternation he spoke with certainly. "I know this is not what you want to hear but every prophecy points to this generation as the last. Life as we know it is about to change forever."

Chapter 7

After several moments of dead silence, allowing the Professor's words to mentally process, the team all began to chatter at the same time.

"Are you absolutely sure?" Faith asked. "Could you possibly be wrong?"

A deluge of questions bombarded the Professor from each team member and he finally just held up his hand meaning 'enough'. They all leaned back in their leather chairs and did as instructed but with questions and fears swirling in their minds.

He pulled a file from his briefcase as the team waited in silence. He laid it on the table unopened. "Before I read the prophecy from the Dead Sea Scrolls you need to understand that according to the Holy Scriptures the two hundred fallen angels, the Watchers that rebelled against God, were bound by God's Holy angels after they sinned and are being held in a place of darkness, called the abyss, in the underground chambers of the earth. They're imprisoned until the end days when they'll be released upon the earth for a short time. It will be a time of great tribulation and great judgment for the rebellion of both humans and angels. The prophet Daniel tells us it will be a seven year period. At the end of the seven years God's judgment will be completed and the earth again cleansed, this time eternally."

This all sounded like something out of a weird sci-fi movie to Gabriella. How could someone really believe this stuff? However, she knew Dr. Brotman was not a man of fantasy. "You really do believe this, Professor?" Her voice was soft in hopes of not being offensive but obviously showing her doubt.

"Not only do I believe it, but I believe we are living in the time the Watchers will be released and the seven years will begin. Both Daniel the prophet and John, who wrote the Book of Revelation, were given a vision of what would happen at the end of days. Daniel was told it would be sealed until the time of the end when there would be an explosion of knowledge. The explosion of knowledge speaks for itself with the cyber world we now live in. In addition, I believe finding the Dead Sea Scrolls hidden during the days of Daniel, over 2500 years ago, and unsealing them at the very time the nation of Israel was reborn marked the generation in which we live as being the end of time as we know it."

Even though it sounded completely idiotic there was something in the Professor's voice that caused Gabriella to hang on every word. She looked at Caleb and their eyes met in silent conversation. She knew he was thinking exactly the same thing.

Dr. Brotman opened the file he had laid on the table. He put his glasses on and said without looking up: "This is a prophecy written by Enoch that I translated from one of the Dead Seas Scrolls."

I Enoch 11-15

11. And the Lord said unto the angel Michael: 'Go, bind Semjâzâ and the Watchers who have united themselves with women so as to have defiled themselves with them in all their uncleanness.'

The Professor paused in his reading to interject an explanation. "Semjaza led the angelic rebellion and the Watchers referred to here are the two hundred fallen angels who chose to sin with him."

12. And when their sons have slain one another, and they have seen the destruction of their beloved ones, bind them fast for seventy generations in the dark chambers of the earth until the day of their judgment and of their consummation, till the judgment that is forever and ever is consummated.

Again the Professor paused from his reading for further explanation. "The offspring that resulted from the fallen angels intermingling with humans had created a malevolent society where all DNA had been polluted, except for Noah. God decreed the only answer was to cleanse the earth resulting in the total annihilation of all the offspring. The "destruction" referred to here is a prophecy Enoch gave of the coming great flood that would destroy the evil the fallen ones had created."

"After forcing the fallen angels to witness the total destruction brought by the great flood they were then put in chains in the underworld abyss for seventy generations awaiting God's final judgment. I want to read something to you from the Book of Revelation that tells what will happen with the fallen angels in the last seven years of time and just before their judgment." He picked up his bible and turned to the last book.

"This is Revelation 9:1-3: "*The fifth angel blew his trumpet. Then I saw a star fall from the sky to the earth. The star was given the key to the deep hole that leads down to the bottomless pit.* [2] *Then the star opened the hole leading to the pit. Smoke came up from the hole like smoke from a big furnace. The sun and sky became dark because of the smoke from the hole.* [3] *Then locusts came out of the smoke....*"

He got up and went to the blackboard hanging on the wall next to his huge, mahogany desk that perfectly matched the conference table and began to make visual notes for them. "John wrote the prophecies in the Book of Revelation in metaphors and symbolisms that would be understood by the Jews. John knew the Romans who were holding him captive would not understand their hidden meanings."

He picked up his chalk and began his translation. He listed the key words from the three verses:

- Star
- Bottomless
- Locusts

He turned to the team and began his explanation. "The word 'Star' is from Isaiah 14:12. The prophet identified Satan as 'the fallen star' who is the leader of all fallen angels and demonic forces. Any Jew would instantly understand the symbolism."

"The term 'bottomless' is a transliteration from the Greek word 'abussos' and in English literally means abyss. According to Enoch and other ancient prophets this is the place the fallen angels are being held. II Peter 2:4 in the New Testament also foretells this."

"If you read further in Chapter 9 of Revelation, it gives a description of the 'locusts' with human faces and long hair and they have a ruling king over them. The following verses of the chapter clarifies this is a metaphoric term."

Eschatologists, those that study the prophetic events of the end times, agree the 'locusts' are the Watchers, the fallen angels, that were bound for the seventy generations. They are the only creatures the Holy Scriptures tells us are held captive in the abyss. Genesis, II Peter, Jude and Enoch all agreed on this. And they will be released upon the earth at the end of days to join with Satan and all of his demonic forces."

The team listened intently as the Professor continued from the Book of Enoch.

13. In those days they shall be led off to the abyss of fire and to the torment and the prison in which they shall be confined forever. And whosoever shall be condemned and destroyed will from thenceforth be bound together with them to the end of all generations.

15. And destroy all the spirits of the reprobate and the children of the Watchers, because they have wronged mankind. Destroy all wrong from the face of the earth and let every evil work come to an end: and let the plant of righteousness and truth appear: and it shall prove a blessing; the works of righteousness and truth shall be planted in truth and joy for evermore.'

He looked up and his expression was grave. "Enoch tells us, as does the Bible which is the true Word of Yahweh, a day of judgment is coming when both evil men and evil spirits will face a final and eternal judgment."

Then the Professor's voice became excited. "I began to do the math, team. According to Enoch 6 and Genesis 6 the angels fell during 'the days of Jared'. The Bible gives us the generations from Adam forward and how long each lived. Jared was the sixth generation from Adam and through calculating his birth and death he lived from 460 to 1422." The Professor stopped long enough to take another puff from his pipe and observe their expressions. "How would you like to live 962 years?" The Professor chuckled.

Gabriella thought of the many times the team had used the board when they were mind mapping their projects and wondered just where he was going with all of this.

The Professor erased the board and with chalk in hand explained as he wrote: "According to Enoch 10 the Watchers will be held in captivity for seventy generations and then released on the earth at the end of days, during the final generation and just before their eternal captivity. Now how do we determine what 'days' that will be?" He turned and looked at the team. "Do any of you know the biblical time frame of a generation?"

"According to Psalms 90 seventy years is a generation." Aaron quickly answered him.

"Correct, Aaron." The Professor affirmed as he wrote seventy on the far left of the board. "Now if we multiply seventy years, that's a generation, times seventy generations we have 4900 years. Right? Right!" He answered himself as he finished the math.

"We know by biblical calculations if we go back 4900 years that would put us right in the middle of the days of Jared." He drew a big circle around the numbers and then continued, seemingly without taking a breath. "I know we have a lot of variable years in the life of Jared so I followed it up with two more timelines."

He moved to a blank space in the middle of the board preparing to write again. "Both Jews and Christians believe God created the heavens and the earth in six days and rested on the seventh." He wrote the numbers one through seven in a vertical line down the middle of the board."

He turned and briefly faced the team. "II Peter 3:8 tells us a day is as a thousand years." He then turned back to the board and added three zeroes to each day. It's been six thousand years since God created time for man to live on this earth. Before that there was no 'time'. Now is the time for the earth to rest. After the seven years of great tribulation Yahweh will set up his Kingdom on earth for a thousand years. Then, according to Revelation 10:6, 'time will be no more'." The Professor circled the seventh day and put a large exclamation marking it as extremely significant.

"I get it!" Faith exclaimed. "Use the analogy of six days and rest on the seventh day compared to six thousand years and the seventh thousand being rest!"

"Exactly, Faith! And we are at the end of the sixth day or six thousand years now which biblically points to the fact *again* we are at the end of days." His expression left no room for doubt. He was totally convinced of every word he was saying.

Gabriella was captured by the information and looked at Caleb. He raised his eyebrows at her and she knew the gesture. He was finding the information fascinating as well, but was not convinced.

Dr. Brotman went to the last empty space left on the far right of the board. "This to me is the most compelling of all the prophetic proof of the time in which we live." He wrote in big letters 1948, drew a circle and put multiple exclamation marks beside it.

They all knew he was referring to the rebirth of the State of Israel as he began to explain. "Numerous bible prophets both in the Old & New Testaments give prophecies of the re-gathering of Israel, after the Diaspora, when the Jews ran for their lives to numerous nations. Might I say, it happened just as it was prophesied." He again was stressing his point of the validity of the ancient prophets. "*But*, never in the history of mankind has a nation been scattered all over the world for almost 2000 years and then come back to their same country, speaking the same language and having a pure blood line. That in its self is a miracle! But it is only the beginning of a multitude of prophecies that have already been fulfilled since 1948... and many more that will be, especially during the last seven years of time as we know it."

Faith's eyes filled with tears. "My family is part of the prophecy of the re-gathering. As you all know when the cold war with Russia was over we were allowed to come to Israel. I was only five years old but I remember my father bowing on the runway when we got off the plane in Tel Aviv and kissing the ground. He told us we were finally home. We all felt it even though we had never even visited Israel."

Faith took a deep breath in an effort to veil her deep emotions. "In Russia we were not allowed to openly practice our religious traditions. Many Jews were put in prison or even killed just because they were Jews. Every religious Jew knew there would come a day our people could return home and each generation prayed they would be the one that would see it happen." She picked up her napkin under her coffee cup and wiped the tears. "My family lived the answer to that prayer."

Aaron also had tears in his eyes which was rare to see. He took a deep breath and shared his personal story. "As you know I was born in Israel. But, my family came from France. They had moved to France from Poland when Hitler declared he would exterminate every Jew from the face of the earth. They escaped Hitler's gas chambers just in time. Had they not left when they did none of my family would have survived."

Dr. Brotman had never told them how he came to Israel and it brought tears to Gabriella's eyes as he opened his heart in remembrance. "My mother and I were the only members of my family that survived Hitler's ovens. My father, grandparents, and all my relatives were taken prisoners in Germany and sent to Auschwitz. I was only a baby when my father took me and my mother to an underground Christian organization that was helping Jews to escape to Holland."

The Professor took a deep breath obviously struggling to continue. "My father had planned to follow us but was captured before he could get out of Germany. We didn't know until the war was over that none of my family survived." His strong voice was edged with deep pain. "All my family was killed—-simply because they were Jews."

Gabriella could not hold back the tears. She could not even imagine what it would be like to live constantly in fear for your life especially when you had done absolutely nothing wrong. These were people she loved and to hear their stories of such deep sorrow broke her heart.

Caleb sat quietly without saying a word. His eyes met Gabriella's and she knew he also was feeling their sorrow, but a very different kind. Being German he was well aware of his country's history even though attempts had been made over the decades since WWII to downplay Hitler's atrocious acts.

Caleb felt he had to make an apology. "You all know how deeply it hurts me that my country slaughtered over eleven million people during the war. Six million of them were Jews! Living in Israel and hearing so many families's stories of persecution during Hitler's war has made the Nazi's horrendous acts very real and personal to me. It seems there isn't a Jewish family in Israel that wasn't affected in some way."

The Professor cleared his throat continuing his personal story. "My mother told me stories of the Christian family we were taken to in Holland and how they had unconditional love and peace even in the midst of the horrors that surrounded them. This family could have died for giving a safe haven to a Jewish woman and her baby. And yet they were willing to take a chance for people they didn't even know. That, my young friends, is a love beyond understanding."

He paced the floor back and forth as he recounted a few of the stories his mother had told him of the acts of heroism this family had taken to hide and protect them until the war was over. "I was about five years old and I remember vividly hiding in the secret attic of the home in Holland and my mother warning me to be completely quiet while the Nazis searched the house. I can still feel her body shaking as she held me in her arms with her hand over my mouth until we could hear the soldiers leaving. We lived in constant fear from 1941, when we first arrived in Holland, until the Americans and western allies invaded Germany and the war ended in 1945. My mother waited to hear from my father and, of course, she never did. Each Jew that went to the death camps was tattooed with a number on their arms which coordinated with their names. A list was eventually released with the names of those that died in the concentration camps. In 1947, she finally heard the dreaded news that every living relative we had was dead."

The Professor stopped pacing. His voice changed to joyful as he turned to face the team with a smile. "There is a silver lining to this agonizing story! It was during those years of living with a loving, Christian family my mother and I came to know the true Messiah of Israel, the Messiah of both Christians and Jews. Christians call him by his Greek name Jesus. We Jews call him by his Hebrew name Yeshua."

"King David wrote in Psalms 30 a song of praise to the Heavenly Father: '*You have turned my mourning into joyful dancing. You have taken away my clothes of mourning and clothed me with joy*.' We experienced this joy in spite of losing everything and everyone. When Israel declared their statehood in 1948 we made aliyah to Israel and became part of the prophecy of the return."

The Professor waved his hand toward Aaron and Faith. "The three of us are examples of Jews all over the world that were persecuted for no reason except the fact we were Jews. And when the prophecy was fulfilled that Israel was again a nation for her people after two thousand years, Jews started flooding back to their land exactly as the prophets said they would. And this was to be the sign of the last generation and herald the return of Yeshua our Messiah!"

There was not a dry eye to be found in the room. Each person had relived with the Professor the agonies of his childhood as he poured out his heart. As a result of the atrocious acts of Hitler, the prophetic truth of the Nation of Israel was born into the spiritual hearts of the Professor and his mother.

The Professor picked up his bible and held it to his chest. "Starting as a young boy, I studied the prophecies of this book. Plus, I studied all the apocryphal writings, the Mishnah, the Talmud, and the Zohar. I have even studied the historical writings of Josephus and every historical book about Israel I could find. I was fascinated with the prophetic silver thread that ran through all of them revealing the plan Yahweh had for his people.

The One and Only God carved out a period of seven thousand years from eternity and called it time on earth. The only place that time even exists. And time as we know it is coming to an end."

He laid his bible back on the table and sat down with the look they knew so well when he would talk about their project. "As I translated the Dead Sea Scrolls and the prophecies of the end of days I knew Yahweh had set me on a mission. When I was commanded to keep silent about the Dead Sea Scroll translation, The Omega Watchers project was born. My purpose became exposing the end time deception that Yeshua spoke of in Matthew 24:24. I truly believe we have the prophetic truth and can prove it!"

The Professor went back to the board and wrote 'Three Prophecies" right in the middle with multiple exclamation marks. He then listed them:

1. Enoch Chapter 10 (70 generations)
2. 6000 years
3. 1948

"Any one of these three prophecies is debatable when standing alone. The Word tells us that out of the mouth of two or three witnesses let every word be established. When you have three prophecies that all say the same, it can only mean one thing. We're at the end of days, my friends!"

He rejoined them at the conference table and spoke with a stern voice they were not familiar with. "Listen close to my words. The tablet that the Prophet gave me was a warning that we are quickly approaching the end of the prophetic timelines I've been working on." He picked up another paper from his file. "There were two tablets given to me by the Prophet. The one I could translate was written in Ge'ez and reads as follows:" '*The Fallen Watchers will soon be released. They will come as angels of light and will deceive many. Only the elect shall not be deceived. The gates of Tartarus will soon open.*'"

Gabriella gasped her question as the rest of the team just stared at the Professor. "Do you believe this place called Tartarus is real? It's the same place the Bedouins in Saudi Arabia warned us about!"

"It's very real!" The Profession proclaimed. "According to Enoch and other ancient writers it's the place the two hundred Watchers are held captive until their release at the end of days."

A foreboding saturated the air as the team relived the ominous feelings in the lava cave. Caleb reached over and took Gabriella's hand. She leaned against him needing his security and strength. This was something that only a few days before she would have laughed about but she realized this was not a joke. If the Professor believed this, and was spending his life trying to prove the validity these prophecies, then she knew it was to be taken seriously.

"What do you think the great deception is, Professor?" Gabriella questioned.

The Professor only partially answered her question. "I have the major parts of the prophetic timelines already determined. However some important details involving the last segment of the end times are still missing. I do believe I know what the great deception will be after piecing the prophecies together but I have to have more proof."

The Professor sat down and looked at Gabriella as he spoke: "Now to answer your question about your morning visitor. You have just perfectly described the Prophet who brought me the clay tablets. We must take his warning seriously."

"Professor, do you have any idea why he would call me "chosen" or what "time and untime" is?" Gabriella asked almost afraid to know the answer.

"Let me explain it this way, Gabi. We live in a three spatial dimensional world...height, width and depth. Time is our fourth dimension and that is our earthly existence, but scientists know other dimensions exist. In fact, it's commonly believed the universe was created with ten dimensions, some of these being where time does not exist. Thus, we have the dimension of 'un-time'. Everyone is familiar with Einstein's theory of relativity. To put it simply he believed there were alternate dimensions we cannot see with our natural eye but it is possible to move in and out of these dimensions through quantum physics. In the last one hundred years scientists have been discovering what has existed as paranormal experiences since the beginning of time."

"I'm still confused as to what this would have to do with me." Gabriella admitted.

He went to his multitude of books and knew exactly where to pull from. He opened the book and began to read from an ancient Cherokee Indian prophecy:

'The Stars above and its configurations hold Time Untime within its grasp upon all life. As all cultures sustain a Zodiac system written upon Time Untime so also the Chickamauga Cherokee of the Americas hold also an Ancient Zodiac of the heavens.

Within the Zodiac of the Heavens of the Chickamauga Cherokee are etched Ancient designs written upon and within the lines of seeing. The Cherokee Zodiac is alive and moves and spins upon the rings of Time Untime. As the main outline remains its hold and is stationed in the sky of stars its movement within that frozen outline does indeed change with the movements of the other elements. It is a place where there is no time. Always alive, breaths, lives, and takes upon each constellation its own deeming of things, Time, Untime, and among those things, Prophecy."

Dr. Brotman looked up from the book of ancient prophecies and said, "The prophecy continues but it tells that before time as we know it ends the 'Time Untime Feathered Serpent of the Sky Heavens' will return and time as measured by man will be no more. In my opinion that prophecy tells us Satan will be released upon the earth, along with the fallen angels, marking the end of time as we know it. What is interesting, as I have studied prophecies of various cultures, they all begin and end the same way."

Gabriella was beginning to understand as the Professor continued the explanation from the ancient Cherokee writing. "They also believe through understanding the zodiac and the movements of the heavenly elements that a shaman, a chosen one that had inherited spiritual powers, could move back and forth in these alternate dimensions from time to untime. These powers of the Cherokee have been studied by many scientists of all persuasions and not one of them can explain these supernatural occurrences which appear to be true. And all religions have similar beliefs of doorways to the supernatural. People want to believe in something beyond this mere human existence."

"Now this is really strange!" Gabriella gasped. "I'm a descendent of the Cherokee Indians from both my father's and mother's ancestry. Don't laugh! I know that's odd with my blond hair and blue eyes but actually it's not that uncommon with the intermarrying and blending of genetics over centuries."

"So that's where your wild spirit comes from." Caleb said teasingly, trying to lighten the atmosphere that had grown heavy with trepidation.

The others chuckled with Caleb but Gabriella was very serious. "The last place I lived with my father was in Cherokee, North Carolina, where he was researching our Indian heritage. We spent endless days exploring the caves of the Great Smokey Mountains. I loved every moment of it, too."

Just as she was starting to connect some dots in their project there were many more unconnected dots appearing. "Do you think there's a connection here, Professor?"

"There are definitely some major parallels in this Indian prophecy when compared to the ancient Hebraic writings." He replied with concern. "Listen to the warnings you were given this morning, Gabi. It seems your worlds of religion, science and the paranormal have come to a crossroads and it can be a very dangerous place for the mind to be dwelling."

The professor looked each team member straight into the eye and firmly stated: "Now you know the complete mission for our project. The missing links in my timeline are exactly when and how the Watchers will return. We know from the prophets they will come as deceiving spirits. But what form? The closer we get to finding the truth the greater the danger. So, if you want to bow out, now's the time. I will totally understand."

The portentous circumstances were causing each team member to reevaluate their involvement but deep down they all knew they had come too far to back out now.

The spitfire attitude common to Gabriella boiled up. She pulled away from Caleb's protective arm, stood straight up and addressed the team. "This is what we've been working for! This is what an archaeologist dreams of! We can't change what might be getting ready to happen but we can be part of discovering ancient truths! That's what we do, team!"

Caleb laughed a nervous sigh of relief. His Gabi Girl had rekindled her spunk. But, he knew now this was no longer just exploring caves and looking for artifacts. This could be a dangerous mission and there were still many unanswered questions. He would stay closer to her than ever before. They all circled around the Professor and swore an oath they were all in this together until the end...literally.

Chapter 8

It had been a very long day for all the team. Finally knowing the purpose of the project was an eye-opening experience.

The team realized Dr. Brotman was levelheaded and did not jump to conclusions on any matter. He always worked from evidence and not assumption. So, as strange as his assertions were, the team had to approach it with the hypothesis that it was reality and their job was to help produce the proof. Although the possibility of it all being true opened a Pandora box of questions.

Gabriella repeated the Professor's words over and over in her mind. She kept coming to the same conclusion. Who would believe fallen angels were soon going to reinvade the earth? Really? The general public might believe in a UFO invasion, vampires, or dead men walking; but an angel invasion wouldn't be on the paranormal agenda! It really didn't matter that the project was top secret, because no one she knew would believe it anyway.

Dr. Brotman interrupted her thoughts. "It's been a long exploration for all of you and I think a rest is needed. Take the weekend to relax and we'll meet again on Monday morning to begin the next phase of the project."

They all agreed their bodies needed to re-energize but they seriously doubted if their minds could rest. Each team member was lost in their individual introspection. It was both frightening and exhilarating to think they had just totally committed to a project that could change life as they knew it. Just thinking about the possibility of the prophecies being true was overwhelming.

Gabriella was deep in her thoughts as she was leaving the Professor's office. "I have a box for you, Gabi." Sandee said. "While you were on exploration our office had a call from someone in the U.S. trying to locate you. He said something about being a former landlord. Naturally, we wouldn't give out your personal information but I affirmed we could get the box delivered to you."

A large box was sitting on the floor next to the exit door. Gabriella looked at the return address and realized immediately it was from the landlord of the last house they rented before her father passed away in North Carolina.

"What in the world? It's been twelve years since I moved from there." Confusion was evident as Gabriella read the return address marked Cherokee, NC. "I sold everything before leaving Cherokee. I only kept my personal items, my father's book collection and a few of his personal items. There was nothing else left."

She did not want to open the mysterious box in a public office so she asked Caleb to take it to the car. It was much too large and heavy for her to carry.

"You don't have any idea what it could be?" He asked as he picked up the box.

"None." She stated emphatically. "But I'm sure anxious to find out!"

Caleb drove Faith and Aaron to their apartments leaving, Gabriella's for last. He carried the box to her apartment and set it on the tile floor next to her couch. He had hoped to be present when the mystery was unveiled but he was sensitive to her every emotion and saw quickly she wanted to be alone.

"Okay, I'm out of here, Gabi Girl. Try to get some rest and if you need me all you gotta do is call." Caleb's words were light but sincere. He gave her a tender hug and whispered in her ear, "I'll always protect you, Gabi." And she knew he would.

As soon as Caleb was out the door, Gabriella cut the tape from the shipping box and opened the lid. On the very top was a letter addressed to her.

Dear Gabriella,

I hope this letter finds you well. Recently I decided to sell the property where you and your father were living when he passed away. After the last renters had vacated the home, I was making final inspections before listing the property. In the closet of one of the bedrooms I noticed some loose boards. When I pulled them up for repair I found this box hidden underneath. It has your father's name engraved in the leather and since it was locked I did not attempt to open it.

The last I had heard you were at the University of Haifa and by contacting them discovered if I shipped it there it would get to you. I hope the contents are something that will bring you joy in remembering your father. He was a very good man.

Sincerely,
Bob Donald

A flood of memories came rushing through her mind when she saw the black box inside. She ran her fingers gently across the engraving on the tarnished brass inlay that read 'Dr. Edward Gabe Russell'.

This was her father's personal journal and he had always kept it locked in this mysterious box. She would sometimes find her father late at night in his study penning their explorations.

As her mind drifted back to their last home, she could still visualize his massive oak desk by the window in his study that looked out on the breath-taking Smokey Mountains. The walls were like Dr. Brotman's office, lined with hundreds of books for research. Every time they moved, each book went with them with the addition of new ones he would discover in their travels. His temporary positions, filling in for professors on sabbatical, allowed him the flexibility of moving from university to university as often as he desired.

The fireplace would have a smoldering fire late at night as he finished his work for the day. The fragrance from his pipe saturated the air while she curled up on the couch in front of the fire and watched him work. She would often see a worried look on his face as he wrote. When he realized she was watching him his expression would quickly transform into a big smile. He would reach out his arms and she would crawl into his lap as he reminded her over and over again of how much she was like her mother.

Gabriella wished she could have known her. She only had vague memories of the beautiful mother that would tuck her into bed and kiss the tip of her nose goodnight, but she remembered vividly her mother whispering, "I love you, princess", before she would leave her room. Most of Gabriella's memories were more the reminiscing of her father as he would tell her stories about their life together.

She stared at the box almost afraid to open it. She never knew why some of her father's documents were locked in the leather box while others were neatly filed and labeled in his desk. She was sure he had his reasons and did not question him. She had looked everywhere for the box when he died and the disappearance had always been a mystery. Now the lost box appeared out of nowhere and was sitting in her living room almost as though an unseen hand had guided its path.

"Hmmm, what are you hiding?" She asked the silent box wanting desperately to plow in but remembering the box was always off limits. "Is it alright if I open you now?" The thought crossed her mind the contents could be articles he was writing for publication and never submitted. As he grew older it seemed he wrote more but published less.

Her father had been in his early forties when Gabriella was born. Her parents had met in college and her mother loved exploring as much as her father. They had spent years of caving and digging on many different continents before Gabriella was conceived. When her mother passed away her father was reminded of how precious life was and how quickly it could fade like a vapor. He was determined to enjoy every moment he possibly could with his beautiful, inquisitive daughter. They were always together as she grew up moving from place to place exploring. Then he, too, suddenly died leaving her totally alone.

The memories were pouring like rain into her mind. She had suppressed them for years because reliving the past was just too painful. For the first time since her father's memorial service she allowed herself to let the tears freely flow. Knowing she was about to hold the pages in her hands that he had poured his life into unearthed emotions within her that she had kept buried through the years.

She went into her bedroom and from the back of her closet pulled out a box that held her father's personal items she would never part with. She had not opened the box since she moved to Haifa. It took everything within her to remove the lid and face the items that linked her to the past. She dug quickly through the box and found a ring of keys, closed the lid and pushed it back into the closet.

With keys in hand she sank into her white, comfortable sofa, positioned the soft sea-blue throw pillows behind her back, and pulled the black box towards her. "Get a grip." She told herself as the tears continued to flow relentlessly.

The locked box seemed to stare at her, waiting to be resurrected. Gabriella held her father's keys in her clenched hand. Each one was a symbol of the precious times they spent together.

She forced herself to open her hand and allow the memories to flood from each key. The large gold key was to his office and it brought back all the memories of their nights of sitting together by the fire and dreaming of far away places. The long, silver key was to his truck. The tarnished key reminded her of loading up their digging gear and heading out every weekend to discover secret wonders hidden in caves. The round, bronze key was to their last home. The reminder of all of the different places they had lived, each one full of love, joy and laughter. The small gold key was to this black box that sat silently waiting and held his mystery writings that she had watched him lock safely away night after night throughout their years together.

The only key missing was the key to her heart that she had given her father for Valentine's Day when she was thirteen years old. She had placed it in a card she made for him that read: "Keep this key with you all the time no matter where you are to remind you that I will always love you." When her father passed away she removed it from his ring of keys and gave it to the funeral director to place next to his heart in the casket.

She forced her self to focus on the small gold key. This key would open his black box and she was convinced it embodied both his journal and the secrets of years of research. They were the only things in his life he would not share with her.

The leather bands on the box were cracked from age and temperature change exposures, but the weathered essence seemed to speak of the written treasures that were hiding within. She ran her hand across the top caressing it as she wished she could just one more time caress her father's face.

As she inserted the key and turned it she heard the click of the lock. She pulled slightly at the lid and it would not open. The years of humidity had rusted the metal hinges on each side and they held tight against her grip as though they were struggling to keep the secrets held in darkness.

She pulled harder and harder until finally the rusty hinges released their strong hold and allowed the lid to reluctantly open.

The first thing she saw was an envelope in her father's handwriting. All that was written on the outside was "To My Princess Gabriella".

Her breath caught and for a moment she could not breathe. He had always called her 'his little princess'. She pulled the letter to her heart and held it tightly against her. The tears cascaded off her long eyelashes, down her cheeks and onto the envelope that she clutched as if it was life itself. She was embracing a piece of her father and she felt his spirit was actually with her. Maybe she was losing it but it did not matter anymore. The feeling of her father's love was washing across her like waves of warm water caressing her skin. The tears were cleansing her very soul that had held her inner pain for so long it had become a part of her to the point she could no longer separate the emptiness from her daily life.

It was one of those moments that you see yourself with crystal clear vision. She realized she never allowed herself to grieve. She always told herself she was not like other women. She was strong and could take care of her self. The loss of both parents hurt so deeply she had built walls around her heart preventing her capability to feel love again. Yes, she cared about people, but she would not allow herself to truly love. At that moment a picture of Caleb's face appeared in her mind. She realized she had feelings deeper for him than she had ever admitted and this time of soul cleansing was clearing her vision.

How strange that just seeing her name written in her father's handwriting could open her eyes to her inner truth and release such vibrant emotions. She thought she would never allow herself to deeply love again and risk the horrible pain of loss. She realized, also, that was an emotion that could not be totally controlled, only camouflaged.

It was at that moment that the phone rang and she knew it was Caleb's nightly call to check on her. She tried to bring her voice into control before answering. Would he hear the raw emotion? She tried to sound light hearted when she said, "Hello, Caleb". But strangely it was the same as the call the night before. There was dead silence. Then a soft masculine voice that sounded very familiar whispered, "Gabriella?"

"Who is this?" she demanded, but there were no other sounds and the line went dead. She felt a rush of fear, anger, and exasperation all at once.

Just as she started to pick up the phone to call Caleb it rang again. "Who is this!!!" She cried.

Caleb's voice came through loud and clear. "Gabriella, what in the world is going on? Are you alright?" She could hear both passion and concern in his voice.

"Oh, I'm so glad it's you," she sighed with relief. Caleb's mind was spinning trying to figure out if it was the day's events, the box that was delivered, or what had caused this emotional turmoil. Gabi never admitted she was glad he called every night but he knew for certain she was on this night.

Gabriella began a rant of inconsistency. "I just had the strangest phone call, and I had another one last night, and I didn't want to tell you because I know how you are...how you worry. I just knew you'd get all upset, come running, and there's no reason for you to, and there is absolutely nothing to worry about...I assure you." He could hear her take a deep breath and she seemed to be fighting back sobs.

This was not Gabriella. She did not babble on like that. She was always in total control and bluntly to the point. With all of the warnings of danger he had to know she was safe. "Please, tell me," his voice was coarse and passionate. "What is it, what's wrong?"

She pulled herself out of the couch and walked to the balcony doors as if changing her position would change the circumstances. Looking out over the bay brought her back to reality. "Really, Caleb, I'm okay." She tried to convince him and herself. "It's just been a rough day with so much to digest."

"I understand." He said with tenderness in his voice. "But what about the phone calls?" She did not reply right away. She simply did not know what to tell him.

Finally she spoke. "I don't know what to tell you. I had a phone call last night and the caller said nothing. Tonight another call and the caller spoke my name but then said nothing else. Both showed 'unknown caller'. I thought last night's call was a wrong number. Now I'm not so sure." She hesitated but then reluctantly admitted. "The voice sounded so familiar."

Caleb's concern for her safety overwhelmed him. "I am coming over there and nothing you say will change my mind. I'm out the door right now." She did not try to argue with him. She finally admitted to herself that she needed him. She would wait to read the letter from her father until he arrived. She needed his emotional strength just to open it.

Chapter 9

Gabriella paced the sea-blue tile floor as she waited for Caleb to arrive. The emotions were running rampant in her mind and body. "Get a grip," she kept repeating to herself. "You can handle this on your own!" But lurking deep in the recesses of her mind she questioned if that was actually the truth. She had tried to convince herself she did not need anyone's help with anything. Now she was not so sure.

After her father died, she kept herself busy with school and exploring, totally ignoring the fact it was normal to need a relationship. When she joined Dr. Brotman's research team she continued to work on her master's degree, allowing her job and study to be the center of her life. Through the years she had become closer and closer to Caleb but she always defined it as friendship. Her fear of being hurt again kept emotional walls of protection around her. Finally admitting her strong feelings for Caleb was the biggest emotional step she had made since losing her father.

Just as she was allowing her true emotions for Caleb to surface the face of the beautiful stranger clouded her mind. Why would she think of him! "What is wrong with me?" She spoke out loud to the empty room. "Why would I be thinking about a man I will never see again?"

She heard the knock at the door and ran to let Caleb in. She felt her heart would beat out of her chest before she could get to him. When she opened the door she fell against him and his arms encircled her with an embrace of protection that penetrated to her very core.

Caleb kissed the top of her curly blond head and whispered in her ear. "It's all right, Gabi, I'm here now."

She did not say a word and just rested in the strength of his arms. He could feel her shaking body begin to relax then he led her to the couch and sat down beside her, holding her hands. "Okay, tell me what's going on and about the box that came today."

She quickly turned her thoughts back to the black box. She and Caleb sat side by side as she explained to him the mystery of the box disappearing and now finding its way to her. She would never have imagined that she would share such a private moment with anyone but she wanted Caleb by her side as she picked up the letter ready to begin.

Little did she know that the envelope she had held to her heart, now stained with tears, was waiting to reveal past secrets. Her fingers shook as she pulled open the sealed envelope. She unfolded the letter that had weathered through the years. She took a deep breath and began to read aloud.

September 12, 1996
My Darling Gabriella,

As I write this letter I am hoping against hope that you never read it. If you are, that means I am no longer with you and you are alone in the world. The very thought breaks my heart.

I have tried to hide from you the events that have taken place since your mother was taken from us. I wanted you to enjoy your childhood and teen years without any apprehensions or fears. I knew there would come a time you would have to know the truth. When this box finds you, you will know it was divine timing.

As you are aware, my beautiful Angelena and I explored for many years before you were born. On our last exploration before your mother passed we were exploring the caves in northern Israel. There we made an unusual discovery that ultimately changed our lives. When we arrived back home we began research on the discovery and also found out that Angelena was expecting a baby...you. We were ecstatic as we had waited so many years and deeply wanted a child. We decided we would work on our research and not travel or explore during her pregnancy.

The further we got into the research the more we realized the magnitude of what we had found. We documented all the evidence and researched corresponding information available from top scientists, geologists and ancient historians, compiling it into a dissertation to prove our hypothesis. You were five years old by the time we had reached our conclusions and preparing to present the discoveries to the scientific world.

I had first thought I would release it for publication as I had done many times before but we decided, since it could be a matter of national security, to meet with top officials in our government for review first. It wasn't easy getting a meeting arranged and I had to present a synopsis of why we had requested such a meeting. When we finally were invited to make our presentation it seemed the national security agents were highly impressed with our findings and said they would contact us for a follow up meeting. We were asked if we had told anyone else of our findings and we assured them we had not. We were informed to not allow the information to be published or to leak the information to any other sources. We left our dissertation with them to pass to higher sources. Of course, I retained my original copy.

We continued to research, gaining additional evidence, and waited to be contacted for a follow-up meeting. We were never contacted. Any attempts we made to contact them were never accepted, so we decided to move forward to publish our findings. I made a call to set up a meeting with a major scientific journal I had published with previously.

On the Saturday morning that your mother was taken from us we were packed and ready for our routine Saturday family outing. Angelena decided to make a quick trip to the store for some picnic items while I was finishing up some work details.

I heard the truck door shut and the engine start and then...an explosion! I could see out my office window our truck going up in flames. No words can describe the anguish and horror that overwhelmed me. You ran to me screaming as if you instantly knew mommy was gone. "NO, NO, DADDY, NO!" At that moment we both went into a deep shock. The next few days were a blur. I arranged for a counselor to help us work through the grief, but it was as though the shock had already blocked it out of your mind and we never talked about it. Afterwards you clung to me in fear I would leave you, too, and we became inseparable.

The tears were falling so hard and so fast Gabriella could no longer read his heart-breaking words. Caleb's heart was breaking for her. In all the years he had known her she never talked about her mother's death. She put up a front that she was tough. She gave the impression she was unaffected by her childhood pain, but he could see clearly how deep the emotional scars were. He took her in his arms for a brief moment wishing he could absorb her pain. He realized there was nothing he could do but let her grieve.

She handed the letter to Caleb and asked him to continue reading. His voice was tender as he resumed where she left off.

The police investigated the accident and their report said it was due to a faulty ignition. I never believed it, and after my own research I came to the conclusion that someone wanted us out of the picture. It didn't matter if you, my darling princess, would have been with us. Had your mother not broken our normal routine we would have all been in the vehicle, as we always were on Saturday morning. Someone had been watching us, I am sure of it.

It was then I decided to leave my permanent position and began taking temporary professors positions. It was important to me to constantly be moving and keep my research project secret.

There were times that I felt we were being followed. And you may remember the time our apartment in Utah was broken into and things turned upside down but nothing was taken. Even my office at the university had been broken into. I always kept my research well hidden...just in case.

No one from the government contacted me again but I believe they were constantly watching. My greatest concern was for you and I wanted to make sure you never knew there was potential danger. For that reason I never published my work. For years I wouldn't even talk to anyone about it. I trusted no one.

I took the money from your mother's life insurance policy and made some major stock investments that would be put in a trust fund for you. In the event something happened to me I wanted to make sure you would not be financially limited. If you are reading this letter you know I made a good decision.

In this box you will find my research papers and documentation that I spent years compiling. I did not want you to even know of the existence of this information until you were old enough to understand. As you read through it you will understand the magnitude of what is now in your hands. I have made my personal notes to you as you journey through the writings of the explorations your mother and I took and, further, the research I continued after losing her. It also could be dangerous if certain people realize it wasn't lost with my passing and discover you have it in your possession.

I can almost hear your voice asking why I didn't tell you all of this while I was still with you. But as I write this letter you are only a young teenager and I would not put the burden of something so profound on your innocent shoulders.

I can visualize your big blue eyes filled with tears as you read this. I know you well, my little princess, and I know the tender heart you have that you try constantly to cover with an attitude of independence. No matter what happens I will always be watching over you with undying love. My greatest desire for you in life is that you find someone that is your soul mate as your mother was mine. The greatest joy in life is giving love and truly being loved. I regret that I will not be able to walk you down the aisle when you give your life and your heart to that special man.

I had hoped to someday present this research to people that could use it wisely. Now it is in your hands and you will determine what is done with my discoveries. I admonish you to start at the beginning and do not jump to the end. Entry by entry the truth will be revealed to you. Use this information with great wisdom. It will open to you great spiritual truths and can change how the world views the past, the present and the future.

You have always been the best part of me and I love you with all my heart,
Dad

Caleb's voice had become coarser as he read through the remainder of the letter. He did not have to look at Gabriella to know the effect this was having on her. When he finished the letter he laid it back in her hands and gently put his arms around her. She laid her head on his shoulder and allowed the sobs to flow from her shaking body. She did not care anymore if expressing her emotions made her look weak. She hurt through and through and she had to release it from her throbbing soul.

Caleb pulled her closer and tightened his hold. He could not imagine what it was like growing up without a mother and then losing her father so young. The letter gave him a glimpse into the relationship she and her father experienced and he now understood why it was so hard for her to get close to anyone. The kind of hurt she had known, and then carried all alone, was more than any one person should have to endure. He vowed to

Chapter 10

Caleb held Gabriella in his arms all through the night. She would continually make sounds of whimpering that were barely audible. He knew, even though she slept, her subconscious was emerged in grief from the past. He watched her with waves of emotion flooding over him, like the pounding surf before a great storm.

He could not sleep either. He was still mentally trying to piece together the events of the previous day. It just did not make sense they could be connected; and yet there seemed to be a sinister, unifying thread that ran from one foreboding event to the other. He looked down on the beautiful woman nestled against his chest that had finally fallen into a deep sleep and he knew without a doubt he would do anything to protect her.

The light of morning was filtering into the room when the sound of thunder awakened Gabriella. A storm was moving inland from out to sea and the winds were starting to gust through the open balcony door. The white linen curtains swayed and caught in the breezes in shapes and motions that seemed like mystical spirits dancing to the rhythm of the rain that had started to fall. The darkness of the stormy morning matched the portending thoughts in Gabriella's mind.

She began to stir and realized she was still in Caleb's arms. She turned her face upwards to look full in his eyes.

"Morning, Gabi." He said softly.

"You didn't sleep at all last night, did you?" Her voice was filled with concern as she sat upright.

Caleb stood up to stretch. "Had a lot on my mind, I guess. I'm worried about you, Gabi. Can't help but wonder how you're going to emotionally handle going through your father's work."

The thought of her father instantly brought back the pain and realization of the task ahead. She truly wanted to know what he and her mother had discovered. But she knew there were more personal notes awaiting her and the emotional pain of his words was cutting deep into her heart. She did not know how to separate the two.

The winds outside were blowing with a ferocity that matched the gloomy reality of the previous day. She got up and walked to the window to hide the tears forming again in her eyes. As hard as she tried, she just could not hold them in.

Caleb pulled the French doors closed to block the winds, somehow feeling it would help to stop the turmoil blowing through her soul. Caleb moved towards her from behind and wrapped his arms around her waist as she looked out the window. "We will get through this, Gabriella, and we will do it together." She knew without his strength she could never face the journey ahead.

Gabriella brewed coffee while Caleb brought the box to her dining table to begin their journey through her father's years of exploration and research. He sat down at the white wicker table with his oversize mug filled with hot, caramel coffee and cleared a space to work. The rain was picking up intensity and beating on the large, scenic view window. He could see the boats of the Marina bobbing up and down in the water as the waves washed over the walkways. No boats were venturing in or out, when normally on a Saturday morning the marina was very busy.

He tried to make light conversation to ease her concerns. "A few brave mariners are trying to tie down their boats. The waves are fierce. Pretty sure they're fighting a loosing battle."

"I'm sure glad we don't have to be out in this weather and thank you for staying with me last night, Caleb." Gabriella said as she brought her coffee to the table to join him.

He knew it was difficult for her to admit she needed him so he teased her to make her feel more comfortable. "Yeah, it's really hard to look at you first thing in the morning. But I made the sacrifice, hard as it was."

She ran her hand through his thick, sun streaked hair and joked back, "You don't look so good yourself, big guy." Caleb got up from the table and gave her a playful hug then brought her father's black box to the table. He pulled her chair closer to his as she sat down. On this day they would begin a journey both into the past and into the future. What they were about to discover was beyond anything they could have imagined.

Gabriella tried to pull open the top of the box that again held tight. It seemed the rusty hinges were warning her once again to keep the secrets hidden.

"It's stuck, Caleb," she said in frustration. She pulled again and it would not open.

Caleb gently moved her hands out of the way for his hands to take control. "Let me try," he said in a voice to sooth her.

The weathered lid could not hold against his strength and with a strong jerk the lid surrendered. Gabriella gently removed her father's journal from its twelve-year-old grave and held it to her heart fighting back the tears.

"This is it, Caleb. This is the journal I would see him writing in late at night. What's in this book may have cost my parent's lives and now we are going to know what it was." She clutched it in her arms as if it was the most valuable treasure on earth. In the weeks to come, she would find out just how valuable it was.

Caleb put his arm around her shoulder and pulled her to him. "I know this is painful but I'm with you every step of the way. One step at a time, Gabi Girl."

"Do you realize I'm holding in my hands the research my father hid from me to keep me safe? Secrets so important that even the government didn't want them known?" Gabriella would not even allow her mind to speculate on what this box would promulgate.

"You can do this, Gabi." Caleb encouraged her and it gave her the strength to pull the cover of his journal open.

The leather binding was worn from her father's constant opening and closing as he added and reviewed his writings. As her fingers touched the edges to begin her journey into the past she could visualize him opening the book with his strong hands that were rough and calloused from years of exploration. The hands that were also tender and loving that would often cup her face as he kissed her forehead and reminded her how much she was cherished.

She looked at Caleb and saw both affection and concern in his eyes. He winked at her and she knew it was time to begin. Immediately upon opening the journal cover she saw another handwritten note addressed to her.

Gabriella,

I am writing these personal notes on the assumption that something has happened to me and you are now in possession of my journal and research papers. You are about to begin a journey that will reveal information extremely vital to the future of both our nation and our planet...and to you personally.

I have often wondered if there are others that may have discovered these truths (or parts of them) and have also been silenced. I am convinced there are life-altering changes coming to the world. I don't know at what time in the future you will read this. It may be these truths are already being revealed. Perhaps information is already surfacing from others with the same discoveries. If so, you will immediately make the connection once you understand.

The journey begins here and I pray the Lord of Spirits guides you.

I love you more than words can say.
Dad

Gabriella looked at Caleb and they were both anxious to begin studying his work but apprehensive on what would be revealed.

"My father referred to the 'Lord of Spirits' several times toward the end of his life but I was never sure what he meant. We were never a religious family but being part Cherokee I studied their spirit world beliefs. The natives believe there are shamans who are guided by spirits of what they call the Upper World. I figured Dad had picked up on some of the Cherokee spiritual clichés."

She paused for a moment trying to reason it out. "It's a phrase I've heard Dr. Brotman use, too. Even the Prophet asked this spirit to protect me. Surely, we'll find some answers in here somewhere." Gabriella was trying to convince herself more than Caleb.

He did not respond immediately. He got up from the table to stretch his long legs and walked to the French doors. The rain was pounding harder against the outside balcony. Finally he spoke. "I wish I had an answer for you, Gabi. As you know my family wasn't religious either. But I have to admit all of the spirit stuff makes a person wonder. If so many people believe it, they're all either terribly confused or understand something we don't know."

Gabriella leaned back in her white wicker chair. "I really want to know, Caleb. I've studied this for years and it just gets more complicated. There are so many different beliefs and many of them are pretty convincing. But nothing can offer any proof. I'm a scientist and I have to prove it to believe it. Do you think my father found something he really believed and thought I was too young to understand? "

Caleb refilled their coffee cups and sat back down next to her at the table. "There's only one way to find out."

They moved their chairs even closer together to begin reading the first pages of her father's journal. The winds from the storm continued to howl outside and the rain was beating even harder on the window. As the force of the storm intensified so did the ominous feelings the couple was trying to suppress.

Underneath the journal were mounds of his research papers. Recalling how her father structured his research, the journal would probably first give them an overview and then they would have to read through the documentation he had found to support his conclusions. They knew this was not going to be just a weekend venture but days and days of intense concentration. They also knew they were just getting into the heat of the project that would demand most of their attention. Gabriella was already feeling torn by the desire to devote her time to both projects. So much for relaxing their minds!

Gabriella held the note to her heart again for a brief moment before placing it back in the front of his journal where it had lain for years. Just holding it gave her the feeling she could reach somewhere into the spirit world and let her father know she was continuing this odyssey he had left behind. She began to read out loud.

The Personal Journal of Edward Gabe Russell

May 8, 1982

I am beginning a new journal that will relate to our exploration of Mt. Hermon.

I had decided to take a sabbatical from teaching and explore caves in the Middle East which seems to be the current hot spot of archaeology. Angelena and I have spent a year exploring the area and especially the caves of Mt. Hermon. This beautiful mountain range borders Syria on the east and Lebanon to the north. The southern slopes extend to the Israeli occupied border of the Golan Heights. 'Hermon' means the 'chief of the mountains' and is five miles wide and twenty miles long. The tallest peak is 9,166 feet above the Mediterranean Sea and the view is spectacular from the highest point we could reach. The Jordan River springs from the southern slopes and flows through Israel to the Dead Sea. The mountain range has the aura of being transcendent and captures the very imagination of events that have occurred here throughout the millenniums. Angelena and I both are captured in our thoughts regarding the myths and legends of this mysterious mountain.

We have leased a wooden cottage for this year near the Rimonim Hermon Village in the North Golan. We have breathtaking views of the mountain terraces to our front and a spectacular view from our back where the highest point of Mt. Hermon looms and seems to beckon us to come and explore her hidden secrets. The quaint cottage is close to the Mt. Hermon Ski Resort, the only ski resort in Israel. We enjoyed a few days of relaxation during the winter months on the slopes.

It has been a magical trip in many ways. Just spending time with my dear wife is always an adventure and together we have explored the grandiose caves and caverns of this magnificent mountain range that is full of both fact and myth. The two have been so interwoven it is hard to discern where facts die and fiction is birthed. The name 'Hermon' is also referred to as the "forbidden place" which adds to the mystique and essence as we pass through its underground world.

This trip has not been for our personal enjoyment, although we certainly have enjoyed it, but an attempt to separate through archaeological proof what secrets this mountain may hold from ancient times and may still lay waiting to be discovered.

Mt. Hermon was the central area of pagan worship in ancient days. It is a mountain of many altars for the worship of numerous mythical gods. The altars, used thousands of years ago, have been documented by explorers for centuries.

As I have traveled and explored many continents through the years it has become obvious to me that religion was a major part of every culture and had many similarities even though they were not in any way geographically connected. Since Mt. Hermon is situated in the area known as the cradle of the world and also is known for its hundreds of altars of pagan worship, I thought this mountain should be the beginning of this new research project. There must be some reason it has been crowned with the name "Gateway of the Angels".

Archaeologists have a difficult time determining the age of most of the worship structures. To further confuse the age, the Romans built altars to their gods over the original altars when they ruled Israel at the turn of the Common Era. We plan to do some research of our own concerning the dating.

In our months here we have explored many of the mountain caves.. We wanted to see firsthand what had been documented by other archaeologists. We were in awe when we ascended the mountain to the ruined temple of Baal, which was constructed of Herodian masonry dating to approximately 200 BCE.

What impacted us greatly was the low place near the northwest corner of the temple of Baal. There we saw excavations that had uncovered huge mounds of ash and burnt bone that had been dumped there as a refuse from sacrifices. There were other altars throughout the mountain with similar sacrificial discoveries dating back thousands of years.

It is hard for one to imagine the sacrificing of human beings, especially innocent babies, but it was very much a part of the pagan rituals. We have personally found evidence of many of the same rituals in other parts of the world. It is well known by archaeologists that human sacrifice was practiced on all continents. It's often gone through my mind that America is doing the same thing under a different guise called abortion. Innocent babies are sacrificed everyday to the god of self.

(On a personal note: It's especially hard for me to imagine aborting a child. Angelena and I have desired children through our sixteen years of marriage and the heartbreak it has been for her not to conceive.. Her heart's desire is to be a mother and words cannot express the longing I have to hold a child our love would create. I guess it just wasn't meant to be.)

Gabriella stopped reading and stared closer at the journal page. "Caleb, do you see that?" She pointed to a stain in the middle of her father's last entry. "That's a tear stain! I'm sure of it! I can almost see tears filling his eyes, cascading across his cheek and splattering onto his journal as he wrote those sad words."

A single tear escaped from Gabriella's eyes, cascaded across her cheek and fell on the very spot stained with the tears of her father. "At least we know their heart's desire eventually came in the form of me." She smiled remembering the many times her father told her she was the joy of his life.

"Enough down memory lane." Gabriella said reluctantly turning her attention back to the journal.

The strange thing about the altars of worship on Mt. Hermon is they are built around the mountain and circle higher and higher to the summit. They form a pattern that points to a sacred building of hewn blocks of stone on the summit known as Qasr Antar. It was the highest temple of the ancient world sitting at over 2800 feet above sea level. It was first documented in 1869 by the explorer Sir Charles Warren. He described the temple as a rectangular building sitting on an oval, stone plateau without a roof. He brought back from his discovery a limestone stele with an ancient inscription that translated to read, "according to the command of the greatest and Holy God, those who take an oath proceed from here."

Gabriella stopped reading and looked at Caleb with eyes wide open. "Did you catch that, Caleb?" She spoke with a voice of almost unbelief. It was more of a statement than a question and he did not comment. She looked straight at Caleb with piercing eyes and could tell his thoughts had gone exactly as hers had.

"This is eerily similar to the Omega Watchers Project!" She got up and walked to the window and looked to the northeast where on a clear day she could see the highest point of Mt. Hermon from her balcony. She tried to imagine her mother and father exploring together the caves of a mountain that was often in her view. She knew her parents had explored in Israel and her father often talked about the beauty and the ancient findings. She began to realize he planted in her at an early age a desire to explore those secret places in this ancient land and discover it for her self. When she was offered the scholarship at Haifa University she did not hesitate.

The rain was starting to slow now and the winds were calming. She turned back to Caleb who was watching her and waiting until she was ready to continue. He knew her contemplative looks and was not going to interrupt her personal thoughts.

"Yes, I do see some strange parallels in your father's entries and the project." He observed trying to bring her thoughts back to the journal. "But there may be nothing at all beyond mere coincidence. Ready to keep going?"

She nodded and turned the journal towards Caleb. "Will you read now?" He began reading with a strong, certain voice without any defining emotions.

May 9, 1982

An explorer's dream is to find what no man before has found and new caves are being discovered every day here in Israel. There are already over a thousand known caves and that is just the beginning. We think of caves being created by the natural formations of the earth. But many caves were created by man carving out spaces for quarries, living quarters, burial sites, places of worship and even hiding places. It is in these places we often discover links from our present generation to civilizations that lived millennia ago. The exploration possibilities are endless!

Caves that I have explored throughout my life have had many myths and fantasies. But the legends of the caves of Mt. Hermon all dealt with pagan worship and pagan gods. It was all the things that would seem to connect to the spirit world and the paranormal.

There is an archaeological site on the southern terrace of Mt. Hermon on the Golan Heights known as Banias. This is in Caeserea Phillippi and is the location of the Cave of Pan. An enormous statue stands at the entrance, symbolic of him being the "gateway" to the supernatural world. Some legends believed the god Pan was born in this cave and he was the Guardian of the Threshold. He was believed to be the conductor of the souls of the dead and allowed them to go back and forth from the natural world to the spiritual world. He was half god and half human and stirred up "pan-ic" from which the word derives. His worship is always associated with sexuality which was very much a part of all pagan religions.

Gabriella interrupted Caleb's reading. "This is just weird!" She said. "Dr. Brotman talked about Mt. Hermon being the gateway to the supernatural world. Now my father says the same thing! Even that explorer,

Warren, dad wrote about found an ancient message on the mountain that said so. Do you believe this, Caleb?" She watched his eyes for signs of doubt.

"Maybe it's just part of the legends that have evolved from the ancient religions." He answered her. "May not be a shred of reality connected to any of it."

She thought a minute and shrugged her shoulders displaying her confusion. "Keep reading. I've got to know if my father really believed this or was just repeating myths."

Caleb continued to read hoping for a revelation into her father's research:

The mystical world of the gods would allure most to desire to understand if they were real or the fabrication of human minds that felt the need for something more powerful than themselves. I have found myself needing an answer to that very question. The more I explore and discover, the more confused I become on what is real and what is not. This should not be the state of mind for a scientist who builds on mere fact and nothing more. But I must know if there is such a thing as a spirit world or another dimension of time and space that we cannot see.

Caleb thought it ironic these had been her father's next words. It was as if he was with them trying to answer their questions. He was sure Gabriella felt the same way as he continued:

Today we entered a cave in the southern part of the mountain range near the Jordan River. We climbed over the fallen rocks and kept going deeper. We both felt an unseen force was pulling us inward and our curiosity was the engine driving us. We squeezed through small openings and pushed deeper into the cave. We had found an area of stalactites and stalagmites that hung from the limestone bedrock that were up to fifteen feet long. The beauty was breath taking! We thought we had met a dead end when we noticed a small opening behind one of the stalactites. We were barely able to squeeze through. It was cold and damp as we surveyed the area around us. Trickles of water were falling through a crack in the limestone. The constant dripping became a hypnotizing, melodic background to what we were about to discover.

Our lights revealed cave drawings that appeared to be from the Paleolithic Age which was before the great flood. It was difficult to tell how the drawings had been etched. It didn't appear to be with the stone tools normally used during the period. Nor was it a paint that would have been derived from berries, soot or charcoal. It appeared to have a precision cut similar to a laser etching. But that would have been impossible!

A series of pictures were scattered throughout the cave walls that seemed to tell a story. There were drawings of flying people but looking closer appeared more like angels. Some of the drawings were similar to what we would think of as UFOs and one in particular looked like a spaceship (some might say a flying saucer) that was sitting on top of Mt. Hermon at the place of the altar. This circular craft carried the angelic creature.

There were many drawings that appeared to be in a heavenly setting. The discs were ascending and descending into the clouds. The flying objects would be situated in precise areas in the heavenly elements as if it was a gateway or entry point. Some of the vehicles had both the angelic looking creatures and humans flying together.

How could someone thousands of years ago have any idea what a spaceship would look like and have a living being inside it flying through the universe? Was someone trying to reveal secrets of the mountaintop and connect them with the shrines of worship? IF there were visitations from another dimension or from alien beings, naturally humans would worship them as gods. And it would make sense the main altar would be at the place they ascended and descended.

It all made perfect mythical sense but made no common sense. The science world would laugh at such a hypothesis. But all scientific quests begin with gathering as much information as possible that will support your hypothesis, then test the hypothesis and come to a conclusion. I knew we were at the beginning of a long journey in the proof of paranormal reality.

We also found, in the midst of the cave drawings, ancient writing. It was in a language I had not seen previously in explorations but I am totally aware of my limitations in that area. Angelena took close pictures of the writings and all of the cave drawings for future research. We believe we have found evidence that will only grow in truth as we have time to do further research.

We gathered our equipment to begin our retraction from the cave, mapping each step. We realized we had gone deeper than we planned and there were strange feelings associated with the area neither of us could explain, but both of us felt.

Angelena who usually chattered all the way out of the caves was very silent. I knew she was excited about the cave drawings and the story they seem to tell but she didn't say a word until we got to the mouth of the cave and the light of day reappeared. Her words echoed all through the cave as she turned towards the darkness and yelled back in, "I'll be back!" The echoes vibrated over and over and over.

Caleb paused to watch Gabriella's reaction. He could see a far away look in her eyes as if she was physically with them in the cave.

"Do you think they were feeling what we felt in the lava cave in the desert?" She was thinking out loud and not expecting an answer.

"It seems to me Dad believes the cave drawings they found are proof space travel existed in ancient times. Is that what you're getting from this, Caleb?"

"Sure seems like it. It would make sense the government wouldn't want this sort of information known to the public if your parents found any type of hard proof, although it's pretty hard for me to believe they could have.'

"But what explanation could there be?" She pondered. "Many times as my father and I explored we would find strange cave drawings that were hard to explain. Things like men flying, space crafts, alien looking creatures, really weird stuff that caught my imagination as a child. I've always wondered if maybe we were put on this planet by another civilization as kind of a test tube existence. I would fantasize they were watching us."

"Or," Caleb interjected, "it was man's wild imagination built on ancient myths and legends. If thousands of years ago they believed in superhuman fallen angels, among other crazy god myths, then man's imagination could create all kinds of possibilities."

She nodded her head. "I'm sure you're right."

June 10, 1982

As I am sitting in our mountain cottage reminiscing of the events of this exhilarating sabbatical, I feel like I am on the verge of beginning to understand that there is more than just life here on this earth. I am now of the opinion that there is some type of intelligence beyond our own. It is really unimaginable that in the vast expanses of the universe that we are the only intelligent beings.

My beautiful Angelena is sleeping.. I love to watch her beautiful face in rest and her long, golden hair that falls across the pillow. I love my work but she is my reason to live.

Caleb looked up at Gabriella. He knew exactly how her father felt.

Chapter 11

Caleb had ended the last sentence in a whisper. So many times he wanted to tell Gabriella how he felt about her but the time was never right. He wanted to now but knew the time still was not right. The tears were still flowing from her beautiful blue eyes and he could feel tears of compassion filling his eyes, too.

He remembered the first time he saw her. It was the first day of Ancient History 101, the fall they began classes at the university. She came through the classroom door with Faith and every guy in the room turned to look at Gabriella. She was totally unaware and uncaring of the male attention. That was what initially intrigued him about her. She was chattering away describing to Faith her last exploration. When Caleb heard the word "exploration" she had his full attention. Could a woman so enchanting also be interested in exploring, which was his passion? Quickly he was captured by her bubbling personality, blue eyes and long, curly blonde hair that framed her beautiful face.

She and Faith sat down across from Caleb and Aaron. Gabriella hardly took a breath in between her sentences directed to Faith and was totally unaware that Caleb was listening. This was when he first nicknamed her 'Gabby Girl'. When Dr. Brotman entered the room and greeted the class Caleb struggled to focus his attention to the front of the room. Never had a woman made such an impression on him. But Gabriella just glanced at him, smiled and turned to face the Professor. He realized he had not caught her attention whatsoever. For Caleb, it was love at first sight.

At the end of the first class session Dr. Brotman instructed them to divide into teams of four. The teams would be working together on various research projects during the semester. Immediately after class Caleb turned to Gabriella and Faith and introduced himself and Aaron. This was his chance to meet her and he suggested immediately they team up.

They not only became a team for the semester but were still together as a research team twelve years later. And with every passing year Caleb fell deeper in love with Gabriella. With every passing year he felt the frustration of her being so involved in her work and studies she took no time for a relationship. He had tried to date other women but no one compared to Gabriella. He knew there was no other man in her life. She was married to her research.

His thoughts came back to the present when she spoke. "My father loved my mother so much, Caleb. I can't even imagine that kind of love. I've never even been in love and just hearing his words makes me realize how much I've missed."

He wanted to take her in his arms and tell her then and there that he loved her just as her father loved her mother and he would protect her from any danger that would ever find its way near her.

Instead he reached over and took her hand feeling her fingers wrap tightly into his. For several minutes neither said a word. Caleb looked toward the balcony and saw the rain had finally stopped. Slivers of sunlight were reflecting on the bay waters that were beginning to calm. The clouds were breaking and soon the sun would be shining through the windows dispelling the shadows.

Caleb thought to himself. "If only my love could shine through like the sunlight and dispel the dark memories haunting Gabriella."

Gabriella was thinking about how truly in love her parents were and how short their time together. She felt cheated her mother and father both had been taken from her and she was now anxious to find out what they discovered that was so threatening that it may have cost their lives.

Determination began to rise up from within her. She had allowed the pain to release through hours of tears and felt there were no more tears to cry. In a few hours she liberated years of pent up emotions. In the midst of the anguish she realized her life could not remain an island.

She leaned towards Caleb and kissed his cheek as she got up from the table. She had often done this teasingly through the years but Caleb knew this was different. He would not press it but just let it flow naturally. He had decided long ago he would wait forever for her love.

She walked to the balcony door taking a moment to clear her mind. "The storm is over. How about we have brunch on the balcony and get some fresh air? I think it'd do us both good." Gabriella opened the French doors to allow the cool sea breezes to filtrate the room.

Caleb got up and stretched. "Excellent idea!"

After a short lunch break Gabriella went back inside, retrieved her father's journal and proceeded back to the balcony to rejoin Caleb. She felt she could deal with the somberness much better now that the storm had passed. There was something about the feeling of freshness and new hope that came after a late summer storm. Everything appeared brighter.

She took a few moments to watch the sun sparkle across the waves that were now gently splashing against the marina. The raging waters had settled and the mariners were preparing their boats for Saturday afternoon excursions.

"Caleb," she whispered. "Let's get on one of those boats and sail away and never look back." He knew she was not serious but he would do it in a heartbeat and the fact she would even think of them sailing away together made his heart skip a beat.

"Which one do you want, Gabi Girl?" he replied. "All you have to do is say the word." She allowed her eyes to stare into his without darting away as they normally did in moments of closeness. Caleb knew her wall of emotional protection was coming down and he would do all he could to make sure it completely collapsed, never to be rebuilt.

"If only..." She replied allowing her thoughts to drift towards the sea. Then she picked up the journal and turned to where they left off and started to read.

July 1, 1982

We are now home in Oklahoma and trying to settle back into a normal life after having been on sabbatical for a year. My mind is flooded with all of the directions I want to pursue in my quest of understanding the ancient gods. Where did they come from? Did man create idols to worship out of their need for something superior or was it in honor of 'gods' (perhaps extraterrestrial beings) that had visited earth and displayed great powers?

What is strange to me is the fact that cultures all over the world have some sort of god, and as you piece their beliefs together you find they really aren't that different at all. Sure they have different names and they take on indigenous characteristics but there seems to be a binding thread to all religions that tie them to the same umbilical cord of creation.

As I read the accounts of ancient gods I compare what is common to all cultures. All of the gods came from the heavens, were supernaturally strong, had the ability to fly and had mystical powers. And there are always the human 'priests', 'shaman' or spiritual leaders who the gods use as a conduit to communicate their messages to mankind.

As I am reading of the myriads of gods, I replace a god's name with "alien being" and it makes perfect sense that these ancient cultures were worshipping what they thought were gods of the heavens. What is troubling to me is the conflict of the worship of these gods. Many required great sacrifices of torture and even human sacrifice, while other gods seem to be loving and wanted sacrifices that had no evil intent.

This leads me to believe there is more than one group of intergalactic beings competing for the worship of humans and some of these heavenly beings are evil and some are good. I have just written my first hypothesis on the subject as I am researching for my next publication, "Dissertation of the Gods".

Gabriella checked the black box for his dissertation notes and found it on top of the research articles. She opened it to the first page.

July 1, 1982
Hypothesis I

Synopsis of research to date:

It would appear by all evidences that gods truly exist in the form of astral beings (both good and evil) and have been appearing to mankind since the very beginning of human existence. It is even possible that human beings were placed on this earth by alien beings, but for what purposes I do not know yet. I believe these celestial, supernatural beings have constantly visited the earth and man has worshipped them as gods. It appears they may have made themselves visible to a greater mass of the populous in ancient times but are only visible to select individuals today who possess an extrasensory conduit enabling them to connect or communicate with these alien beings.

Also, from my research thus far, it seems since WWII there are increasingly greater numbers of people having encounters with alien beings. There must be a reason for these exponential sightings and why they are so quickly covered up or explained away with irrational reasoning.

To further my study I plan to locate individuals who have had supernatural alien encounters and are willing to share their experiences with me so I can endeavor to formulate some type of scientific conclusion to the matter. My greatest hope is to have a personal encounter with the 'gods' so I will have firsthand knowledge upon which to base my conclusions.

Gabriella stopped reading to let this sink in. "Caleb, he never talked to me about actually believing in UFOs or anything extraterrestrial. This is all totally new to me! How could he have done this research and never told me? When we were exploring caves we would find ancient altars, cave drawings and artifacts that probably connected to his research but he didn't indicate to me in any way what he was doing. Did he keep all of this a secret to protect me? You would think he could've told me something!"

Caleb knew she was venting her frustration that was continually building. He tried to comfort her. "I'm sure he knew if he told you anything at all you wouldn't give up until you knew everything."

Gabriella instantly realized the truth of his words. She also realized how well he knew her. "That is exactly what I would have done and my father knew it. He was convinced the less I knew the safer I was. I sure wish he'd lived to tell me this himself so we could have explored it together. I feel so cheated yet again!"

"He's telling you now, Gabi." Caleb spoke with a caressing tone. "And just maybe now is when you need to know."

"You're right," she admitted again. Part of her wanted desperately to know and part of her wanted to get on one of those boats at the marina, sail away and never look back.

She forced herself to go back to her father's journal and continue reading. She laid his dissertation notes to the side to read at a later time.

July 16, 1982

So my journey into the supernatural world to prove "gods" are really intergalactic beings begins in what I feel is the most logical place...right here in America among the Indian cultures who had their own gods before the white man came and brought his god.

I remember my grandmother telling me that I was a descendent of the Cherokee Indians and strangely enough, Angelena also had some Cherokee blood. This was not too surprising since both of us were born and raised in

Oklahoma where a large number of the Cherokee stayed after their 'trail of tears' forced resettlement by the U.S. Government.

My grandmother passed to me the stories that had been passed to her from her grandmother. The thing that stands out to me as I recall those stories is that the Cherokee were very different from the other Native Indian tribes and she made sure I knew it.

None of the stereotypical images of American Indians apply to the Cherokee. The Cherokee never lived in teepees, never hunted buffalo, and never used smoke signals. They were not savages as many of the Native American tribes were. Many Cherokee today do not have physical features expected of American Indians. Some are blonde, blue-eyed and fair-skinned in large part because of early inter-marrying with Scottish, Irish and German miners that migrated to the southeast. This would explain why my Angelena could be fair skinned and still be Cherokee descent.

My grandmother strongly believed in an ancient Cherokee legend of their ancestors coming from across the great waters from the land of the great sea. The legend says they were part of a great tribe taken captive by an enemy nation. A group of them were able to escape and found passageway to a new country where they eventually settled in what is now known as Georgia, Tennessee and North Carolina.

That is how they explained being different from America's native Indians. The legend says a Great White Spirit from the sky led them to the new land for a place of safety. They strongly believed in spirit guides sent from the heavens. Legends have passed down through the generations that Cherokee are actually of Middle Eastern descent..

The Cherokee believe a spirit of "Fire" was appointed by the sun and the moon to take care of mankind. It was considered as being intermediate to the sun god, and the smoke is symbolized as the messenger of the fire that would make known the petitions of the people to the sun god. The Cherokees believed the morning star was once a wicked priest who killed people by witchcraft. When the Indians planned to kill him, he took all his shining crystals and flew away to the sky where he appeared as the morning star ever after.

As I began to study the religious beliefs of my ancestors, I found that same "god/alien" thread that ran through the other religions across the world. The 'beings' appear to be extraterrestrials coming down from the skies. The 'fire' was a good alien messenger. And an evil alien taking his "shining crystals" and flying away to the sky. We see again the struggle of good and evil that seems to continually appear in the stories of the gods.

The Cherokee (as do most religions) believed in an after life and those who had behaved in a 'good' manner went to a place that was light and pleasant. Those who had behaved poorly would be sent to a bad place and face torture.

It is amazing how the same stories are repeated in different ways through each religious culture, but always with the same story of sky beings (both good and evil) coming down and going back into the heavens. There are also many stories about how the sky gods taught men the medicinal purposes of plants, the use of metals for weapons, how to converse with the spirit world, enchantments, potions and the list of imparted knowledge goes on.

The one thing I discovered in my Cherokee studies was the power of the shaman. I remember my grandmother using this word to describe her grandmother. A shaman is a person, quite often a female, with Cherokee blood that has been chosen to inherit the ability to have supernatural spirit world connections. They connect with spirits while in a sleep like trance. During this sleep-trance they have the capability of moving into another dimension where time does not exist and where they can communicate with the higher beings gaining knowledge, wisdom and supernatural understanding.

It was in one of those sleep-trances my ancestral grandmother died. The folklore was she became one with the spirits and chose not to return.

It seems to me rational reasoning would conclude that certain people have been somehow genetically wired to be able to communicate with the god/aliens. And this would be how they would pass their information as "gods" to those that have been "chosen", who then would pass knowledge to the people of their tribe. The Cherokee call this shaman experience "time, untime".

When Gabriella read those words she dropped the book to the floor and her face went stark white. She was not able to utter a word. Caleb caught his breath and had to struggle to keep his composure. They looked at each other without saying a word.

With a quivering voice she spoke. "In just two days a triangle has formed connecting the Prophet, The Omega Watcher Project and my father's research."

Caleb did not say it out loud but racing through his mind was the thought. "And the common denominator of all of it was Gabriella."

Gabriella fell into Caleb's arms and starting sobbing uncontrollably. "It's like my father is in this room trying to explain to me what the Prophet was saying! And the Professor knew about the Cherokee Prophecy of Time, Untime. If I take this literally then it means I could have some type of supernatural connection with another world! You would think I would know if there was something really weird like that happening. And I wasn't even born when my father was writing this so there was no way he could know this would happen to me. I am so confused and, Caleb, this really scares me. I am an archaeologist not some kind of soothsayer! I look into the world of the past, not the future!"

Caleb had no words with which to console her. He was as confused as she was and his concern kept deepening with each new chapter from the journal. He knew his physical strength and his ability to protect her in the natural world but he had no defense against something he could not see or touch. For the first time he feared for her safety in a way he could not control.

"There has to be more to this." He tried to convince Gabriella. "Perhaps the next chapters will show us that your father found out he was totally wrong in his research and this shaman thing is just a myth." But he knew in his heart something very dangerous was emerging.

"But the thought of aliens being the gods of this earth is just as strange as Dr. Brotman's theory that fallen angels had become earth gods. These are two polar opposite opinions and yet my father and the professor both seem convinced they're correct." Gabriella was speaking more to herself and just allowing Caleb to hear.

Caleb realized their research for Dr. Brotman's project just took on a deeper meaning. He decided he would be doing some studying of his own on the spirit world. For Gabriella's safety he had to understand what he might be battling.

Gabriella was very aware that Caleb was not giving his usual comforting words of protection. He took her into his arms and held her tightly. She knew the messages from the journal had struck deep into his soul as it had hers. There was no way to explain the connections of the Time Untime, except that it must be real. How else could these disconnected events all merge together at the same time unless there was a supernatural connection? She realized they had entered into something beyond her control and she had gone beyond the point of no return.

Chapter 12

All afternoon and into the evening Caleb and Gabriella had dissected and discussed the various elements they had read so far in her father's journal. They kept coming back to the same conclusion, that there was a mysterious link existed connecting the Omega Watchers Project and her father's research. Try as they might, they had no idea how it linked...accept through Gabriella.

The sun was setting into the Mediterranean Sea. A huge sphere of fire was descending into the horizon exploding with a heavenly masterpiece of vibrant colors. As it disappeared deeper into the blue waters dusk began to drop a dark veil. The water and sky blended together in darkness. Slowly and methodically the stars started appearing, manifesting a visual majesty on the black canopy of sky.

The warmer nights of late summer bring panoplies of new stars and constellations to capture the imagination. Leo, the lion heart, appears from the eastern horizon as a solo entry upon the dark stage. Then Virgo soon after makes her debut. Arcturus, with a delayed arrival, makes his grand entrance as the brightest star in the night heavens to be wished upon by star lovers across the planet. As she watched Arcturus make his luminous ascension, she thought it eerily ironic that Arcturus in Greek means "Watcher".

She pointed to the stars and commented, "It's easy to understand how ancient people thought there were god forces connected with the heavenly bodies of the universe. Watching the movement of the heavens and all of the wonder of the universe makes it almost impossible to believe it all just 'evolved'. Do you really think there is life out there somewhere, Caleb?"

He responded solemnly: "I hope there is more than what we can see and touch. If not, we're here a short time and then it's all over…sad thought."

"But extraterrestrials? Don't you think that's really far out? And I don't mean that as a pun." Gabriella snickered. "My father was a man of science and wasn't the type to believe in spiritual folklore."

Caleb just listened and let her vent. "To read in his own words his quest for understanding the gods helps me to understand some of the conversations we had before he passed away. At the time it didn't make much sense to me especially when he would use the term 'Lord of Spirits'. Maybe he was discovering something and afraid to tell me too much. Sadly time ran out."

Exhaustion was beginning to set in on Gabriella and Caleb was fully aware. "I think we've covered all of the territory we can in one day, Gabi, and you need to get some rest. How about I go back to my place and pack some things to stay with you until our meeting Monday? I really don't want you to be alone."

Normally she would dismiss it as a ridiculous notion that she needed someone to stay with her, but she welcomed the thought of not being alone. She was finally admitting to herself what she had always known deep down. She wanted Caleb to be near her.

"Thanks." she finally admitted to him. "I don't want to be alone." He sighed with relief that she was not going to be her independent, flippant self because there was no way he was going to leave her alone until they had a handle on what they were dealing with. He carried the box from the balcony to the dining table then closed and locked the French doors.

"Lock the door behind me," he said as he picked up his keys. She walked him to the door and he leaned down to kiss the top of her head. "I won't be long and I'm sure I don't have to tell you to not let anyone through this door but me…period! I'll call on my way back and I'll hurry, I promise." A quick hug and he was gone.

Gabriella closed the door behind him and made sure it was locked. The emptiness was overwhelming as she turned back around to face the apartment without him. Fear was trying to etch its way into her mind and she was fighting with everything she could muster.

"I'll take a long hot, bubble bath and relax while he's gone," she said to herself. "That's what I need to clear my head."

She filled the tub with warm water and added lavender bath gel. The aroma would help sooth her body and the mind. As she slipped into the tub and closed her eyes to allow her mind and body to relax in the bubbling water, she was immediately overcome with that sensation of another presence in the room. It was what she had felt two nights ago when they first returned from their exploration.

She had made sure everything was locked tight so she knew she was totally alone. "My mind is working overtime!" She closed her eyes and tried to relax. Her thoughts regressed into her childhood, wishing she could remember her mother and wondered if she had told her stories of being part Cherokee. It made her feel proud that she was part of what was considered native Americans but wondered if the Cherokee had migrated from some other country as her father said.

"Something else to study when I have time," she thought.

There was a much bigger question looming in her mind. With the Cherokee DNA did she also inherit some type of "chosen" genetics that she had been oblivious to?

The lavender fragrance was working its charm and Gabriella could feel herself finally relaxing. She felt she was moving into a REM sleep but was still totally conscious. She heard a popping sound and had the sensation she was floating. It was a feeling of liberation as warm winds were moving around her from head to toe. She relaxed in the ecstasy of the moment not knowing what to expect.

In the faded distance she heard the melodic humming of the beautiful stranger and then his voice calling to her. "Gabriella". The humming was hypnotic as it continued. She felt all the turmoil, pain and fear melt from her being. A peace like nothing she had experienced went through her body like the waves of the ocean washing over the sands of the sea.

Then the voice again, "Gabriella, I am waiting for you." The voice was calling to her and even with her eyes closed she could feel light penetrating her soul and pulling her away from her body. Desire filled her to submit to the unseen power when a loud banging pulled her back to reality.

With a jerk she sat up in the tub and realized she had fallen asleep and was dreaming. The banging continued and she could hear Caleb calling her name. She must have heard him calling for her and her subconscious wrapped it into her dream.

She jumped out of the tub, grabbed her robe and hurried to the door. "I'm coming, Caleb!" she yelled.

She struggled to get her mind back into reality fighting the sensations of the weird dream. When she opened the door Caleb took her into his arms and was breathless. "Are you alright? Couldn't you hear me knocking? I was ready to break the door down!"

She pushed him away to look into his eyes. "What do you mean? How long have you been out here? You said you were going to call before you came back."

"I did call," he assured her. "I kept calling the entire way back and it kept going to voice mail. I've been knocking and kept trying to call for at least fifteen minutes."

"That's odd," she said as he entered the apartment and she closed the door behind him. "I took the phone with me while I was bathing but I never heard it ring. I fell asleep in the tub and was having the oddest dream. I think all of this stuff of the spirit world is working on my subconscious. I must have been so deep in sleep I didn't hear anything."

Caleb knew something was not right but discounted it to the emotional upheaval she had been through. "You always hear your phone."

"I know." She looked at her phone and it showed fifteen missed calls. She checked the volume just to be sure. "I had the strange sensation someone was in the apartment. All this alien stuff is working on my mind."

Caleb walked through the apartment checking the bedrooms, the closets and the outside balcony. The apartment being on the tenth floor, however, would have been next to impossible for someone to gain access.

"There's no one here, Gabi. I've checked every crook and cranny." But she could see it in his eyes. He knew there was something she was not telling him.

"I'm exhausted." She said in the form of an explanation. "That has to be what's wrong. We've a long day tomorrow, too. The guest room is ready for you and I'll see you in the morning." She kissed him on the cheek and started towards her bedroom. After a few steps toward her bedroom she felt Caleb moving behind her. When she turned around he took her into his arms and held her close.

"I was so afraid something had happened to you!" His excellent English was overlaid with a German accent which became more pronounced when he was truly emotional. "I feel like I'm fighting some unknown force."

"I think we're both fighting the unknown right now," she said circumspectly. "Tomorrow we will see things more clearly and I'm so thankful you're with me in this journey. I couldn't do this alone." She kissed his cheek and went to her room.

He watched her close the door. He knew there was no way anyone could get into her bedroom without coming through the living area so that is where he would spend the night. He was taking no chances.

Gabriella opened the window to allow the night breezes to fill the room and then pulled back the soft, white comforter and slipped between the linen sheets. The dream from earlier was so burned into her mind that it felt as thought it was a real experience, one in which she could gladly lose herself. The curtains were swaying and she could hear the distant sound of the foghorns from boats arriving late into the marina. She often watched the fog come rolling across the sea laying a blanket of serenity across the bay. The fog seemed to be drifting through the window and filling her room as she fell into a deep sleep. The feeling of tranquility once again swept over her in wave after wave.

The melodic humming again filled her bedroom and she felt the liberation from the stresses of the body. She opened her eyes and through a misty veil she saw the form of a man standing beside her window. She felt no fear as he moved towards her and the hum of his voice penetrated her very being. She blinked her eyes trying to get a clearer view through the foggy mist and then his face appeared. The dark eyes penetrated hers and the shoulder length black hair fell around his beautiful face as he stood over her bed. He took her hand and she felt her soul floating up to him. He did not say a word. The warm winds were blowing around her body again and she had no fear whatsoever of what was happening. An unfamiliar energy pulsated through her body as her hand stayed captured in the hand of the beautiful stranger.

Without opening his mouth she could hear his words. "Don't be afraid, Gabriella. I am here to guide you. You have been chosen and I have come to protect you and lead you into new understandings."

Gabriella tried to speak but no words would form. She discovered she did not have to speak. He could hear her thoughts. "Are you real?" Her mind asked.

"Of course I'm real," he smiled. "I am more real than the flesh and blood that bogs down the human body and holds the spirit captive."

"But I can feel your touch."

"My touch is real. I am real. I know the secrets of stepping from time to untime and as your spirit guide I will teach you. This is where your questions will be answered and your seeking for knowledge will be found."

"But are you real or a spirit?" she asked. In this altered state of mind her subconscious was telling her she was dreaming but it all seemed so real. She did not want to wake up.

He answered her in his melodic voice. "I am real with a body, soul and spirit. The soul and spirit are eternal and can move from the body to travel through time and space. But I have a body I can return to just as you will return to yours after our journey."

She looked down on her bed and saw her body lying there in what appeared to be a deep sleep. She wondered why she was not afraid, but the peace she felt was so overwhelming she was going to give herself totally to the experience.

"Why did you come to me and where are we going?"

"You are of the chosen, Gabriella. It has been passed through your ancestors from generation to generation. Many never learn to move into their spirit realm and use the mighty gift they have been given. But your quest to understand the past and the future has created an opening in your subconscious mind that allows the release of your spirit into a higher level of understanding. And I will be with you to unveil the secrets *and* to keep you safe from the evil ones."

He held her hand tightly as he explained. "You have nothing to fear. Your astral soul has left your human body but you can return anytime. You are traveling in the same world but you will now see it with your spirit eyes. You have moved into the dimension of untime."

"Is untime where the spirits of the dead go?" she asked.

"You are beginning to understand, Gabriella. The body dies but the soul and spirit are eternal. Most do not realize this until their body ceases to exist and their soul and spirit have been released into the universe. But you are one of the chosen few who will be able to experience the dimension of untime while your body is still living."

"Can I see my parents?" she asked. "Can I talk to them?" The exhilaration she was experiencing was vibrating all through her and she realized her human body could not have tolerated it. It was an energy flow that pulsated like constant charges of electricity.

The beautiful stranger continued to hold her hand as he explained. "The flow of consciousness from those that have already crossed over must merge at the appropriate time with one that has not yet eternally crossed. When you have reached your higher consciousness your spirit communication will open."

He pulled her beside him and began moving forward. "Since it is your first astral journey, it will be brief. Your body is not accustomed to being without your spirit. We will build up to longer journeys with time. I will always hold your hand for protection and you must not separate from me."

She had no desire to separate from him and with her hand in his they went from her bedroom through the living area of her apartment. It was not necessary to open doors. They passed through walls as though they were nonexistent. She could see Caleb lying on the sofa. Something in her wanted to call to him but she was instantly on the balcony looking out over the sea. "We are going to the Axis Mundi of the earth, the Gateway to the Heavens. From that point the seven heavens and the entire universe can be accessed with your conscious thoughts. You only have to learn the secrets of astral travel."

"How do we get there?" Gabriella asked. He smiled at her, tightened his hold on her hand and the warm winds picked them up carrying them into the night. She looked down as they soared over the bay, then over the Carmel Mountain range and on to the highest point in the horizon. It happened so quickly she felt she had entered a time warp.

"We are about to enter the Gateway to the Heavens where time no longer exists."

"Where are we?" she asked as she looked in awe at the majestic view of the heavens.

"We are on the summit of Mt. Hermon...the gateway to the eternal dimensions and to the Akashic Knowledge."

"What kind of knowledge?" Gabriella asked trying to mentally get a grip on her mystical surroundings.

"The Akashic Knowledge is the collective understanding of all the events that have happened since creation and is encoded on a non-physical plane of existence. Every event that happens in the human existence is recorded throughout eternity creating either a positive or negative charge in the aether of the universe."

Her mind was swirling and she felt light headed. "Surely", she thought, "I will wake up and this will all be a dream."

"It is not a dream," he said, again hearing her thoughts. "What you consider the real world is only a shadow of that which is eternally true. We must return now. We must limit your first travel."

As instantly as he said the words she was back in her bedroom and could feel her body and spirit reuniting. She looked at the spirit guide and spoke her last question before he vanished. "What is your name?"

"You can call me Arcturus," he whispered.

She smiled and whispered back as he drifted out of the room. "Arcturus, my Watcher." And she went into a deep, restful sleep.

Chapter 13

Gabriella felt she had no more than closed her eyes until the sun was shining through and caressing her face. The sea breezes seemed to be whispering secrets from the night as she tried to gather her thoughts into something that seemed reasonable. The details of the dream began to unfold into what she realized were the events from the last couple of days that tangled into a subconscious imagination.

Everything in the dream had been part of the mysterious happenings. The Mt. Hermon Gateway, her parents being murdered, her being chosen with a supernatural gift, time-untime, even watching the star Arcturus rise were just mumbled subconscious thoughts that had become part of a metaphysical dream. The beautiful stranger, however, was always in the shadows of her mind just waiting for a mental portal of entry. She decided for the sake of the dream he would now be named Arcturus.

Once she settled in her mind why she had such an odd dream, she realized she was rested and ready to face the day. She quickly dressed, brushed her hair into a ponytail and went out to find Caleb. He was on the balcony waiting for her.

"Good morning, Sleeping Beauty," he kidded her. "I thought I might have to come in and give you a kiss to wake you up." She loved his joking. It always brought a smile to her face even in her worst mood.

"Good morning, Prince Charming." She returned the jest. "A kiss to wake me would not have been a bad idea. I can think of no better way to start the day." Caleb leaned over and kissed her cheek as he pulled her chair out.

"There, my princess, now all is well in the kingdom." And somehow she felt it was, in spite of the mounds of secrets still hiding in the black box.

"Why did you sleep on the couch last night, Caleb?" She asked.

His eyes darted towards her with confusion. He had not left any signs he had slept on the couch and she had not been out of her room all night. He was sure he would have heard her.

"How did you know I slept on the couch?" He watched her as her eyes narrowed. He knew her expression all to well. She did not want to answer him.

After a moments hesitation she finally answered. "I heard you through the door. And I know you like a book. You wanted to make sure you were between me and any potential intruder. And I thank you, sweet prince, for your gallantry." Her words were not totally convincing but he could not put a handle on why.

Gabriella was trying to make light of it but how could she explain to him the vision she had as she dreamed of floating through the living room and seeing him on the couch.

She silently asked herself, "How did I know?" She had not heard him, but she could not bring herself to talk about her dream. It was too perfect, too wonderful, and she did not want him making light of it. It was only a dream but she wanted to hold the euphoria of flying through the night heavens. Again she asked herself, "How did I know he slept on the couch?"

It was a beautiful day with the sun sparkling on the ocean waves and a perfect Sunday for the mariners to enjoy their day at sea. She watched the numerous sailboats on the horizon as the wind whipped into the sail and carried them away. It was a liberating thought to follow the winds wherever they might lead, but not at all practical and she knew she had to deal with reality.

"Beautiful morning, Gabi. How about breakfast at the café? The exercise will do us good."

It was a weather perfect day and they needed the walk and fresh air. Gabriella took an outside seat on the stone patio next to the rock fountain while Caleb went in the café to order. There was a long line and she knew he would be a few minutes. She leaned her head back to enjoy the sun full in her face. The humming of Arcturus' voice began in her mind. It was a melody that seemed to pull her from reality as she would lose herself in the sound.

As she listened to the melody in her mind it led her into reliving the dream. She had never before experienced any type of soul connection with the universe, but now she felt a cosmic sense of no limitations to time and space. What a wonderful thought that her mother and father might be experiencing this tranquil dimension of untime. She reminded herself it was a dream. Such a place does not exist!

She opened her eyes and glanced in the café. Caleb was still patiently waiting. Her eyes moved to the picturesque park across the street. She watched people enjoying the morning. It was the perfect setting stretched along the seaside for them to jog, walk their dogs or play with their children.

In the distance, she caught a glimpse of a man that seemed to be looking her way. She squint her eyes to try to get a clearer view of him. Her breath caught as the tall, figure seemed to be moving toward her. Could it be? She could see that beautiful face and a smile that seemed full of pleasure as he watched her intently and moved closer. She could not take her eyes off of him. He was ready to cross the street when Caleb rejoined her.

She felt frustrated at the interruption and Caleb immediately sensed her mood change. She glanced back across the street and the man she had named Arcturus was no longer in view. Did she imagine it? She was struggling with separating reality from her strange dreams.

"Are you okay?" Caleb asked her. "You look like you've seen a ghost."

She could see the concern in his face but she could not tell him about the strange dreams. She simply replied, "I thought someone across the street was watching me but I think my mind's just playing tricks."

Caleb looked around them and nothing looked unusual. He was struggling to get a handle on this new Gabriella with the constant fluctuations in moods. "You've got a lot going on in that beautiful head of yours. Natural to feel uneasy." He reached over and gently squeezed her hand.

"I'm sorry, Caleb. I know I'm not myself. It's going take some time to process all of this stuff that's hit me." Her eyes briefly looked into his but then moved on past him as though watching for someone else to appear.

"Do you see someone?" He abruptly turned looking in the same direction.

"No, there's no one there." Caleb detected what he thought was disappointment in her voice. The feeling inside him began to really root that there was something going on she was not telling him.

She quickly changed the subject. "Do you think we should tell Dr. Brotman about my father's journal? And how about Faith and Aaron? There are definite parallels in the research that actually may help. My only concern is there seems to be a possible danger to anyone connected with my father's research. Dr. Brotman already feels his project has potential danger and this could only make it worse."

Caleb sat quietly for a minute allowing her words to process before he answered. "I believe, Gabi, the danger may be one and the same. It seems that your father was starting to believe in aliens as being the gods with great powers the ancient people worshiped and actually that makes sense.

"Think about it, Gabi. What your father was researching is pretty close to what Dr. Brotman believes. His theory is the gods that were worshiped in ancient civilizations were actually fallen angels that produced children with human woman creating half human and half angel hybrids. That seems a little more far fetched to me. But, the point is they're both looking for the same thing. Perhaps the two parallels will somehow merge and we can be part of the greater understanding."

"That really makes sense." She agreed as she compared the two theories. "Maybe the Professor's been looking into his religion for answers on these so called fallen angels coming to earth and, just maybe, his religion has actually misinterpreted what were really extraterrestrial visits. The Jews believe strongly in heavenly beings, and that sort of thing, so it would be a natural conclusion. I do know the Professor believes it with all of his heart, just as Faith and Aaron do. But then they've all studied the same religious books so, of course, they'd agree on the matter."

"That's my thinking." Caleb nodded leaning back in his chair with a look of satisfaction.

"But are either of them right? Or were ancient gods just man's imagination hoping for something eternal? My father and I traveled all over the North and South America continents exploring caves and finding proof of the gods the ancient civilizations of the Americas worshiped. I always wondered where they came from, could they possibly be real, and did they have supernatural powers? As I got older I chalked it all up to wild imaginations that grew as they became legends passed down from generation to generation."

Caleb stretched his legs thinking back over his years of traveling and exploring in Europe. "You know, it was the same with me. All throughout

Europe there were mythical gods worshiped in ancient times. And that's exactly what I considered them...myths!"

Gabriella agreed. "My father told me stories of the myriad of gods that existed in all parts of the world. It seems from his journal he has found a common thread of cosmic life that ties all of these various beliefs together. And, knowing my father, he's made notes on all of it."

"Religion was not part of my life growing up as you know." Caleb said reflecting on his young years. "My family had no religious affiliation except an occasional trip to the Catholic Cathedral for a Christmas or Easter Mass and that was mostly because of the beauty of the ceremony. I can remember as a young boy staring at the statue of Jesus and wondering why a man would willingly die in such a horrible way when it was obvious so few people even believed in Him. But there was a peace that I felt in the midst of the music and the worship I have never felt anywhere else. There've been times I've longed to feel that again. It's a feeling I can't describe."

She was surprised to hear him speak so openly about religion. In all of the years they had been friends he had not mentioned going to the holiday masses or feeling a religious peace. She saw in his eyes a look that was different from any she had seen before and she felt a closeness to him she could not explain. Maybe it was because they were sharing their common desire to understand the supernatural powers and they both wanted to believe a divine power beyond human life existed.

"Are you ready?" Caleb asked pushing his chair away from the table. Gabriella reached out for Caleb's hand and they both felt a bond that was new in their relationship. She realized they had everything in common and she would never find another man as wonderful as Caleb.

Although she was realizing her deep feelings for him, she kept glancing back and forth hoping to get another glimpse of Arcturus. She realized she was being ridiculous and imagining things. He could be anywhere in the world. Why would she think he was here in Haifa?

She brought her attention back to the present and was content to walk with Caleb feeling his strong hand wrapped around hers. She did not need a mystery man in her life. She was enjoying this new intimacy and conceded it was growing into something much deeper than the friends they had always been. She knew it could have years ago if she had only allowed it. So much wasted time! She squeezed his hand just to let him know she was right where she wanted to be. His hand tightened on hers and that said enough.

Arriving back at the apartment, they returned to the balcony to enjoy the warmth and sunshine. It was only natural on such a beautiful day to enjoy the outdoors while they delved back into the journal. She took a deep breath as she pulled the book back out of the box and opened it to where they left off.

"Would you read first?" She asked Caleb. He took the journal and placed it on the table in front of him and began to read. Gabriella laid her head on the back of the cushioned chair and closed her eyes ready to listen with an open mind.

August 1, 1982

Of all of the things I could possibly write in my journal I am about to pen the most important entry. Angelena is pregnant! She had been having some nausea but we hadn't made the connection. After all of these years we had given up hope of having a child. Our excitement is beyond words! Our precious baby would have been conceived while we were in the beautiful mountain cottage in Israel. That is the crowning event to the entire sabbatical!

Caleb's voice started to break and he immediately stopped reading as tears filled his own eyes. He could feel the passion her father felt emanating from the journal's writing. Caleb could imagine nothing more wonderful than the love of a man and a woman creating a child that would be part of both of them.

He looked at Gabriella and her words were spoken through the tears that cascaded across her cheeks. "Isn't it odd I was conceived in Israel and without knowing it came back to Israel to study? Once I moved here I didn't want to leave. The Jews say the word 'coincidence' doesn't exist in their Hebrew language. But this sure is a big one."

Caleb pulled her chair closer to him and tenderly brushed the tears from her eyes. He put his arm around her shoulder as her head fell against his chest. She barely could speak her next words. "As deep as the pain is, Caleb, it's wonderful to experience through my father's own words how he felt when my mother told him she was pregnant with me."

Gabriella wondered what Caleb's reaction would be if they shared the same experience of having a child and as if he read her mind he whispered in her ear, "I can imagine nothing more magical."

Chapter 14

Caleb held Gabriella giving time for her emotions to process. After a few minutes she raised her head from his chest and Caleb again gently wiped the tears from her eyes. "Are you ready to continue?" He asked her with tenderness that brought more tears to her eyes?

Bravely she sat up and fought back the tears. She nodded her head and Caleb picked the journal up to continue.

The excitement over Angelena's pregnancy had made it difficult to concentrate on our research. However, I must continue and follow up on some important discoveries. My dear wife will be busy decorating the nursery and getting ready for our precious one to arrive in the spring as I continue working. She wants to focus on preparing for our baby's arrival and I understand. After all of this time waiting, I want her to enjoy every moment. We both wonder if it will be a boy or girl. Either way there will be no greater love on this earth than what we will give our child. I must admit a darling daughter that would be like her beautiful mother would be a gift more wonderful than anything I could imagine.

Along with the excitement of the baby, I am very excited about my research. I have read many books and articles trying to connect my hypothesis with what others believe to be true, with the ultimate goal to determine if there is any valid proof to the existence of extraterrestrial life.

In the myriads of information available it is difficult to ascertain myth from reality. Much of it I would have called ridiculous hallucinations before my sabbatical findings. But I have opened my mind to not prejudge any beliefs, no matter how crazy it sounds, and allow myself to look at all evidence before deciding what I personally will hold as truth.

There have been many people that have written of their personal experiences of "the enlightenment", but there is one that set my journey on a definite course. It was the writings of a prophet born in 1877 in Hopkinsville, Kentucky named Edgar Cayce.

Cayce was in his early twenties when he moved to Bowling Green, Kentucky, where he first discovered his 'gift'. He was a spiritual man and wanted only to help others. Supposedly, after asking for divine guidance, a spirit guide and mediator came to impart unlimited knowledge to him as needed. Upon entering a trance, Cayce would deliver medical advice, talk about religious issues, and address any maladies of the body, soul or spirit. He had no medical or formal religious education and did not know what he was saying while in the trance. His spirit guide that had all wisdom and knowledge would speak through Cayce as Cayce's wife would journal everything spoken during the trances. He was called 'the sleeping prophet' and was one of the 'chosen' to enlighten humanity on the worlds beyond our own. It is reported he gave over 15,000 physic readings that were without error.

Instead of his profound work being accepted and embraced by the world, he was considered by most to be a fake. Very few took him seriously, although the people that came to him with sicknesses of the mind and body believed him to be a miracle worker. He gave all credit for his supernatural abilities to the powers endowed upon him by an extraterrestrial civilization far more advanced than we are and he did not use his gift for fame or monetary success.

Cayce wrote these extraterrestrial beings are based in every country on the planet with the purpose of choosing humans in which to channel their information. Their ultimate goal is to be guardians and protectors of man, assisting us in entering the higher consciousness of the universe. The 'chosen' humans possess high vibrational frequencies that allow the chosen to communicate with their extraterrestrial guardians. It is a supernatural gift one is born with and cannot be humanly manufactured.

It is the same type of spirit connection I wrote about concerning the Cherokee Shaman. I realized, yet again, that different cultures have different titles for those that are chosen for spirit world connections. The titles all signify the same purpose...to channel messages from the realm of the paranormal.

Cayce wrote there were both good and evil extraterrestrial forces that fight for control of our earth. I have previously documented in my research that all religions and cultures teach forces of both good and evil. This further substantiates to me the polar forces were birthed in religions through 'heavenly gods' and these gods being extraterrestrials rather than angels, which is the bases of most religious beliefs.

Cayce believed the guardians are from the most advanced civilization in the galaxy and are here for the common good of all. These extraterrestrial guardians taught Cayce to heal through the nonphysical consciousness of vibrational energy frequencies which is the true power of the universe.

The guardians exist in a fifth dimension that only the chosen can enter as natural humans but all humanity will enter when they leave the cage of the human body. The most fundamental ingredient for achieving this dimension of energy is the search for truth and love. Negativity, fear and guilt must be overcome and exchanged for 'the light'. Through a guardian's direction we can eternally enter a dimension where there are no limitations of time and space.

Cayce gave many details regarding this extraterrestrial society ruled by the almighty High Ascended Master, who is the essence of all knowledge. The Ascended Master is also called "The Mighty I AM Presence" and will one day come to earth to reveal the paths to peace and harmony. 'I AM' will teach man to reach into his inner godhood that was always available but few would seek.

Sadly, very few would listen to Cayce and no one of spiritual significance took him seriously. I was among those that thought prophets, faith healers and people who channeled higher powers were all fakes, until now.

Edgar Cayce gave a universal description of the extraterrestrials both good and bad. He said this advanced civilization with their guardians is from the planet Arcturus.

When Caleb read those words he heard Gabriella gasp. Breathlessly she whispered, "Oh, my god!"

Caleb looked up and Gabriella's face had turned a pale white, as though the life had drained from her. "What is it, Gabi? Tell me, what's wrong!" He waited for an explanation but she either could not or would not say a word.

When he tried to take her hand she pushed him away, jumping up from her chair. "It's too much, Caleb," she muttered. "It's all too much for me to process. Here we go again with the chosen, the shaman, and now I think my father really does believe in beings from other planets!"

She stopped short of telling Caleb her biggest shock was Arcturus. She could not tell him about a dream she had just the night before in which the beautiful spirit guide said to call him Arcturus! This was settling in as something much more than strange coincidences! The more that evolved the more ominous it was becoming.

Gabriella paced back and forth across the blue balcony tiles trying to piece it all together in her mind. She would stop, gaze at the sea and then begin pacing again. Caleb sat silently watching her. He knew with all of his physical strength there was absolutely nothing he could do to protect her from the battles of her mind.

He heard her whispering in a questioning voice, "Arcturus".

"Arcturus is a star, Gabi, not a planet. We were watching it just last night. Remember? That is definitely a mistake."

"Of course it is! I just don't know where my father's going with all this nonsense. This isn't like him at all. I never heard him talking about aliens."

Coming to no conclusions she sat back down in the chair and picked up the journal. "I will read now," she said with determination. "I want to know about Arcturus!" Caleb noticed something different in her voice. It sounded as though she was talking about another man. He told himself he was being foolish and dismissed the thought.

Gabriella started reading where Caleb left off.

Edgar Cayce who became known as "the Father of Arcturians" wrote the guardians would come to him while he was in a trance or a dream state. He would have someone write down everything he said since he remembered nothing when he would awake. While in these trance-states there were numerous specific details given to him by his guardian.

In one of his journals he wrote: "The Arcturians are a fifth-dimensional civilization that is a prototype of Earth's future. Its energy works as an emotional, mental, and spiritual healer for humanity. It is also an energy gateway through which humans pass during death and rebirth. It functions as a way-station for nonphysical consciousness to become accustomed to physicality. Of all the extraterrestrial civilizations, I feel most drawn to Arcturus because of their total focus in every aspect of society on the path of God-realization. One of the reasons Earth has not been attacked by warlike negative extraterrestrials has been those civilizations' fear of the advanced starships of the Arcturians. The Arcturian ships are state-of-the-art technology, far beyond anything else in the universe. One of the starships circling the Earth is called the Starship Athena named after the Greek war goddess. The ship exists in an alternate dimension and cannot be seen with the natural eye. But it is there constantly protecting us."

My research concerning Cayce has led me to read many other pusblished articles concerning intergalactic beings. I am keeping all pertinent references in this box with my journal. I truly believe I am on the verge of a life-changing discovery!

Gabriella laid the journal back on the wrought iron table and stared out to sea. "Caleb, what do you think? Could Cayce be right? Could there be Arcturian guardians surrounding us in another dimension and we not even know it? Could this be the same as guardian angels that some people refer to? Cayce said they are here to lead us to God realization. This could be our answer to all the research about gods and myths! It really does make sense, don't you think?"

Caleb heard the pleading in her voice like a person holding on to their last thread before losing all hope. He wondered why she now sounded so desperate when before it was more confusion.

"Gabi, I wish I knew the answer. And yes, it does make a type of sense but what are you not telling me? There's something bothering you. I know it! I want to help but how can I if you won't open up to me?"

Gabriella realized she could not hide her feelings from Caleb. He knew her too well. She also knew she could not tell him about her dreams. Not until she knew if they were just a figment of her subconscious mind. *Or!* Was Arcturus her guardian angel, guiding her through dreams to discover The Enlightenment?

Chapter 15

Sunday afternoon had stretched into late evening. Gabriella and Caleb decided to order in dinner to save time in the pursuit of her father's discovery. After dinner, they put the journal aside and started plowing through the research papers containing additional information about the Arcturians. She was amazed at how many people in different countries had written about their beliefs in aliens, and especially the guardians from Arcturus.

As she filtered through the stack of journals, articles and her father's personal notes she looked up at Caleb in a voice of disbelief. "Caleb, can you believe this long list my father has of books and published articles written about the Arcturians? Look at these schedules of seminars where 'the enlightened' told of their dream visitations. No wonder my father was so excited!"

Gabriella found an article Cayce had used in a seminar in Virginia Beach in 1940 entitled 'Arcturian Starship Athena' and read to Caleb: "*The Starship Athena is an Arcturian Starship that is the most advanced and feared ship in the galaxy. For this reason, Arcturians have been able to protect and prevent any invasion of our planet Earth from Grey Aliens and Reptilian Aliens. Arcturian's Starship Athena quietly resides between the planets Jupiter and Saturn awaiting any invading armada of the Grey aliens. The Greys discovered the plentiful sources of negative energies throughout planet earth and sent word so their entire race could find a new home. As they entered the outer limits of our Solar System the Starship Athena waited patiently cloaked and ready to repeal the unwanted race of Greys.*"

"If this is true, Caleb, it could explain the ancient stories of the good and evil spirits that fought for control of earth. Naturally, humans would consider them gods. I'm beginning to understand how my father's mind was working. Just think of it! Every religion and culture on earth described the same spirits, both good and evil, as coming from the heavens. They applied their own names and descriptions, but my father was right! They could all be alien beings that have been visiting the earth from the very beginning!"

Caleb was in deep thought as Gabriella impatiently waited for his response. "But, Gabi, when was the beginning? Where did the first humans come from and how did they get here? The concept of alien beings just doesn't jive with the theory of evolution, now does it?"

She squinted her eyebrows and Caleb saw her confusion as she responded. "You're right. It doesn't make sense. If man was 'evolving' why didn't the bad aliens take over the earth before man existed? Could it be that man was put here as some type of 'test' by a more advanced civilization and that's why they're watching over us?"

Caleb shrugged his shoulders and intended to respond, but Gabriella kept talking. He listened patiently as he kept looking through her father's numerous collected articles.

"Listen to this, Gabi. This is from a UFO journal. I didn't even know there was such a publication! '*The Arcturians work in close connection with the Ascended Masters whom they call the Brotherhood of the All. They also work closely with what they refer to as the Galactic Command. The Arcturians travel the universe in their starships, which are some of the most advanced in the entire universe*'. This sounds like something out of a sci-fi movie." Caleb flipped the pages infatuated with the numerous articles about alien adventures.

"This is interesting, too!" He continued. "This article says Arcturians live on our planet and they call it 'the Earth plane'. They are among us and we don't even realize they are here. This writer says she personally knows one who has led her into a universal spiritual understanding."

"Caleb, this sounds so ridiculous. Anyone that read this stuff would think my dad had joined a group of scientific quacks."

"As ridiculous as it sounds, these people believe it." He said seriously as he continued: "This article says they can read your mind. *'Arcturians are able to ingest information by means of their telepathic abilities. This process is similar to ingesting food but it occurs on an energy level. They are able to assimilate information one hundred times faster than the average human being on Earth and that is the reason they outgrew the need for using computers/electronics.'* Caleb laid the article on the table and said teasingly, "I wish sometimes I could read your mind, Gabi."

"I'm sure glad you can't." She tried to keep her voice light as her thoughts were being drawn back to the previous night.

In her dream Arcturus knew everything she was thinking. Much of what these papers were revealing, she had already experienced and there was no way she could have known it was in her father's research. She glanced up at Caleb and his eyes were searching her face. She realized when she thought about Arcturus, Caleb instantly sensed something different about her.

"What's the matter, Caleb? Why are you looking at me like that?"

This was the straight forward girl he loved and he was very careful how he answered. He studied her face for a minute before he spoke. "I don't know what it is, Gabi. Since we arrived home I've noticed a difference in you. Often you get a strange look on your face and I feel like you're hiding something."

Gabriella twisted her head around to look out towards the sea which she often did, but this time Caleb got the distinct impression she was avoiding eye contact. He got up to stretch and walked around the table where she would have to look at him. "You know you can tell me anything."

She saw both love and hurt in his eyes and could not endure causing him pain. Just the thought of hurting him felt like a hammer pounding in her stomach. She stood up and wrapped her arms around his waist. Without hesitation his arms encircled her. She whispered in a broken voice, "I wouldn't hurt you for anything. Please be patient while I try to work this all out in my head."

"You *will* tell me if there's something wrong, won't you?" He pleaded with her.

"Yes, Caleb," she promised him. She did not feel like she was lying because there was nothing wrong. She was just confused and needed time to sort her dreams from her reality.

"It's getting late, Gabi, and we have a big day with the Professor tomorrow. We best get some rest."

Gabriella suddenly realized how tired she was. "You're right," she admitted. She neatly stacked the papers they had already gone through and placed them to the side. She gave Caleb a kiss on the cheek and he gently pushed her towards the bedroom door.

She wasted no time snuggling into her bed, hoping Arcturus would come for another dream visit. She closed her eyes, but sleep evaded her. Too many thoughts saturated her mind. She could not escape the confusion and myriad of questions that kept tormenting her.

She heard Caleb closing the terrace doors and knew he was locking up for the night.

Finally she relaxed and her body was asleep, but consciously she was aware of everything around her. She could see the white curtains blowing in the night breezes, making the stars visible as they peeped through the wind tossed curtains. She tried to get up but she could not move. She realized she had entered the astral world.

Gabriella was immersed in an aura of total serenity waiting for Arcturus to appear. She finally decided he was not coming. She kept telling herself, "This is not real. I'm dreaming." The disappointment caused her to ache all over. She wanted to wake up and go to Caleb but she was trapped in her dream state. She could not move.

Then she heard it! It was the melodic humming that could only be Arcturus! She could feel his presence before she could see his form entering the room. He came to her bedside and held out his hand.

"Are you ready?" He spoke with a voice so mesmerizing that she lost all control of her thoughts, totally captured by the music in his voice. She held out her hand and the night journey began.

Again they floated through the living room. She could see Caleb still reading some of her father's journals. For a moment he looked up as though he knew someone was in the room. He looked straight towards Gabriella but obviously did not see her. A strange questioning look was on his face as she and Arcturus floated by him and out the balcony doors.

A smirk spread across Arcturus' face as he looked towards Caleb. For a brief moment she resented Arcturus, but it was only for a moment. Arcturus turned his head towards her and when their eyes met she was a willing prisoner of the night. She knew Caleb sensed something but her thoughts went directly back to her dream visitor, wondering where this astral travel would take them.

"We are going to the most enchanting, mystical place in the universe," he answered her, again reading her thoughts. "But there are some dangers of which I must warn you. The universe has many evil beings and sinister planes. To be safe you must do as I say! There are negative astral beings that would capture soul travelers that are not protected by their guardians. A soul imprisoned is taken to the vortex of the Phantasmagoric Plane, an engulfing black hole from which there is no escape. Do not let go of my hand! I am your protector."

"What happens to the body of the person whose soul has been taken prisoner and can't return to their body?" She asked as the beautiful dream was now taking frightful turns.

"The body cannot live when the soul cannot return. It is 'bangungot', meaning fatal nightmare. Doctors will say it is a sudden heart attack or maybe acute hemorrhagic pancreatitis. They simply do not understand the separation of the soul and spirit from the living body, so they try to apply a medical condition. Don't be afraid! As long as I am with you there is nothing to fear."

She had no intentions of letting go of his hand. Arcturus looked at her and smiled, reminding her she had no private thoughts.

"They drifted up towards the sky and across the moon caressed Carmel Mountains. The harbor lights sparkled in the bay waters, whispering secrets of the night as they slowly disappeared. The huge ships on the sea faded into mere specks and then dissolved away, as the night travelers ascended higher. Gabriella turned her eyes toward the heavens where the sky was filled with millions of stars winking at her, as though each understood the heavenly place she was journeying to.

The winds caught in her hair and blew around her face as hand in hand she and Arcturus soared upward and then descended once again on the summit of Mt. Hermon. Gabriella released his hand and turned full circle to take in the 360 degree majestic view. She saw the lights of Haifa in the distance and wondered if her apartment was one of those distant flickers. She knew Caleb thought she was safely in her bed.

Arcturus turned to her with a look in his eyes she had not seen before. It was close to threatening as he spoke: "You must not think of him! He does not have the high vibrational frequencies you possess! Your powers would be diluted in a union with that man, or anyone that does not possess equal or superior frequencies. You would not be able to see or travel with me ever again!"

"How do you know all this?" She demanded of Arcturus. Even in her dream state she became angry that he would tell her what she could and could not do.

His smile was rapturous as he answered her, "Remember I told you when you leave the dimension of time all knowledge can be accessed. The Akashic Knowledge is the collective understanding of all things and through it I know every detail of your life. I am your Guardian Watcher, Gabriella, and there is nothing you can hold secret from me."

In that moment she lost all thoughts of Caleb.

Gabriella and Arcturus stood at the pinnacle of Mt. Hermon, at the axis mundi, the gateway to the universe. She saw a circular cloud descending. It was a mighty vortex with an open center. It came closer and closer, until it covered them. She felt the exhilaration of being surrounded by the swirling wind, lifted up and swept away.

"We are entering the astral plane energy field, Gabriella. All you have to do is think where you want to be and the energy of the universe teleports you at the speed of thought. As I said, we are traveling to the most beautiful, magical place in the universe. Don't let go!" Arcturus demanded as he once again clutched her hand and they departed the earth plane.

Gabriella felt the winds carry them away, and within the blinking of an eye they were standing in the middle of indescribable beauty! Mountains higher than any on earth surrounded them. Waterfalls cascaded from the apexes over majestic rocks and ledges, splashing into pools of water surrounded by exotic flowers beyond description.

The sounds of the flowing waters created harmonious music similar to the melodic voice Arcturus possessed. The flowers' colors vibrated in majestic tints and hues that glowed as the light from the heavens shone down upon the mountains. The fragrance emanating from the myriads of blooms filled the air with incense, calming the soul into total tranquility.

Groves of trees and enchanting plants covered the mountainsides as sweet nectar flowed from them. Arcturus wiped his finger across the nectar of one of the plants and lifted it to Gabriella's lips.

"Taste and see that it is good." She touched her finger to the nectar and tasted of a blend of almonds, honey and galbanum. A mystifying smile came across Arcturus's face as he identified the narcotic flavor, "It is 'sarara', the nectar of the gods."

"There is nothing on earth like this." Gabriella's words slurred, intoxicated by the flavor.

Her head was spinning as she gazed at the numerous rainbows of vibrating colors covering the mountain tops, overlapping and circling down to the crystal clear lake at the bottom where the two of them stood.

"What are these colors in the rainbows?" Gabriella exclaimed! "This is beyond anything the human mind can conceive!" The ineffable beauty was almost too sacred for words.

"You are beholding the vibrations of the heavenly light that shines upon the mists of the falling waters. Color is vibration. The more intense the color the faster your eyes vibrate. With human eyes when you see the color blue you are experiencing fifty trillion light vibrations. In your astral body the vibrations are increased by hundreds of times and create colors no human will ever perceive. The varying velocities of light contain the splendors of the universe, just as the vibrations of a musical note contain the sounds you hear. That is why the sounds of the waters falling can create music that can only be heard through astral ears.

Everything in the universe is determined by vibrational frequencies. In the astral plane you experience vibration unknown to humans in the cages of their bodies, and you experience senses far beyond only the five known to man. Your spirit and soul are totally free from human limitations. You can be one with the universal harmonics comprised for a higher level of existence."

Gabriella wondered where they had traveled to and without her speaking a word, Arcturus again answered her. "We are on the astral plane called Summerland. It is the pinnacle of human spiritual achievement in the afterlife. It is the highest level, or 'sphere', of the afterlife we can hope to enter. The chosen few are allowed access from the earth plane to gain universal knowledge. Vibrational energy is alive here and moves and spins upon the rings of time untime. Earth plane time no longer exists and the frequencies breathe and live in the vibrations of this chosen place."

"The Cherokee Indians knew about this place. The shamans visited here to get their powers? Right?" Gabriella felt she was beginning to piece together some parts of confusion.

He smiled at her in affirmation. "They called it by a different name, but it is the place where the chosen few upon the earth plane gain their supernatural powers. Edgar Cayce was one of those chosen few because he possessed the highest vibrational frequencies possible to the human body and still be able to remain in an earth existence. He was a channel between the Ascended Masters of the planet Arcuturs and the bodies on earth that were hurting spiritually, physically or emotionally. His desire to be used of the Masters opened the godhood that dwelled within him."

Arcturus turned in a circle waving his hand over his head. "This is the center of the universe and all knowledge and power proceed from this place. The essence of Summerland is its existence as a resting ground where souls can reflect on the life they lived, see if they learned the lessons necessary for the peaceful existence of humanity, and then return to earth and try again in due course. Summerland is not seen as a place of judgment as some religions teach, but rather as a spiritual self-reflection and self-evaluation. It is the place where the soul reviews its earth life and gains an understanding of the total impact of all human actions, while in the cages of their bodies. Each particular life lesson is chosen and planned out by the soul itself while in Summerland and with the assistance of a spirit guide.

Most souls of humankind will return with the hope they will reach a karma balance on the earth plane and eventually create a Utopia. Mankind refers to it as the Age of Aquarius. It will be a final peace, harmony and love for all. It is a realm of untime that will soon come to the earth, but the people of earth will not be able to create it without help from the Ascended Masters, the Watchers of the earth."

"Are you telling me that eventually everyone on earth will be filled with love? How could that be possible with all of the evil and hatred that exists?" Gabriella could not envision the possibility.

"There are those that will never willingly change, Gabriella. They live in their own worlds of self-righteousness and have no toleration for the beliefs of others. In being intolerant they have shut out the possibility of man creating peace on earth. It will be necessary for their guardians to take them from the earth plane and bring them to Summerland for self-reflection. After they have realized the error of their selfish ways they can return and become part of the new age of universal understanding."

"The Arcturian Ascended Master created Summerland as the place of peace and tranquility for the soul and spirit to prepare for the return to earth where they will live in another human body. The trips are repeated until karma balance is achieved."

"You're talking about reincarnation! I never believed it was real! You said *most* will return. Why not all?"

"There are some soul-spirits that refuse the harmony of the universe. They are taken to a separate place and cannot return. Even the Watcher Guardians cannot access that place!" Arcturus spoke the words with a vehemence Gabriella had not heard in his voice before and she instinctively tried to pull away from him.

"Don't be afraid." He soothed her again with his beautiful and hypnotizing voice. "Those souls refused the harmonic convergence and are eternally separated from us. My assignment is to make sure you reach your higher consciousness. Your vibrational frequencies will increase more and more as we travel the universe, and as a result your spiritual understanding will converge with the Akashic Knowledge. You will know all things. You have only begun to realize what ultimately awaits you!"

Gabriella watched the rainbows twist and turn around the mountains. The swaying movement was in rhythm to the musical concert of the cascading waters. The colors vibrated in the light creating a dancing sensation and the melodic waters held her spell-bound. She suddenly realized it was the same melody that Arcturus would hum. Euphoria overwhelmed her as vibrating energy pulsated through her.

He gazed at Gabriella with a knowing stare. "Your vibrational frequencies are increasing. You are becoming one with the universe and there is nothing that can be withheld from you as you are saturated with universal understanding."

Arcturus squeezed her hand. "We must go back now. It is almost morning and your body cannot awaken until your soul has returned. "

As soon as he said the words she was back in her body and Summerland was nothing more than a dream. Her eyes opened expecting Arcturus to be standing there but instead the sun was coming through the window and Caleb was peering down at her.

"I kept knocking, Gabi, and when you didn't answer I was getting worried." Caleb spoke with such tenderness that Gabriella melted inside.

She reached her arms to him and he sat on the side of the bed and held her. Her body was shaking.

"I was dreaming again, Caleb. It was both wonderful and awful. I can't explain it but please don't leave me. I couldn't stand it if you left me!" Gabriella made no attempt to hold back the tears. The raw emotions moved over her wave after wave as she tried to bring herself back to reality.

Caleb did not ask any questions. He just held her close. He knew eventually she would tell him about these tormenting dreams. In the meantime, he felt helpless knowing he could not fight what he could not see.

Chapter 16

"I've got to get ready for the meeting with Dr. Brotman." Gabriella realized Caleb had already showered, dressed and was ready to go. "I'll hurry." She said jumping out of bed. Caleb left the bedroom and closed the door behind him.

Gabriella quickly showered and prepared herself both physically and mentally to face the day. She pushed the dream to the back of her mind and began to focus on the Omega Watchers Project.

She was seeing more and more parallels to the gods vs. alien theory and her mind, being saturated with an overwhelming amount of information hitting all at one time, was causing these crazy dreams about Arcturus. She knew in the light of day her night travels were only dreams reflecting her daytime reality.

She went into the living room refreshed and ready. She looked at the black box containing all the research papers from the night before, and they were exactly as she had left them. She remembered in her dream Caleb had taken them back out to read.

"Did you read anymore after I went to bed?" She asked Caleb.

Caleb looked at her with a strange expression. "Why do you ask?" He had made sure he put everything back in its place just as she had left it.

"Just curious. I heard you moving around before I went to sleep and thought maybe you had." She hoped Caleb would say he had not read anymore and then she could rest in the fact it was nothing more than a dream.

"I tried not to bother you. I couldn't sleep so I did read some of the articles and found some really interesting points we need to talk about. I put everything back just as we left it last night so we'd know where to start."

"No problem." Gabriella tried to sound casual to camouflage Veritas phobia slowly taking control. She was beginning to fear the possible truth. Was she actually seeing things in her dreams? How could she know what Caleb was doing? She decided her subconscious had heard him and translated the sounds into her dream, nothing more.

"Gabriella," Caleb spoke gently, "at one point last night I could have sworn you had come back in the room. I always know when you're close to me even without looking. But you didn't leave your bedroom. I even opened the door and peeped in just to be sure. You were sound asleep. Really weird, huh?"

In her dream, as she and Arcturus were leaving, she had seen Caleb look up from the papers and felt he was looking right at her. Goose bumps crawled up her arms as she struggled to keep her composure.

"That's pretty strange." She was trying with everything in her to not allow her voice to quiver.

She knew he was mentally questioning what was going on and she quickly changed the subject. "We gotta go or we'll be late." She grabbed her bag and headed for the door.

Caleb tried to break the tense atmosphere and joked with her. "And whose fault is that?" He caught up with her and grabbed her hand. She leaned against him and pushed slightly. "Okay, rub it in. I am a woman you know. We usually keep the men waiting."

"I know that! Look how long I've been waiting for you. And I don't mean this morning." Caleb took Gabriella in his arms. A playful kiss quickly became a bond she could not deny. She felt the breath leave her as she melted against him. They both knew beyond a shadow of a doubt how deeply in love they were. Finally, Caleb pulled away long enough to speak.

"Gabriella, do you have any idea how long I've loved you and longed for this moment?" His voice was breaking as he whispered the words. He knew the day would come when he took Gabriella in his arms and proclaimed his love that had been building for over a decade. It was a magical moment beyond anything he ever imagined.

"I have been such a fool." She whispered back. Arcturus and the universal knowledge was the furthest thing from Gabriella's mind. Being in Caleb's arms made all the ominous shadows dissipate.

The moment was interrupted by Caleb's cell phone ringing. He knew who it was without looking and told Gabriella they had to go. "I know that's Aaron calling and they're wondering why we're late."

Caleb answered his phone. "We're on our way, man. Had some interruptions this morning," he said winking at Gabriella. "Be there in about ten."

"So I'm an interruption now?" Gabriella teased him.

"You can interrupt my life anytime, Gabi Girl." Caleb said as he gave her one last kiss before leaving. She was amazed at the foreign feelings. She wanted to put everything in life on hold and stay in his arms. She had wasted so many years running from a relationship, afraid of more hurt, and now she wanted to make up for lost time.

"Duty calls." He spoke in a military type voice and they hurried towards Caleb's car.

Within a few minutes they picked up Aaron and Faith and were on their way to the campus. Aaron and Faith were chattering about research they had done over the weekend and noticed Caleb and Gabriella were very quiet. That was unusual, especially for Gabriella. Faith and Aaron both sensed something very different about them.

When they got out of the car Faith looked from Gabriella to Caleb. "Ok, guys, tell me what's going on?"

Aaron chimed in. "You two are acting really strange. What's up?"

Gabriella flushed and Caleb just smiled.

Faith and Aaron looked at Caleb and Gabriella. Then they looked at each other and started laughing. Faith was laughing so hard she could hardly speak. "Is that all? I thought something was really wrong."

"What do you mean, 'is that all'?" Gabriella looked confused.

Aaron stopped laughing long enough to answer. "We've known for years you two were made for each other. We even had bets on how long it would take for you to realize it! I won the bet! You owe me, Faith!"

Faith playfully pushed Aaron. "Good luck on collecting!"

Faith hugged Gabriella and told her how happy she was for her. Aaron slapped Caleb on the back. "Way to go, man!"

As they hurried to Dr. Brotman's office everyone that passed them heard the laughter and the joy. There was no hiding the love that emanated from Caleb and Gabriella.

They entered Dr. Brotman's office and Sandee looked up. "Hey, Team, how are you today? Hope you were able to rest." Then she looked at Caleb and Gabriella. She looked at Aaron and Faith and raised her eyebrows. Faith just said "Yep" and Sandee started laughing. About that time Dr. Brotman came through the door. He looked at everyone in the room and then his eyes stopped on Gabriella and Caleb. He peered at them for a full minute without his expression changing.

"It's about time," he said dryly. Then the whole room broke in laughter.

Gabriella asked laughingly, "Am I the only one that didn't know?"

The Professor gave her a fatherly hug. "We have all known how Caleb felt about you and we knew you would wake up one day and realize it, too. You just had to get your head out of work long enough to see love was waiting for you."

Just to seal the fact for everyone in the room Caleb leaned down and kissed Gabriella smack on the lips. She was surprised at his public display of emotion but it was wonderfully satisfying that he wanted everyone to know. The rest of the group broke into applause and Gabriella embraced the moment with a willing heart.

"Okay, we have to get to work, team." The Professor pushed his office door back and directed them in. "As wonderful as love is, work goes on." The Professor gave Gabriella another hug as she passed him. "I know your dad would be so happy for you."

Quick tears stung her eyes as she whispered, "He would have loved Caleb."

"I'm sure he would." The Professor motioned toward the cart with morning drinks and pastries. Sandee always thought of the small details that made the team feel really special and created a personal environment for their work.

"Help yourself and we'll get started soon." They had all just settled into their comfortable, leather chairs with their notes in front of them when Sandee knocked on the door. She peeped in and said to the Professor, "He's here. Are you ready for him?"

The team looked at each other in confusion. No one else was ever included in these meetings.

"Send him on in." The Professor instructed.

A young man in his mid-thirties came into the room carrying a briefcase. He looked American and when he spoke to the Professor it was in perfect English with a slight southern accent.

The young man went over and gave the Professor a quick hug and they exchanged a few personal words. The team watched them, realizing their relationship was more than business.

"Team, I want to introduce you to Kian Jameson. He is from the States and is joining our research team. He's been here the last few weeks while you were finishing the exploration." The Professor introduced each of the team members to their newest addition.

"Call me KJ. " He went around the table and firmly shook hands with each one, smiling with excitement. "I can't tell you how much it means to me to be part of this project."

The team was friendly but confused. Why would the Professor be bringing someone else in?

The Professor waited for KJ to sit down and the team to refocus. "I know you're all wondering why we need another team member. As I told you on Friday we have reached a new level in our research and this requires adding a computer specialist. KJ is highly qualified in technology specializing in ancient languages. He'll be taking care of the technical part of the research we're going to need going forward. He's the son of a longtime friend of mine from the States and I have followed his achievements for years."

The Professor paused and lit his pipe filling the air with the familiar, cherry fragrance. He took a puff and then continued: "KJ has both the spiritual understanding and the brilliant technical skills we need for research, project planning and future communication. We had a meeting over the weekend and I've brought him up to date on what we've done so far. We've also discussed in length the project's objectives and the prophetic reasons for our research. He's totally on board with us."

KJ leaned forward at the table briefly addressing the group. "I'm honored to be part of this elite team and you'll find as we go forward this is a project that I am totally dedicated to. I join you not only technically but spiritually. I've no doubt this project could have a world wide impact."

Gabriella realized they had another team member that had strong religious views and she admired their willingness to stand for what they believed. She really wanted to believe something but she needed proof. It was a growing agony in the pit of her stomach. A longing for supernatural truth that was consuming her but she was more confused than ever before. The Professor, Aaron and Faith...they all believed in an Almighty God, King of the Universe. Now their newest team member apparently held the same belief.

Gabriella was opening her mind to the probability the 'almighty' was actually far advanced extraterrestrials being perceived as gods throughout millenniums of time. She knew whatever happened going forward it would be anything but dull.

Caleb spoke for the team: "We're glad to have you, man. And you'll make our work a lot easier. Welcome aboard!"

"Now it's time to get down to business." The Professor left no doubt time was of the essence. KJ pulled his laptop from his briefcase, put on his glasses and began to focus. The rest of the team had their notes ready and they embarked on a mission they all knew could be both dangerous and life changing, no matter which way the wind of truth would blow.

Chapter 17

Dr. Brotman pulled the notes from his briefcase and placed them on the conference table. Another puff on his pipe and once again the fragrance was saturating the room. Gabriella closed her eyes and for a moment remembered her father smoking his pipe and sitting next to her telling stories of far away places. Reading his journal had brought back so many memories she had tried to suppress through the years. Her nostalgic interlude was interrupted when the Professor addressed them.

"I've spent the weekend reviewing all my notes up to the point of your discovery of the ancient writing. When KJ and I met this weekend he scanned the picture of the writing you found on the cave wall. He also scanned the writings from the Dead Sea Scrolls and took pictures of the fragments that the Prophet gave to me. KJ called me late last night with some very interesting insights. KJ, please share with the team what you told me."

KJ looked at the team before he spoke. "I know you all have invested years of research and work into this project, and you'll be gratified to know it hasn't been in vain. I've run a database search comparing the images of the clay fragments given to the Professor and what you found written on the cave wall. I was looking for some type of link to cuneiform, commonly believed to be the earliest language known to man. Although a few markings were similar, it's obvious to me what you discovered is a much earlier language, the existence of which has been either lost or altered over millenniums of time. I've searched the universal databases and, so far, found nothing we can match to."

"How do you plan to do the translation if there's nothing to match to?" Aaron being the ancient writing specialist asked the question the rest of the team was also wondering.

"The closest thing we have is Ge'ez which the professor is fluent in. Actually, Ge'ez is still used in the liturgy of the Ethiopian Church. I think it's also a notable point that the Ethiopian Bible has always contained Enoch's writings as a canonized book. So has the Eritrean Orthodox Tewahedo Church and Beta Israel."

"Let me add to what KJ is saying." The Professor interrupted. "This fact makes it obvious to me that the Book of Enoch was originally part of the biblical manuscripts and used both before and after the coming of Yeshua. Enoch's writings were later removed just as many other books when the scriptures were canonized. The Catholic Church still has the Books of the Apocrypha but the Christian Bible does not. We have to study their history to find out why, but we can't dismiss something just because it isn't part of today's 'traditions'. The Bible tells us 'to study to show ourselves approved'. We are to thirst for knowledge and understanding and be open to what truth reveals."

The team knew he was about to focus back on the Dead Sea Scrolls just by the passionate look on his face. "When we were translating the Dead Sea Scrolls many of the texts long removed from the canonized books were discovered again. It was as though Yahweh had hidden them for this final generation to make sure Enoch's words were heard."

The Professor got up from the table and started slowly pacing the floor in contemplative thought. Then he continued: "There's archeological proof the Ge'ez language began in the area of Mesopotamia, the area now known as Iraq. Mesopotamia's literal meaning is 'land between the rivers' and refers to the Tigris and Euphrates Rivers. In the Book of Genesis it states this was the location of the Garden of Eden, the cradle of the world. The fact this ancient writing was found in the area where we know life began makes it very possible it was the language used during the great flood in the days of Noah. We just need proof."

The Professor continued to slowly walk back and forth across the tile floor. "Any thoughts, KJ?"

"I totally agree with your thinking," KJ confirmed. "We'll use the earliest form we have of Ge'ez to look for symbols also found in the language we're trying to match. And then try to form a translation. I'll run the symbols one by one in the universal databases to find any known matching symbols on the worldwide web. If we get enough matches we can start working towards a translation."

"I need to regress for a minute." Faith interrupted. "Why do you think the Ethiopians still use the Ge'ez and no one else?"

The Professor stopped pacing and looked at Faith. "After the flood, Noah's son Ham migrated with his family south of the Mesopotamia area which included Ethiopia. That would explain how the language got there and could also be further evidence it was the language that was used at the time of the flood. Somehow it was preserved there through the millennia."

The Professor turned to KJ. "Have you thought about researching the latest archeological finds in Ethiopia to see if there's anything close to the cave writings the team found?"

"That's the next thing I plan to do," KJ confirmed. "If we can find any writings in an earlier form of Ge'ez, it could help us bridge the gap between what we can translate now and what is totally foreign at this point."

Gabriella entered the conversation. "What do we need to do, Professor, while KJ's working on the translation?"

"I have a strategy in mind, Gabi. You're all aware our research focuses on comparing today's society to the days of Noah. That is one of the major prophecies determining the timeline for the end of days. We know it was an evil, perverted society in total rebellion against Yahweh."

The Professor rejoined them at the conference table, picked up his pipe and laid it back down without even a puff concentrating on the importance of his next statement. "The prophecies also tell us in the end of days there will be a great deception that will parallel the days of Noah. In other words it will be the same evil society. However, it will not appear to be evil. In fact, it will appear to be very good. Deception propagates beliefs that are not true and causes people to believe a lie. Something evil is coming! This I know with certainty, and it will be so convincing all people will believe the deception instead of truth."

KJ biblically confirmed what the Professor had stated. "Yeshua, who had warned about this dreadful time, prophesied saying, 'Even the very elect would be deceived if it were possible.'"

"The elect? Who is that?" Caleb asked.

"Anyone who has chosen to believe in Yahweh as the One True God and in His only Son, Yeshua. Most Christians call him by his Greek name, Jesus." KJ looked directly at Caleb and then at Gabriella as though he discerned their doubts. "Anyone can be part of 'the elect'. You just have to believe."

Out of respect for both the Professor and their new team member Gabriella kept her mouth shut. But she wanted to shout: "Maybe you're the one deceived!" Her father's journal was a polar opposite to everything the Professor, Aaron, Faith and KJ believed. She and Caleb were the only ones with an open mind to find real truth.

The Professor got up from his black leather chair with his pipe in hand and walked to the window gazing toward the peak of Mt. Hermon. He was silent for a minute and the team was all waiting for their instructions.

Finally he continued. "I believe the deception is already here." He turned and looked at the faces of the team. "You all know I am a man of science and work from a hypothesis to find truth."

"Those are the very words of my father," Gabriella thought. The Professor believed the ancient gods were fallen angels with supernatural powers. Her father believed the ancient gods were extraterrestrials with supernatural powers. Both had their merit or maybe it was neither. Maybe it was all just myth and no real gods ever existed at all. Just maybe, this life is all there is and when we die it is over. After all of her years of searching to understand the truth of the gods, she was more confused than ever!

"There is another prophecy I want to share with you." The Professor returned to the conference table and picked up his bible. The Prophet Isaiah sheds some light on our research project concerning the future return of the fallen angel Watchers. In the Jewish Septuagint version of the Old Testament the prophet Isaiah wrote over 2700 years ago in the thirteenth chapter: '*Open the gates, you ruler, I give command and I bring them. Giants are coming to fulfill my wrath.*'"

The Professor closed the book and looked at the team. "Isaiah is writing about the end of days. When the prophet said 'open the gates', I believe he is referring to the gateway where the fallen angels came to earth and ascended back to heaven. It's the same place they swore their oath to sin. It is the entry point for the fallen angel Watchers to enter the dimension of the physical earth and then return to the spiritual realm. It's a spirit portal, so to speak."

The Professor walked back to the window and pointed to Mt. Hermon. "According to the prophet Enoch, the summit of Mt. Hermon is that gateway...the axis mundi, the center of the earth, the portal to the spirit world."

The Professor turned around and looked directly at Gabriella. "It's the gateway between time and untime."

Gabriella caught her breath as she remembered Arcturus referring to Mt. Hermon as the axis mundi and the portal to the heavens. The Prophet had warned her about being caught between time and untime. Goose bumps once again were crawling up and down her arms. "What could one thing possibly have to do with the other?" Her mind was questioning.

Gabriella stared speechlessly at the Professor. He had told them in their previous meeting Mt. Hermon was the place the fallen angels had sworn their oath. Her father wrote about his exploration there. Gabriella was detecting more clearly the reason she was dreaming about Mt. Hermon. She discerned she had simply wrapped her beguiling, beautiful stranger into the dream. Her subconscious had to be twisting everything she was hearing and reading into a night fantasy. It made perfect sense!

"Are you alright?" The Professor asked Gabriella. "You look upset."

"I'm sorry, Professor. My mother and father had explored Mt. Hermon years ago and it brings back memories of them." Gabriella was not ready to reveal her father's research. She had to know the details for herself first. Caleb reached across the table and took her hand to comfort her. She could not admit the truth. The Professor's information reminded her of the mesmerizing dreams about Mt. Hermon and Arcturus. Not telling Caleb about her dreams of Arcturus caused a sting of guilt in the pit of her stomach. She soothed her guilt, reminding herself it was only a dream.

"I understand," the Professor said compassionately. "Memories are the mirror to our past and bring us both joy and sorrow. Do you need a minute before we continue?" Gabriella felt a special love for this father figure in her life. He really cared about her and it touched her deeply. She wished she could confide in him, but the dreams were too personal. She had become a solitude prisoner of her own subconscious thoughts.

"No, go ahead, Professor. I'll be fine." Gabriella said as she felt Caleb squeeze her hand confirming his support.

The Professor took a moment to form his next words. "I want to summarize and recap the most important points as we go forward. The

Prophet Enoch wrote that there were two hundred angels called the Watchers that swore the oath to sin against God with the daughters of men and willingly relinquished their heavenly estate. As a result they were bound in the place called Tartarus until their final judgment. At the end of days these fallen angels, the Watchers, will be released from captivity in the abyss for a short time. At the same time a powerful, religious leader will rise up from out of the nations and have the ability to work great miracles. People will trust him because he will demonstrate supernatural powers. He will lead the released Watchers and together they will prepare the way for a mighty leader on the earth. This man will deceive the entire world. This leader is the one the Bible calls the Anti-Christ."

The Professor paused in contemplation and took one more puff from his pipe before he continued. "I believe I know what the great deception will be. I'm going to share my hypothesis with you and then I want you all to research on your own while KJ starts working on the language translations. We'll meet again at the end of the week to assimilate the information you've found." The Professor laid his pipe in its tray. He pulled out some documents and told them it was an excerpt from an Israeli newspaper in 1987.

"On the evening of September 28, 1987, a 27 year old auto mechanic was driving south of Haifa when he saw what he thought might be a helicopter in distress hovering just above the Mediterranean Sea on Shikmona Beach. He stopped his car and to his utter amazement saw a disc-shaped craft which emitted a bright red flash before disappearing.

Two days later he returned to the site with an UFOlogist the police referred him to, Hadassah Arbel. What they discovered were remains of the most lasting proofs of physical evidence ever left by an unidentified flying object. The flash of light emitted by the craft burned its image into the sands of Shikmona Beach. A fifteen meter ellipsoid disk was burnt black into the sand but what was more interesting was what wasn't burned. In the vegetation which wasn't burned was a clear image of the pilot of the craft facing a control board."

Gabriella's hand tightened around Caleb's as she listened to the professor read from the newspaper. They were both amazed at what they were hearing! Gabriella was wondering how the Professor would connect this with fallen angels.

He laid the article back down and looked at the team. "I know you think I've lost my mind in a world of science fiction. But keep an open mind here, team. A sample of the burnt sand was sent to a laboratory for tests. The sand melted in the laboratory lights which the scientists could not explain. They discovered the sand was covered by a hydrocarbon material which does not exist on this planet. These are facts, my friends!"

The team was silent, trying to digest what the Professor was telling them. Aaron finally spoke. "Are you telling us you believe in UFOs, Dr. Brotman? And, even if you do, what could this possibly have to do with our project?"

"Allow me to continue, Aaron, and then I'll answer your questions. This incident was followed by repeats of other UFO crafts in 1988 and 1989. They came to the same site on Shikmona Beach. This is significant because there's an ancient spiritual connection to this beach area. It is within a few yards of the biblical shrine called 'Elijah's Cave'. Elijah is another prophet that substantiated over 2700 years ago what would happen at the end of days. In fact, he was taken by Yahweh in a 'chariot of fire' which many would probably call a UFO."

The Professor chuckled slightly at his own humor before continuing. "This same area of Shikmona Beach is where Elijah challenged the Canaanites in a dual of the gods. Canaan was the land of the giants, who were the nephilim descendents of the fallen angels. The challenge was to tie two bulls to separate altars and pray to their gods to supernaturally burn them and prove the true god. The Canaanite god failed to produce fire, but Elijah's God, Yahweh, sent fire down from heaven. It didn't only burn the bull but also burned the altar, the rocks and even burned into the ground. In Elijah's Cave is an ancient drawing on the wall of this event which shows the ground burned into a disc shape. It is the spitting image of the craft burned into the sands in 1987."

Gabriella and Caleb both immediately thought of the cave drawings her father had found in the deep recesses of Mt. Hermon that appeared to be craft images in the form of discs. Apparently, something from the heavens had appeared in ancient times to this area and Gabriella was even more determined to know what it was.

The team all had questions to ask but waited until the Professor finished.

"Through the 1990's there was an outbreak of UFO activity in Israel and around the world. So I began to study the connections of supernatural occurrences in our Bible to current day UFO incidents. My curiosity started with Elijah's fire and the Shikmona Beach incidents. I asked myself why aliens would come to the exact same place and leave the exact same burning image as the ancient drawing on the cave wall. Could that be some sort of sign? This question eventually led me to my hypothesis and the pivotal point of our research!"

The entire team leaned forward in their seats in anticipation. You could hear a pin drop in the room as they waited for his next words.

"I believe, my friends, the craft image burnt into Shikmona Beach was a counterfeit of the fire that God sent down when Elijah prayed. It was the same place and the same image. Remember the meaning of deception is to believe a lie."

"My hypothesis is the great deception, the prophets warned us of at the end of days, is the return of the nephilim in the deceptive disguise of extraterrestrials. Also, the two hundred fallen angel Watchers that have been held in the abyss will be released as super powers to lead the deception. The people of earth have been purposely conditioned over the years to believe in the possibility of life on other planets through movies, books and, supposedly, actual encounters. It would be easy for them to accept intergalactic beings and never suspect what is really happening."

The Professor leaned back in his chair and picked up his pipe. He watched the faces of the young team and received exactly the reaction he had anticipated...disbelief. He especially noticed that the color had drained from Gabriella's face. Caleb had moved his chair closer to her and embraced her with one arm in an obvious gesture of protection.

Aaron broke the silence. "Your hypothesis astounds me, Professor! I know the story of Elijah and have visited his cave and seen the cave drawing. I'm even aware of the UFO sightings on Shikmona Beach but I never put the two together as part of the end of days deception!"

"Think about it, Aaron," the Professor challenged him. "Does it make sense, or not?"

Aaron leaned back in his chair with a stunned look on his face. "I'm going to have to let this process." They all knew Aaron never jumped to conclusions.

Faith's voice was quivering as she tried to talk. "When I was about six years old my parents took me to the beach to see the place the craft had crashed. Everyone in Haifa was both amazed and concerned about it, especially when there were two more sightings in exactly the same place the following two years. There was never an explanation for where it came from or what it was. I've grown up believing there could be an extraterrestrial existence because of that very event."

"Exactly my point, Faith!" The Professor said.

Caleb made his thoughts known as he was enthralled with the Professor's conjecture. "I need to understand what your prophets say about this deception. If this is proposed to be a real event that soon will take place, what's the purpose? Why doesn't your God just wipe these evil beings off the face of the earth and destroy them all? You say He is all powerful?"

The Professor smiled, understanding Caleb's lack of biblical knowledge. "That's a very good question, and one you need to understand as you research UFO activity. Yahweh God created man with free will and everyone has to make their personal choice of who they will follow. The choices they made before the flood were so vile they had corrupted the entire earth. God repented He'd made man and decided to cleanse the earth. He started again with Noah who possessed the only pure bloodline. Just as God gave man a chance to make a choice for righteousness in Noah's day, before He judged the earth with the great flood, God will again give man the opportunity to make the right choice before He judges the earth the final time."

The Professor looked directly at Gabriella and continued: "The powers of both good and evil exist in the supernatural realm and constantly battle for the possession of people on the earth. The great deception is an attempt to seduce mankind into believing a lie to enable the powers of evil to take control of the earth. Our prophets tell us most will believe the lie. Every person will have to make a choice as to whom they will serve."

"What happens to the people that don't believe the deception, Dr. Brotman? You called them the elect." Caleb continued to question.

"Isaiah the Prophet tells us Jehovah will send a Righteous Judge to rule over the earth. The evil forces will be forever chained in darkness along with the people that chose to believe the deception. The earth will be the paradise that it was created to be and the elect will remain on the earth, just as Noah did after the first judgment.

The Professor's voice was filled with emotion as he spoke the next words: "I believe we are very close to seeing these events take place." His words were so potent it cut through to Caleb's very soul. He felt drawn to a personal understanding of these prophecies and not just an academic knowledge.

Gabriella was thinking the Professor's story about his God sending a supreme power from heaven to cleanse the earth and return it to the Garden of Eden sounded just as unbelievable as aliens coming and setting up their utopia. Both seemed ridiculous!

"KJ, you have just joined us and I have laid a pretty heavy hypothesis on the table. I want to know your reaction," the Professor said.

KJ laid his glasses on the table and leaned forward. "I have a very good friend that has studied UFOs extensively. He has a PhD in astronomy and has observed the skies for years. He documented sightings, time tables, and even interviewed people that claim to have been abducted. He's compiled extensive research and is convinced it's a real phenomenon. The fact it could be a satanic counterfeit he has also considered. In his research he found the modern day activity really increased around the time Israel declared their statehood in 1948, which he believes has a definite spiritual connection."

The Professor nodded his head in agreement. "All of the end time prophecies are connected with the rebirth of Israel. I don't think it's a coincidence the alien encounters started the same time. You know the word 'coincidence' is not in the Hebrew language."

"We know," the team all chimed together. They could not count the number of times he had stated the fact throughout the years.

Aaron was beginning to understand the Professor's reasoning. "KJ, it's apparent you have a good understanding of spiritual things. The Professor and your friend may be on the right track. This requires some serious contemplation on my part."

It was apparent they were waiting for Gabriella to enter the conversation. She normally was the one leading on every topic. Caleb knew the emotional battle going on inside of her and tried to break the tension and lighten the atmosphere.

"After all these years Gabi has just realized she is and has always been in love with me and she can't think straight right now." Caleb gave her a playful hug and they all laughed. Gabriella tried to smile, but she knew the room was saturated with so much speculation concerning the Professor's hypothesis that she had to make an observation of some sort.

"Professor, I'm not as surprised as you might think, but have you considered the possibility that it could be exactly the opposite of what you believe? Maybe the aliens are the real truth and your God is the counterfeit to that reality? Perhaps what you call the nephilim are actually extraterrestrials and not hybrids of angels and humans. Maybe it was aliens that mated with humans and created the giant, powerful beings. If you replace the word "alien" when you read about the mythical "gods", it makes just as much sense, maybe even more so." Caleb knew she was reciting from her father's journal, but did not say a word. Gabriella held her breath knowing she would probably offend the Professor with the very idea. She respected him too much to be defiant.

The room was silent as they all waited for Dr. Brotman's reaction. Surprisingly, he leaned back in his chair and smiled. "Gabriella, you have just described the perfect deception! That is exactly what I believe this earth will accept as the absolute truth. That is the ultimate counterfeit. That is the flip side of my hypothesis!" There was no animosity in his voice. Neither did his voice have a scolding sound.

"And that," the Professor declared, "is your assignment, my friends! Discover the truth! I want each of you to research all the information you can get access to...past and present."

Gabriella could not believe they had just been assigned a job that would allow them to devote full time going through her father's journal and research papers. This was exactly the information the Professor wanted and maybe they could prove to him the flip side of his hypothesis was actually the real truth!

"Let me end our meeting with this." The Professor was very solemn. "KJ will be working on translating the writing. If I am right, and the UFO sightings are really the return of the nephilim to deceive the world into believing they have come to help mankind, then we have a lot of work to do quickly."

The Professor lowered his voice as he spoke. "This is the reason the founders and financial backers of the Omega Watchers Project have been so dedicated to our success. It is vital to warn people the end of days is upon us, but we must have proof. It is also the reason I have been told to keep silent."

A sad countenance spread across the Professor's face. "People do not want to hear the truth of a coming judgment. They only want to hear things that make them feel good, and there are a huge amount of ministers more than willing to 'tickle their ears'. Sadly, most people will be blindsided by what is getting ready to take place." He exhaled a deep sigh before continuing.

"It is imperative you understand you're entering a spiritual realm of research where there are evil powers." The Professor's voice was filled with deep emotion and concern. "These spirits will lie, deceive, and seduce in an effort to catch you in their trap, so you will not believe the truth. Not only do we face a danger of human powers but, also, the supernatural powers that would destroy our mission and even destroy us individually, if possible. I pray the Lord of Spirits will protect you and lead each of you to His Truth."

Chapter 18

"Well, my young friends, we all have much to do the next few days," the Professor said as they walked through the outer office. "We will meet back on Friday at noon to compare notes. Hopefully, KJ will have some breakthroughs for us."

Gabriella gave the Professor a hug before she left. "Thank you for listening to me. I don't want to be offensive. I just have to know the truth."

"If you seek the truth with an open heart you will find it, Gabriella. That is promised to us. As I have always told you, I am here if you need me." The Professor gave her a kiss on her forehead and then looked at Caleb. "I know you will take good care of her."

"You never have to worry about that, Dr. Brotman. I've waited too long and I intend to make every day count for as long as we have." Caleb put his arm around Gabriella's shoulder as they left the room wondering just how long that would be.

When the team had all left his office and the door closed behind them, Sandee asked the Professor, "Will you ever be able to tell her?"

With a sad voice he responded as he walked back towards his private office, "I truly wish I knew." With that his office door closed and Sandee exhaled a long sigh as she went back to work.

The team now consisted of five members and they all walked together retracing their steps along the stone walkways toward the parking lot. Gabriella was too engrossed in her thoughts to enjoy the scenery.

"Can we give you a ride, KJ?" Caleb asked. "Where are you staying?"

"Thanks for the offer. The Professor arranged for me to have one of the faculty apartments on campus while I'm here. I can walk back but let me get your numbers so we can stay in touch." Faith offered to give KJ a tour of the campus and the team felt an immediate bond with their newest member.

On the way home Gabriella sat silent while Caleb and Aaron were engrossed in conversation regarding the meeting.

"The Professor really blind-sided me with the alien theory," Aaron admitted. "But the more I think about it, he may really be on to something."

"Yeah, man, it does make sense." Caleb responded. "But how do you know which is the truth...or if either is? Seems to me if it has to be one or the other, aliens or fallen angels, aliens makes a lot more sense. In fact, it makes perfect sense."

It was obvious Aaron did not agree. "As the Professor said, Caleb, that's why it could be the great deception. Just because it does makes sense. We live in a society that more people would accept some super human straight out of a movie more than an actual divine Creator." Aaron was totally convinced the Professor was right and Caleb wanted that confidence, too, but where was the proof?

Aaron made one last statement then rested his case. "Science has taken the position of evolution and genetic engineering. That would go more with the alien theory of earth being a human test planet. That is what people will *choose* to believe. That does not make it truth!"

Gabriella wanted so badly to tell Aaron about her father's research but did not feel it was time yet. Aaron held his religious views without any other possible interpretation and she did not want to take the chance of offending him without being able to prove her father's hypothesis.

They dropped Aaron at his apartment and stopped for a late lunch before going back to Gabriella's apartment. They drove to a small bistro overlooking the bay. The sky was clear and the gentle waves were swishing against the boats in the harbor. The patio tables had a perfect view of the crystal blue sea with the familiar backdrop of the Carmel Mountains in the distance. Caleb went in to order while Gabriella chose a table next to the water. She sat down to relax in the cooling, late summer sun.

She closed her eyes, listening to the serene sounds of the waves. They were repetitive and peaceful. She could not help but compare the sounds to her Summerland dream. The water vibrations were nothing like the mystical, musical sounds in her dream. Was it really possible that vibrations, when multiplied exponentially, could make moving waters sound like an orchestra? She could not remember ever hearing or reading anything like that and decided to do some research to see if that was even plausible.

While she was lost in her thoughts she heard a voice addressing her. "Gabriella." She opened her eyes to the bright sun and could barely make out the form of the old Jewish man looking down on her. Squinting to focus, he partially came into her view as the sun reflected around him.

"It's you! The Prophet! Please, I have so many questions!" She sat straight up in her chair ready to start asking.

"No questions." He said firmly. "The great deception has begun and the project must move quickly. In your pursuit of truth and understanding you must ask the Lord of Spirits to keep you from the evil place." He handed her a scroll and then quickly walked away.

She stood up to follow him as Caleb came out of the restaurant. "Caleb! That was him! That was the Prophet again!" She exclaimed and pointed in the direction he had gone. Mysteriously, he was nowhere to be seen. The other people sitting around her looked towards where she was pointing and then looked at her questioningly. She felt like an idiot as she sat down and waited for the atmosphere to return to normal. The Prophet had simply disappeared into mid-air.

Gabriella sat silently clutching the scroll and Caleb knew it was proof someone had visited her. "What is that?"

"I don't know. The old man handed it to me and told me the deception had already begun and he had come to warn me. Then he said the strangest thing. He told me if I asked the Lord of Spirits he would keep me from an evil place. Then he was gone as quickly as he appeared. What evil place, Caleb? Does it make any sense to you?" Gabriella was trembling as she handed the scroll to Caleb.

"Do you want to open it here?" he asked.

"No. Let's take our lunch home. I need privacy."

Caleb went inside the restaurant and returned with carry out boxes. Gabriella watched every person coming and going, hoping to catch a glimpse of the Prophet. It was apparent he was not returning.

Gabriella and Caleb wasted no time returning to the apartment. They both were anxious to know what the mysterious scroll would reveal. Neither was concerned about lunch as they entered the apartment, put the food on the counter and sat down to unroll the scroll.

Gabriella untied the brittle, leather string and broke the wax seal that kept the scroll rolled. She gently tried to pull back the end but the paper was old and stuck together. She was afraid she was going to destroy it when she tried to gently pull it apart. She pulled it down just far enough to see the script was in a language much like what they had found in the cave. Caleb looked as frustrated as she felt.

"Now what do we do?" She asked him.

Caleb grabbed his phone. "I'll call Aaron and you try to get the Professor."

They each made their calls and both were disappointedly greeted by voicemail. They left messages and would just have to wait.

Caleb put his arm around Gabriella. "I know you're frustrated, Gabi, but I'm sure we'll hear back from one of them soon? Let's have lunch while we're waiting."

They took their sandwiches to the balcony and Gabriella tried to force herself to eat. She just nibbled at her sandwich as she thought about what message the scroll would reveal and the warnings of the Prophet. But what captivated her thoughts the most was the evil place he warned her of. She did not know of any evil place in her life.

"I wish the phone would ring, Caleb." Gabriella paced the floor, wondering why the Prophet had warned her again about danger.

Caleb could tell the fear she had experienced after the Prophet's first visit was descending on her again. "Gabi, I am not going to leave you. Too much is going on. I am parking myself right in your living room until we get some answers."

She knew he would not leave her alone. Even knowing he would be there to protect her did not totally calm her anxiety. If they were dealing with a spirit realm, she had no idea how anyone could fight it. Her deepest hope was her father's journal would give more answers. She looked through the balcony window to where the black box was sitting on the coffee table, silently beckoning.

"Let's read, Caleb. We need some answers!" Caleb got up and pulled her out of the balcony chair and into his arms, the place that had become her safe haven. In the back of his mind he kept questioning how he could fight what he could not see, touch or feel. He recognized his need for a power source beyond himself, but had no idea how to find it.

He kept his arm of protection around her shoulders as they started back inside. "I want to show you some of the articles I read after you went to bed last night." Caleb commented pulling back the balcony curtains for Gabriella to enter. "A lot of it goes right along with what the Professor was talking about but I didn't want to say too much until you'd had a chance to read it."

Gabriella made coffee while Caleb found the papers he wanted to read. The fresh, ground fragrance filled the room and a feeling of home settled over them. Gabriella's apartment had always been a place to sleep and work. She had not felt a sense of home since her father passed. It was so natural for Caleb to be with her day and night. She did not ever want him to leave.

Chapter 19

It had only been an hour but it seemed like an eternity when Gabriella's phone rang and Dr. Brotman was returning her call. She could not wait to blurt it out. "I've had another visit from the Prophet and we really need to see you, Professor!"

Dr. Brotman could hear the urgency in her voice. "I'm not too far away, Gabriella, I can come by your apartment in about ten minutes."

"Please hurry, Professor," she said breathlessly. "It's really important!"

"I'm on my way."

"He'll be here in a few minutes." Caleb could hear the relief in her voice. "Stack the papers and put them back in the box before he gets here. If they're scattered everywhere I know he'll want to know what we're researching. I don't want any questions until we have some answers."

Within minutes there was a knock at the door. Gabriella let the Professor in and was recounting her visit from the Prophet when he saw the scroll. His face drained of color.

"What is it, Professor? What's wrong?" Gabriella detected that just the sight of the scroll had an immediate impact on him.

"Can I have a glass of water, please?" The Professor asked as he dropped into one of the wicker chairs. Gabriella rushed to the kitchen while Caleb sat down next to him, making sure he was all right.

Gabriella set the water in front of the Professor and sat down next to Caleb. The color was returning to his face as he drank. They had never seen the Professor totally without words.

Gently the Professor picked up the scroll. "Was the seal broken when this was given to you?" He asked Gabriella.

"No. I broke it open. It was so brittle I barely pulled and it snapped in two. I just assumed when the old man gave it to me I was to read it. Shouldn't I have?" She was concerned she had done something really wrong.

The Professor explained to her: "In ancient times when scrolls were sealed it was only to be broken by the person the document was intended for. When the recipient received it, they knew it had been kept private by the seal. Since it wasn't previously broken, it means we are the first to read it. You say the Prophet gave you this? The same man you saw a few days ago?" She detected doubt in his voice.

"I'm sure it was the same man." Gabriella stated emphatically. "The sun was in my eyes but it was the same Hasidic clothing, dark glasses, and beard. He looked exactly the same."

Ever so cautiously the Professor turned the scroll and surveyed it without attempting to open it. Then he laid it back on the table. He looked at Gabriella and Caleb and they could perceive in his eyes the scroll was of exceptional value.

The Professor cleared his throat. "There's no doubt this is an ancient scroll. I can tell by the paper and the condition. It's exactly the same condition as the Dead Sea Scrolls discovered in 1947 at Qumran. When I worked on the translation the paper had been mutilated from time and humidity. Some of the sheets had become so badly stuck together that years passed before we could decipher the writings. Digital infrared technology helped in some cases, but some writings were a total lose due to the condition of the scrolls. I hesitate to even touch this one."

Gabriella nodded her head in understanding. "When I tried to pull the page down it stuck so badly I was afraid I would damage it."

"That was a smart move," the Professor assured her. "We won't be able to do anything with it right now. It will take a special process of separating the pages without destroying them."

"So we have no idea what this is all about?" Gabriella's frustration was mounting. "Why didn't he just bring the scroll to you? Apparently he knew that's where it would end up? He had to know I couldn't do anything with it since he seems to know everything else about me!"

"I can honestly say I'm at a total loss, Gabi." The Professors voice was filled with obvious confusion and she also detected a veiled apprehension.

"Professor, do you have any idea what he could mean about the evil place? I don't go anywhere evil!" Gabriella's mind was spinning, trying to discern the Prophet's warnings.

"Maybe it's not a physical 'place' as we think of it, but a 'spiritual' place. Do you realize, Gabi, there are 'familiar spirits' that are passed through the generations from ancestors? We are constantly being watched by our guardian angel and also by a demonic familiar spirit. When we die those spirits move on to watch the next generation. They see everything we say and do. That's the reason when people have séances and they think they're talking to dead loved ones, they are actually communicating with a familiar spirit. The spirit can answer the most intimate details of their lives because they were always watching that person."

Gabriella's eyes grew wider as she listened to the Professor. "I've read about stuff like that but never believed it to have an ounce of truth. I thought it all a big fake just to make money."

Caleb who had only been listening to this point commented. "Really, Professor? Do you really believe that?"

"It's definitely true if you believe the Bible, which you know I believe every word." The Professor pulled a notepad from his shirt pocket and made some notes. "Here, Caleb, these are bible verses from Leviticus 20:27, Deuteronomy 18:11, 2 Kings 21:6, 2 Chronicles 33:6 that explain familiar spirits. You don't even need a Bible. You can Google it and you'll find many more, too. This is nothing to be taken lightly. These spirits are very powerful and very real!"

"If that's true, what kind of power do they have over us...if they see and know everything we do?" Caleb's question showed a leaning toward believing the Professor.

"It's very simple. The only power they have in your life is the power you give them! A ghost, aka familiar spirit, will not visit you unless you have opened a door to them through your curiosity or seeking to find them. A voice from the dead cannot be heard unless you enter a séance or use some source of conjuring. That is why God specifically demanded in His law, the Torah, you are not to be part of these acts, which He calls abominations. You are opening a door to an evil place! And once the door is open it becomes very dangerous."

The Professor turned to Gabriella. "Perhaps that is the place the Prophet is warning you of. You said you had a shaman ancestor that communicated with a familiar spirit. That puts you in a higher possibility of paranormal activity. But you have to give access to the spirit for it to manifest."

Gabriella just shook her head. "You know I have the greatest respect for you, Professor, but this is just too far out for me."

She could tell the Professor was not offended but he was very concerned. "Just be very careful, Gabriella. As the Prophet told you, the Lord of Spirits is stronger than any spirit that exists. His name is Yeshua and He will answer when we call to Him."

The Professor hesitated for a moment and then looked from Gabriella to Caleb. "I warned you this project could take some dubious turns and could become dangerous. It's not only the powers of man on earth that would stop our project but the spiritual powers of darkness."

The Professor took Gabriella's hand in a father type embrace. "The human psyche is a tremendous intuitive gift granted to us by our Creator. You can feel when something isn't quite right. Follow those intuitions."

He gave her hand a gentle squeeze, got up from the table and looked out the balcony doors. "You have a beautiful view, Gabriella." But she knew he was not interested in the view. He had seen it many times. It was obvious he was checking it for safety. "Caleb, I assume you are staying here to protect her?"

"Yes, Professor," Caleb quickly affirmed. "I'm not leaving until we have things under control."

The Professor turned and looked at Caleb with an expression that did not need defining. "That day may never come. If the Prophet is correct, and I believe he is, the deception has already started. We could be getting very close to exposing the truth and that is where the greatest danger lies."

Caleb's eyes turned to the woman he loved. If by some outside chance the Professor was correct in his theology concerning the familiar spirits, Caleb realized his need to understand how to call upon the Lord of Spirits. He was fully aware his own strength would not be enough to protect her. Not if they were dealing with evil powers beyond this earth.

"May I take the scroll with me, Gabriella?" The Professor asked as he walked from the balcony doors.

"Of course you can. I know the Prophet intended for you to have it anyway. I wish I knew why I was the go between."

"Hopefully we will all have some answers soon. I have to go. I have some important work to do." The Professor moved quickly to prepare to leave. "I must get started on the scroll. I never expected this."

Gabriella sighed in relief that the Professor did not notice her father's black box. He was obsessed with the scroll. She carefully picked up the scroll, gently caressing the parchment as she passed it to the Professor. He opened his briefcase and cautiously slid the ancient treasure into a leather sleeve kept for fragile documents, storing it for protection from further damage.

"We may need to meet before Friday," he said as he hurriedly left the apartment, with not even his normal hug of good-bye.

Gabriella closed and locked the door and turned to Caleb. "Did that seem a bit odd to you? His whole countenance seemed to change when he saw the scroll. I'm not quite sure what to make of it."

Caleb assured her with his usual confidence, "You're reading too much into every little detail, Gabi Girl."

Gabriella was sure he was right and together they sat down to begin more investigation into the mysterious journal.

Caleb reopened the black box and took the journal out to begin. He turned to the marked page where they had left off. She motioned for him to read first.

January 1, 1983

It is New Year's Day and Angelena and I are anxiously awaiting our new addition in the spring. We have discussed all through the holiday season what it will be like next year to have our child with us and how much our lives will change...for the better. The nursery is finished and she is buying all the baby necessities we will need to welcome our precious one.

As she has prepared for our baby's arrival I have continued research on Edgar Cayce's work and I am documenting my findings with an open mind. My scientific wisdom tells me I am losing my hold on reality, but there is something inside me that drives me daily. I am determined to know once and for all the total truth.

Caleb paused to see if Gabriella had any comments. He knew reading about her parents' anticipation of her arrival would be an emotional moment for her. He looked up at her and she was smiling in spite of the tears that had escaped and slowly drifting across her cheeks.

"It's wonderful to know how much I was wanted." She said after a few moments of gaining her composure. "His journal makes me realize how much like him I am in wanting to understand the gods. There were times he'd make statements that seemed odd or disconnected but I had no concept of what he meant. In his later years he often spoke of the shaman powers of the Cherokee. I think he really wanted to discuss it with me but was afraid to let me know too much. Oh, Caleb, how I wish he could sit down with us and explain his research in person!"

"I know," Caleb said soothingly. "But he did have the foresight to document everything. And it must have been an act of the 'gods' that it got to you right at this time." His hand reached for hers and he gave a gentle squeeze knowing she would understand his questionable reasoning.

"Keep reading," she said continuing to hold his hand.

In studying Edgar Cayce's writings he often related there were elemental beings, which consisted of vibrations (similar to electrical energies). Under some conditions, these vibrational forces could manifest into physical forms which were always amazingly beautiful. He was of the opinion they often appear and are not recognized as being extraterrestrials.

So I have continued my research and feel I am getting closer to truth. I have articles written by highly respected professionals that I have included with this journal to support my hypothesis.

Caleb looked up from the journal. "I was reading some of those last night." He reached for the pile of neatly stacked articles and filtered through. "Listen to this article!"

"A medical practitioner, Dr Stephen Greer, supports a disclosure program and owns videotape of hundreds of hours of testimony from high ranking military personal. They all confirm that UFOs are real and there is a systemic and deliberate cover up by government agencies. Retired American Army and NATO Command Sergeant-Major Robert Dean in the 1960s and 70s guarded COSMIC-classified files which showed that government agencies were fully aware that extraterrestrials and UFOs regularly penetrated our airspace."

Caleb laid the article to the side picking up more. "There are several interesting articles in here from the A.R.E. Journal. That's the 'Association for Research and Enlightenment'. It's a resource center in New York that has continued Cayce's work. "

They read through several articles all of which reported, what the writer considered, the undeniable truth of alien existence and interaction with earth's civilization. After several hours of reading and discussing they went back to the journal.

Caleb read the last paragraph of the New Years Day entry.

Now to my favorite part of the day, the time I spend with my soul mate. Our little one is kicking like crazy! Angelena will sing to our child as I lay my hand on her stomach and wait for movement, wondering if our little one will be a kicking football player or kicking cheerleader. Either way our lives will be complete. Life is wonderful in spite of this agonizing research.

Chapter 20

Caleb pulled Gabriella out of her chair and held her close. "Let's take a break and get some fresh air." They went out on the balcony to a perfectly enchanting evening. The rain had stopped and the clouds had drifted away, revealing the resplendent horizon of the Mediterranean Sea. A fresh, exhilarating breeze was blowing across the balcony helping to expel the dark shadows surrounding her. She watched the sea gulls soaring around the harbor boats as the sun slowly descended into the sea. She leaned against Caleb and felt his arm go around her waist, pulling her close as they watched the sun descend into the darkening sea. The evening was sublime and Gabriella, for a brief moment, pushed everything out of her mind, but the closeness of Caleb.

Caleb pulled slightly away from Gabriella and reached into his pocket and pulled out a small black box. "When I went to my apartment Saturday I brought this back with me. I've had it for years hoping one day I would be able to give it to you." He pulled open the lid unveiling the most stunning, antique diamond ring Gabriella had ever seen.

Caleb spoke with a tenderness that melted her heart. "I've waited over a decade for you to realize we destined to be together. When you finally did, it's in the midst of total chaos and uncertainly of what the future holds. That makes it even more important we waste no time."

"This was my grandmother's engagement ring. When she died she left it to me to give to the woman I would marry." He got down on one knee and held her hands. With the backdrop of sparkling harbor lights and stars twinkling approval Caleb spoke in a quivering voice. "I wish we could be in some enchanting, magical storybook place to ask my princess this question, but when you're with me every place and every moment is magical. We don't know what will happen or how much time we may have. If I only have one day, and it's with your love, it's better than a lifetime without you. Will you marry me, Gabriella?"

She could see love saturating his eyes. His hands were shaking as he held the ring poised to put on her finger. She knew they were born to be together and she would love him until the day she died.

"Yes, oh yes!" She exclaimed. "Why did I waste so many years?" He kissed her hand and then gently slid the ring on her finger. He stood up and took her fully into his arms. Joy was sweeping over her in wave after wave and she realized her dream had come true. Caleb loved her the way her father had loved her mother. It was a rare love that most people never experienced...a love that transcended the earthly realm of time and space.

Caleb wanted to immediately call his parents and let them know. Gabriella wished desperately she had family she could call. The Professor was the closest thing she had to a father and he had too much on his mind to bother him. Of course, she would call her dearest friend Faith, who in many ways was like a sister, but it just was not the same as being able to call her mother and father who would have understood totally what they were experiencing. That feeling of being cheated by life swelled up inside her once again.

As she watched Caleb place the call with his face gleaming, she realized she would have family again. His family would now be her family, too. She had spent time with them on many occasions over the years and they were warm and loving. They had come to visit Caleb in Israel several times and he always invited her to be part of their visits. She thought at the time it was because they were best friends, but she realized he had always known someday they would be together.

She could hear the excitement in his voice as he talked with his mother. "Mom, I have some news for you. Gabriella and I are going to be married!" She watched the emotion in his face as his mother replied. Caleb wanted Gabriella to hear her reaction and put his phone on speaker.

"Caleb, how wonderful!" His mother exclaimed. "It certainly took you long enough to ask her! Your father and I could tell how you two felt about each other. We will have a daughter and I am so excited. You do know we will spoil our grandchildren rotten!"

"You're moving pretty quickly, Mom. We have to have a wedding first." But Caleb laughed as he winked at Gabriella. "Gabi can hear you, Mom. I have the phone on speaker."

"Gabriella, my dear, welcome to our family!" His mother's voice was filled with love and reminded her of her own mother's voice that she vaguely remembered.

"Gabriella dear, I am thrilled our only child is finally marrying. I have always wanted a daughter and you will be like our very own. When will the wedding be?" It was obvious his mother was ready to start making plans.

Caleb answered for them. "I've just asked her tonight. Mom, I gave her Granna's engagement ring. It is beautiful on her hand." He reached out to Gabriella and pulled her next to him, kissing the hand the precious ring now graced. "I know Granna would have loved Gabi." His voice was filled with emotion as he looked into Gabriella's eyes. "But about the date, we haven't discussed it yet. As far as I'm concerned tomorrow is not soon enough." He smiled at Gabriella and she actually felt a flush sweep over her. How could she feel this depth of love and all these years never realize it was deep inside just waiting for the chance to surface?

"Oh, no, Caleb!" His mother's German accent was humorous as she let him know that would not be acceptable. "You have to give us enough time to plan to be there. We can't miss your wedding!"

"I'm just kidding, Mom. Of course we want you at our wedding."

Gabriella interrupted Caleb. "I would have it no other way. We'll coordinate everything with you. As soon as we decide when and where, you'll be the first to know."

"Thank you, Gabi, and I will do anything I can to help. Just let me know, dear." Gabriella's heart melted as she heard his mother's sincere desire to be part of this special time. "Caleb, your father wants to speak to you. Hold on."

"Caleb, my boy!" His father's voice was deep and kind. "This is the very best news I could imagine. I was beginning to wonder if you would ever get the nerve!" She could hear his father laugh with heartfelt joy. "Perhaps we should plan a quick trip to Israel to spend a few days and help with plans. Since Gabriella's parents are no longer with her, I insist on paying for the wedding. I will hear no arguing about it! Understand?"

The gesture of kindness pushed Gabriella over the emotional cliff. Tears began to cascade down her cheeks as the feeling of family bonds began to settle in her heart. Oh, how she had missed this! The tears flowed even more when she realized she could have had a family again long ago if she had not been so stubborn and independent!

"Thank you, sir." She was barely able to mutter the words. "That is so kind."

"Sir?" His father corrected. "I insist you call me Dad. You are about to become our daughter. From now on we would love to be Mom and Dad to you."

Gabriella leaned against Caleb as she sobbed openly, allowing the years of loneliness to release from her heart. As much as she missed her own parents she felt the void quickly filling in her life. She could not wait to be Caleb's wife and a part of his wonderful family.

"We'll start making plans right away and keep you posted on every detail." Caleb assured his father.

"Very good and we love you, son. Your mother is blowing you kisses."

"I love you both and see you soon." Caleb disconnected the call and took Gabriella in his arms.

"How does it feel to have parents again? And you don't have to answer that, Gabi. I already know." He held her close and whispered in her ear. "I can't wait for you to be Mrs. Caleb Timothy Ahrberg."

In the midst of her joy Gabriella could hear in her mind the melodic voice of Arcturus, telling her she could not be with Caleb. She would no longer have the power for the night astral journeys that would lead her into harmonic convergence with the universe and total spiritual truth. Nor would she see Arcturus again. She quickly pushed the thoughts aside and reminded herself once again they were just mystical dreams reflecting the ominous events surrounding her. In fact, the dreams had to stop! She would allow nothing to destroy this wonderful life that was just beginning.

Gabriella and Caleb decided they needed an evening out to celebrate with their friends. Neither of them wanted to dampen the excitement of their engagement with the doom and gloom of aliens and evil angels. They called Aaron and Faith and asked if they would like to join them for a late dinner. Both agreed.

"Can I invite KJ? "Faith asked. We've been going over lots of notes on the project and he could use a break, too."

"Absolutely! Meet us at the Harbor View Restaurant at nine. We have some big news." Caleb disconnected the call before Faith could ask any questions.

He turned laughing and gave her a quick hug. "This is our night, Cinderella. Let's get ready to celebrate."

Gabriella took a quick shower and dried her hair allowing the long, natural curls to fall gracefully around her face and down her back. A slight amount of make-up was all it took to compliment the natural beauty of her face. She slid on a black dress for evening wear and black high heels. Her ensemble was completed with a string of translucent colored pearls that had an undertone of soft blue. The necklace was a high school graduation gift from her father. He told her the soft blue reminded him of the color of her eyes. He had died shortly after that and she had only worn them once....to his memorial service.

She looked at herself in the mirror and hoped Caleb would be proud to have her officially by his side. She walked out of her bedroom and stood waiting for his approval. His eyes told her all she needed to know.

"Wow! Cinderella has made her grand entrance! Where have you been hiding, you beautiful creature?"

She giggled like a teenager and replied, "I have been waiting for my Prince Charming to come." As she said the words she thought of how unlike her to talk like that. She had never been a romantic.

"All kidding aside, Gabi, you are breathtaking. I will be the envy of every man that lays eyes on you! I may even have to fight a few off."

She was all smiles as she went to the table to pick up her keys to leave. Caleb had already closed the balcony doors and she could see the lock in place. The curtains were open allowing a view of the harbor. As she started to turn back around to leave she saw the outline of a man standing on the balcony staring at her. She knew instantly who it was. The words of her father's journal rang in her ear. "*Under some conditions, these vibrational forces could manifest into physical forms which are always amazingly beautiful.*"

Dizziness came over her and she felt her body swaying. When her keys dropped to the floor Caleb realized something was terribly wrong and caught her as she passed out.

She was immediately submerged into darkness and felt she was falling into a deep pit. Down and down she was going and there was no bottom, no end to the plunging depth. She could not breath.

Arcturus appeared to her and caught her hand and as soon as she felt his touch the breathing became natural again. She saw light at the end of the tunnel. A glorious light filled with the majestic colors of the rainbows of Summerland.

In the distance was the mesmerizing music of the water falls blending with Arcturus' melodic humming. Peace settled through her like penetrating light saturating the darkness. She relaxed and was wondering where this travel would take her. As the light became brighter, the peace became sweeter. She was ready to immerse herself totally in the illumination when she heard Caleb calling her name in the distance.

"Gabi, are you alright. Gabi, wake up!" She felt Caleb's arms holding her close as her eyes opened and began to focus. Immediately her eyes darted toward the terrace but no one was there.

"Are you alright, Gabi? Do I need to call a doctor? What do I need to do?" She heard sheer panic in Caleb's voice.

The color was returning to her face and her breathing was steady. Caleb was in a state of panic. "Can I get you anything? Tell me, Gabi. I was afraid I was losing you. I thought you had stopped breathing! I'm going to call for help!"

The vision of Arcturus standing on the terrace was branded in her mind. She was wide awake, but yet she saw him there. Or did she? She was overwhelmed by the excitement of their engagement and that layered on top of the alien stories and mystical dreams apparently was all too much. Plus, she had hardly eaten anything all day.

She sat up, still light-headed. "I'm alright, Caleb. I must have fainted. I think not eating today caught up with me, and in the midst of our engagement excitement it was overwhelming. I'll be fine." He helped her to her feet. She was a bit unsteady but was regaining her strength.

"Do you feel like going out? We can always cancel."

"I'll be fine. This is our perfect evening and nothing is going to change that!" She glanced one more time towards the terrace just to be sure. Caleb watched her eyes and felt that deep churning in his soul there was something she was not telling him.

She forced Arcturus out of her mind. "Come on, Caleb. Let's begin our celebration."

He kept his arm around her waist to steady her as they left the apartment and took the elevator down to the parking garage. Caleb opened the sunroof as they drove to the restaurant. The warm night breezes surrounded them with a hypnotizing tranquility. He held Gabriella's hand adorned with the sparkling, antique diamond ring he had placed upon it.

"I still have the handwritten note that my grandmother included with the ring, Gabi. One of her final wishes was someday I would find the woman of my dreams and this ring would be our symbol of a supernatural bond." He ever so gently squeezed her hand and saw a smile spread across her face.

Gabriella leaned her head back and looked out the sunroof enjoying the beauty of the heavenly skies. "Caleb, how could something evil come from something so beautiful? I've tried to weigh it out in my mind and it makes so much more sense that my father was right. In this beautiful, vast universe surely we are not alone and it would seem extraterrestrials have tried to let us know that."

Caleb squeezed her hand. "I'm sure if there are millions of other planets with other beings, none is more beautiful than you. Now, let's forget all the paranormal for one night. Let's just be two people in love discovering and planning our life together. No one's guaranteed how long they have and we'll all face our end of days in one way or another. I want every moment we have to be magical, Cinderella."

She turned her head toward him and smiled. "You're absolutely right. Tonight we will celebrate with our friends. No work and no fear."

They finished the drive in silence each lost in their thoughts of their future together. When they arrived Caleb parked the car and came around to open the door for Gabriella. He pulled her to him and for a brief moment she had a flashback of the image of Arcturus standing on her balcony. She quickly pushed the thought away. She would not allow anything to destroy this wonderful evening! They crossed the parking lot holding hands and entered the restaurant lobby.

"We would like a private table with a nice view of the bay, please." Caleb instructed the

maitre d' and placed a sizeable amount of money in his hand.

"Yes, sir!" He responded and showed them to an area with a panoramic scenic view. As they waited for the rest of the team to arrive, they held hands and began to plan their future. Within minutes they saw Faith, Aaron and KJ weaving in and out of tables to join them.

When they sat down at the table Faith, who already suspected she knew the big announcement, could not wait any longer. "Gabi, Caleb, what's going on?"

Caleb stood up and tapped his water glass with his spoon. "I have an announcement to make! This beautiful creature has agreed to be my wife!" Gabriella blushed as she held up her hand to display the engagement ring.

"Wonderful!" Faith exclaimed. "Congratulations! That certainly was quick. You just decided this morning you were a couple."

Caleb laughed. "We've been a couple for years, she just wouldn't admit it!"

"I'm not at all surprised and wish you the very best. I assume I will be your best man?" Aaron stated it more than asked it.

"I will be the 'best' man, Aaron! If you were the best she would be marrying you!" Caleb joked. "Kidding aside, of course you will. You've encouraged me for years to not give up. You kept telling me she would come around eventually." He looked at Gabriella and back to Aaron. "I'm so glad you were right."

KJ had just met them but it was obvious their love had been brewing for a very long time. He lifted his water glass to them and proposed a toast. They all lifted their glasses as he spoke: "May your love for each other be combined with the love of God, that you may enjoy the fullness of your earthly love as it is blessed from the perfect love of our Heavenly Father!" They all joined their glasses and sipped.

"What a beautiful gesture," Caleb said being drawn more towards understanding this heavenly love.

"So when is the wedding going to be?" Faith asked expecting Gabriella to let her know she would be part of the wedding party.

"We haven't set a date yet. Faith, you know I want you to be my maid of honor." Gabriella watched a smile spread across Faith's face.

"You know it." Faith could not control her excitement. "Behind your back Aaron and I have said for a very long time someday you two would get married and we'd be standing right there with you. We just didn't think it would take this long." The group laughed and all looked at Gabriella. She knew she had been the hold-up, but it was full speed ahead now!

There was a wonderful atmosphere of celebration. It was a perfect dinner and being with friends was the crowning touch to a perfect night.

Chapter 21

The team left the restaurant and walked together to the parking lot. Caleb was going to drop the rest of the team at their apartments on their way back to Gabriella's. They were almost to the car when Aaron's phone rang.

"Who could that be this late? Hello." The team waited while Aaron answered.

The expression on his face told them there was something very wrong. "Yes, I know him." Anxiety was growing as he looked at each of them with fear on his face. "Yes, of course. I'm on my way."

Aaron disconnected the call and with a quivering voice said, "Let's go!" He could barely speak. "It's the Professor. He was in a car accident and he's in the emergency room at Bnai Zion Medical Center. We have to go now!"

"Is he going to be okay?" Gabriella was in tears as they rushed to the car.

"I don't know all the details, but apparently it's pretty bad. They found my number as the last call on his cell phone. I just talked to him a couple hours ago when he was telling me about the scroll you gave him today, Gabi. Come on, guys, we gotta hurry!"

"Someone needs to call Sandee. The Professor would want her to be there." Faith said through her tears.

Aaron made the call to Sandee while Caleb drove speedily to the hospital. He dropped the rest of the team at the ER door and rushed to park the car. By the time he had gotten inside they were already talking to a doctor. The news was not good.

The Jewish doctor's face was very somber. "We're taking him back for surgery now. There are injuries causing internal bleeding and must be stopped, if he's to survive. It could be a lengthy surgery so you may want to go to the surgery waiting room where you'll be more comfortable. I'll talk to you as soon as the surgery is over.'

After the Professor's wife had passed in the late 90's, having no children he buried himself in his work and his team had become his family. In many ways, he had been like a father to them.

"He can't die, Caleb!" Gabriella was sobbing desperately. "I can't lose him, too. I wanted him to give me away at our wedding. We haven't even had a chance to tell him we're engaged. Life is not fair!" Caleb held her close and wondered how much more she could take.

They made their way to the waiting room for what would become long hours of agonizing suspense. Aaron paced the floor praying in Hebrew. Caleb sat next to Gabriella with an arm of protection constantly around her. KJ and Faith sat next to each other, both silently praying.

Gabriella wished she knew who or what to pray to! She left Caleb and walked to the large window that looked out towards the heavens and whispered to an unknown god, "If you're out there somewhere, please let the Professor live."

They were the only people in the surgery waiting room and could talk openly. Aaron asked first, "What will we do about the project if something happens? We don't know enough to keep it going. The Professor is the hinge on which the whole project hangs!"

"We can't think that way!" Faith cried. "We've got to believe he's coming out of this! He IS going to be alright! Don't even..."

Faith's words were interrupted as the door opened and Sandee came in, followed by two Israeli policemen. "I met these policemen on my way in. They have some questions to ask us."

Caleb stood up and did not hesitate to ask, "What's going on? What do the police have to do with this?"

The older of the two policemen introduced the two of them. "I'm Detective Richards and this is my partner Detective Harold. We just need you to answer a few questions."

"About what?" Caleb questioned.

Detective Richards pulled out a pen, a pad of paper and started asking questions, without any further explanation. "I need each of you to tell me how you know Dr. Brotman."

They each in turn told who they were, gave their addresses and phone numbers and told how they knew him.

"So you all work with Dr. Brotman?" He asked in a voice that was on the edge of suspicious. "What kind of work do you do?"

They all looked at each other and wondered how much they should tell him, since the project was not to be discussed with anyone. If they did not answer his questions, they could be in serious trouble. If they told them about the project, they could be in serious trouble. They felt they were out on a limb that could break at any minute.

Caleb became the spokesperson for their team. With his tall stature and strong countenance he would be less intimidated by the officers. The rest of the team allowed him to take the lead.

With a strong voice that did not waiver at all Caleb answered. "We are all scientists. We conduct research for the Professor. Detective Richards, can you tell us why you're here?"

The policeman was cordial but stern. "All I can tell you is the circumstances of the car accident are questionable."

"Questionable?" Caleb echoed in shock. "What do you mean questionable?"

The policeman could see the young group was very upset and it was apparent they were all shocked at the news. Detective Richards relaxed slightly.

He motioned for them to sit down and he pulled up a chair to continue the questioning. "Now one by one, please tell me what kind of research you do for Dr. Brotman." In turn each told what science degree they had and the type of research work they did. None mentioned The Omega Watchers Project.

Caleb was the last to address the question and finished with a question. "We're all earth scientists and we work with Dr. Brotman on finding ancient artifacts and determining their period of history. What does that have to do with the accident, if I may ask?" Caleb was very polite and the detective obviously appreciated his attitude.

"I'm trying to determine if his work could have anything to do with the accident. Do you know of any reason someone would want to harm Dr. Brotman?" The detective asked.

Silence filled the room as his words settled in. The Professor had warned them the project could become dangerous. No one said a word and simply shook their heads no. They simply did not know what to say. They did not even know who the founders and financial backers of the project were so they surely did not know who would try to harm him. Everyone in the group was thinking that if it wasn't an accident they could all be in danger.

"Do you know of any students or fellow professors that had issue with Dr. Brotman?" Again they all shook their heads no.

"Apparently you worked closely with him. Are you aware of any project he was involved in that someone would want stopped?" The detective could tell immediately he had struck a nerve. He watched their faces as they struggled to try to hide their emotions. Yes, he was convinced they definitely knew something!

"Listen to me," he said with compassion. "I am not the enemy. This is serious, very serious. The brake lines had been cut in Dr. Brotman's car. We have no idea where he had been, but he was coming down Mt. Carmel when he hit a rock wall along side of the road. If it had been just a little further down the mountain he would have gone over a cliff. I think that's what was planned. Someone wants him dead."

The gasps of disbelief could be heard from everyone in the room as they fought back both anger and tears.

Aaron blurted out. "I just talked to him a couple of hours before I got your call, detective, but he didn't say where he was. We were setting up a meeting for first thing in the morning to go over some, uh, paperwork."

"What kind of paperwork? What was it pertaining to?" The detective watched Aaron's reaction closely.

"I really don't know. I haven't seen it. I would have found out in the morning." Aaron looked at his watch and realized it already was well into the morning hours. "Well, in just a few hours from now we were to meet."

Gabriella was trying to decide about the scroll and just how much she should tell the detectives. She looked at Caleb and saw from his eyes to not say anything. She remembered the Professor warning them there were people in high places that wanted the project stopped. She remained silent.

As the detective was making notes the doctor came in the waiting room. The look on his face was not very promising.

"He's out of surgery. The impact of the accident was so forceful it compressed his internal organs and ripped open a main artery in his stomach.

The soft tissue lining of the spleen and liver were torn from the trauma and blood had filled the abdominal cavity. We were able to stop the bleeding but he's still unconscious and lost a lot of blood. We've started a transfusion. This type of injury normally results in shock to the organs and they stop functioning."

The doctor's voice became more compassionate as he continued. "The ultimate outcome from this type of injury is usually coma, stroke or death. All we can do now is wait and hope for a miracle. If you know how to pray, I would suggest you do so. It's up to a higher power now. We've done all we can do."

"Can you give us any idea what his chances are?" Caleb asked the doctor.

"Rarely, do we see patients fully recover from these types of injuries. If he makes it through the next twenty four hours we'll have a better idea what the prognosis will be. I'm sorry I don't have better news. Is there someone named Gabriella here?" The doctor looked around the group.

"I'm Gabriella." She replied as she stepped closer to the doctor.

"Just as Dr. Brotman was being sedated, he asked for you. He said he must let you know, but the sedation took over before he could finish. It sounded very important whatever it was. I hope he'll have another chance to tell you."

The doctor was turning to leave the room. "There's nothing more you can do here. I suggest you go home and rest. The nurse on duty will call Aaron if there are any changes."

With that the doctor left them. Sandee began to cry uncontrollably. Gabriella and Faith also could not contain their emotions. Aaron and Caleb struggled to keep calm but they were losing the battle.

"I wonder what he needed to tell me." Gabriella was sobbing out loud. "What could have been so important that it was on his mind, when he could have been dying?"

Sandee looked at Gabriella wanting to comfort her but knew she had promised silence to the Professor. Instead she gave her a hug and whispered, "It'll be all right. Don't worry, honey."

"No! It won't be all right. Not if he dies!" Gabriella was not one to raise her voice but she did not care who heard her.

KJ took control of the situation. "Well, I know how to pray! Sandee, Aaron, Faith, you do, too. I suggest we do exactly what the doctor said."

KJ's voice rang with a certainty of belief that made them all feel a little more hopeful.

KJ looked at Gabriella and Caleb and spoke in a very sensitive tone. "The Professor has told me you both struggle with what you believe. He's convinced you will find the truth in your own time. Because you're still seeking, don't let that stop you from asking. I serve a God that says, "Seek and you shall find. Ask and you shall receive."

The detectives took off their hats in respect as the group gathered in a circle and KJ led the prayer. "Father, we come together asking for a miracle. The Professor is your child and you have a plan and purpose for his life. There is work for him to finish and we ask you to bind every evil power that would try to destroy him. We ask it in the name of Yeshua Ha-Mashiach, Jesus the Messiah, and thank you that you have heard us. Amen."

With that simple prayer a peace began to saturate the room. The tears were replaced with hope, and fears were replaced with faith. Even the detectives sensed something supernatural had just taken place. There was a holy silence that engulfed them.

Gabriella heard Aaron say, "We thank you, Yahweh, you have heard us."

KJ also was expressing his faith. "I know you have heard our prayers and you are able to do exceedingly, abundantly above anything we can ask or imagine."

Both Gabriella and Caleb were wondering what just happened. They felt an unknown Presence enter the room as they listened to the others pray. It was something they had no explanation for. Gabriella thought perhaps it was just the emotional upheaval affecting her mind, but it was something she had never experienced before.

They all sat quietly, not wanting to disturb the atmosphere of serenity. The detectives said they would be in touch later and silently left them to their prayers. For over an hour no one said a word in reverence to the Presence that surrounded them.

Gabriella closed her eyes and let peace flow through her. How could she feel this way when her father figure was fighting for his life? She was immersed in a peace that passed all understanding.

Caleb, finally, fully embraced the fact there are supernatural powers that exist. He felt it inundate the room. He could not deny it! He wanted to understand where it came from and what it meant.

KJ broke the silence. "We've touched the throne of God. I know it! What you feel in this room is not just human emotion. It is the Presence of Almighty God's Spirit!"

Immediately after he spoke the words, the doctor came rushing through the door.

"Oh, I'm so glad you're still here! I can't explain it and I've never seen this happen before! His vitals just stabilized, his breathing is normal and he opened his eyes. It looks like he might just pull through! We're going to sedate him so his body can rest and heal from the trauma. We'll monitor him in ICU for the next 24 hours. If he continues to improve we'll consider moving him to a room tomorrow."

The doctor stopped and took a deep breath. "But I can assure you, what just happened was not the result of anything the medical personnel did. This is the work of a higher power! We've just witnessed a true miracle!" The doctor left the room shaking his head in unbelief. They heard him mutter as he exited, "It's a miracle, a true miracle."

The room that had been filled with agony just a short time before was now filled with jubilation. They were hugging and rejoicing as they heard KJ say, "Nothing is impossible with God!"

Aaron and KJ gave each other a big hug. Aaron exclaimed, "We serve a mighty God!"

Caleb stood a head taller than both of them. He put an arm around each one and looking down confessed, "And I want to know more about Him!"

Gabriella could not believe what had just happened. She had read about the supernatural healing powers of Edgar Cayce, the shaman and other faith healers; but KJ was praying to Yahweh God.

She asked herself under her breath. "Are they all the same God?" There was no denying a supernatural healing had taken place that baffled even the doctors. Now she *had* to know where that power came from!

Chapter 22

It was evident everyone was exhausted and Gabriella stepped into her role as team leader. "You all go home and rest. There's no need in all of us waiting for the Professor to wake up. I'm staying." They all knew that tone of voice and she was not to be argued with.

"You're not staying alone." Caleb insisted. "In case you've forgotten you're not really dressed to sleep in a waiting room. I'll go back to your apartment to change clothes and pick up whatever you need. Will you be all right for a little while? I'll hurry."

"Of course I'll be all right," Gabriella retorted as she listed what she needed for him to bring back. "What could happen here?"

Aaron interjected: "After we get some rest we've got to decide how to proceed. There's lots of work to do and we don't know how long it'll be until the Professor can rejoin us. Plus, now we have to deal with the safety factor!"

"Let me make a suggestion," Gabriella said as she was thinking it through. "I have plenty of room at my apartment. Caleb, take Faith, KJ and Aaron by their apartments to get what they need for a few days. We'll all stay together until we know for sure what's going on. Faith can sleep in my room with me. The spare bedroom has twin beds for KJ and Aaron, and Caleb can take the couch. If we're together we can get more work done, plus we know each other is safe. Someone needs to stay here with the Professor. He can't be left alone."

"I'll stay starting tomorrow morning," Sandee said emphatically. "With all of you working together you should be able to accomplish a lot of the translation work quickly. I'm familiar with the entire project and have access to the Professors notes, if you need anything."

They all agreed it was a good plan. Caleb gave Gabriella a quick kiss on the cheek as they were leaving. "I'll be back as soon as possible. I'll let the nurse know you're here." He pulled a blanket and pillow from the storage cabinet and laid it on the couch for her. "The nurse's desk is right outside if you need anything."

"I'll be fine," Gabriella assured them. "Now the rest of you get some rest. I'll call if there's any change at all." Faith and Sandee hugged Gabriella as they left. Caleb kissed her one more time and then the room was empty.

She slipped off her high heels and stretched out on the couch allowing her mind to replay the events of the last few hours. Could it really have been a miracle? The doctor said it was nothing they did. But then the power of the human spirit could do miraculous things and she knew the Professor was very strong willed. "He will be all right. I know he will." She muttered to herself.

As she tried to rationalize the events of the night and the 'Presence' that seemed to saturate the room when KJ prayed, she began to drift into a slumber. The room was quiet. Occasionally she would hear faint noises from the nurses talking outside the waiting room door, and carts moving up and down the hallways.

Totally exhausted she finally went into a deep sleep. The sensation of falling began to repeat. Down and down into the abyss. Darkness swallowed her. She was choking and could not breathe. "Arcturus, where are you?" She screamed in total fear. "Catch me!"

Immediately Arcturus' hand caught hers and a bright light appeared. This time Caleb was not there to call her back to reality.

"What's happening?" She could hardly whisper the words as Arcturus was guiding her flight towards the light at the end of a long, black tunnel. She was no longer afraid.

"It's very simple, Gabriella. Your soul is responding to your high vibrational frequencies and moving naturally into untime, traveling without me. You *must* have me with you at all times. I've warned you of the evil ones that are waiting to capture unguided souls."

"I wasn't trying to! It just happens. How do I stop it? It scares me, Arcturus!"

"All you have to do is call upon my name. I am always listening and I'll be there to guide you. Are you ready for a new journey?" His hand was holding on to hers, but she sensed something was different.

"What's wrong, Gabriella? Do you not want to understand the shaman powers working through you? You can help many people with the knowledge I give you!"

"Do I have the shaman powers my father wrote about? What do I do with them? How can I help people?"

"Your father wrote in his journal about the ancient shaman powers, so you would understand the gift you inherited. You have not read it yet. But you will. Powers that are supernatural and few people possess. Don't you realize YOU just healed the Professor with your powers?"

Shock came over her and she blurted in unbelief. "I healed the Professor? You can't be serious! That's totally ridiculous!"

"It was your deep love for him that released the god powers within you. Those powers merged with the powers of the universe and created vibrational frequencies that intensified to the level of supernatural healing. Every person has inner god powers they can learn to release. But you, Gabriella, have a rare harmony with the cosmos. For a moment you became one with the Akaisic Knowledge that knows all things and can do all things. You healed him!"

"But KJ prayed to his God and they all think that God healed the Professor. Even Caleb thinks so."

The look on Arcturus' face turned dark. His countenance of beauty changed to a vileness she could not explain. "THAT god does NOT exist!" His voice became loud and demanding. She had never heard him speak that way and she tried to pull away as fear gripped her.

His hand tightened around hers and immediately his face reversed back to one of beauty and his voice again became the hypnotic, mesmerizing sound she had become so familiar with.

His soothing voice as he explained, "The true god is the one within each of us. When we converge with the universal powers all things are possible, if we only believe. The human understanding limits the god consciousness. Very few recognize it in the human cage. It is not until they are released their true power is realized. But soon, Gabriella, this earth plane will receive an Ascended Master who will lead them to this truth. Those that refuse to receive the transformation will be removed. It is the dawning of the new age of peace and love. We have this on our planet. And we will bring it to the earth plane before humans destroy themselves with war and hate."

Arcturus' dark eyes looked deep into Gabriella's. "You must understand who you are and what you are. Your father learned the secrets of the coming new age. That is why your mother was killed by sinister earth leaders, who also intended to kill your father. When they were able to silence him they left him alone. He stayed silent to protect you. These powerful men control nations and do not want humankind to understand their inner, eternal powers. They would lose their control. Power and greed separate the human spirit from the godhood within them. Soon it will all come to an end and the people of earth will be led to truth. Your father discovered this truth."

Arcturus' face scowled and his voice became angry. "Elders from our planet have tried to guide the leaders of the earth plane to a higher consciousness, but love of self dominates them. The earth leaders were willing to accept our technology but turned it into more power and greed! They will soon learn that true power comes through the inner spirit finding synergy with the universe and not through weapons. Gabriella, soon the whole earth will find what your father found to be true."

"That is what my father knew? That is why my mother was killed? How do you know all this?" Gabriella was trying to assimilate the information and balance the reasoning of how this could be!

"I am your Watcher and I possess the universal knowledge. I know all things! If you will stay pure to your vibrational frequencies you can know as I know. As you journey with me, your frequencies will increase and so will your powers that can do good for the people of the earth. You can be one with the Ascended Master and be part of ushering in this new age on earth. Don't you want to see love abounding and others healed as the Professor was?"

Arcturus waited for her to realize fully what he was offering before he continued. "There would be no limit as to what you could do, but only if you separate from Caleb. He does not believe! He will dilute your vibrational frequencies and ultimately destroy your power. You are chosen, Gabriella!"

"Chosen? Is that what the Prophet was trying to tell me?"

"Do not trust him. He has come to deceive you! Trust only me, and the knowledge of what is good and what is evil will be yours eternally."

Darkness began to swirl around her and Arcturus' voice was fading away but echoes continued in her mind. "You must separate from Caleb... you must separate from Caleb."

Gabriella felt arms wrap around her and hold her close. She felt a warm kiss and heard the words "I love you" whispered in her ear, erasing Arcturus' voice. She opened her eyes to Caleb's loving gaze.

Chapter 23

"Gabi, wake up." Caleb's voice was gently calling her back to the real world. "The Professor is awake and asking for you."

"I've got to go to him." She sat up and struggled to her feet. Caleb helped her from the couch and held her until she was fully awake.

"Are you going to change first?"

"No, I'll change later. Just give me my shoes."

Caleb pulled the black house slippers out of her bag and she was trying to put them on as she rushed towards the door.

"Is he okay? Did they say how he's doing, Caleb?"

"They just said he was awake and asking for you."

They exited the waiting room where a nurse led them to ICU and back to the Professor's room. "Don't stay too long. He's really weak and needs to rest. He lost a lot of blood. It's amazing he's still alive." With those words the nurse left the room and closed the door behind her.

The Professor opened his eyes when he heard them enter. Gabriella went straight to his bedside and took his hand. "I'm here. I've been here all night. Are you in pain?"

He shook his head and it was obvious he was still heavily sedated and too weak for conversation. Gabriella continued to hold his hand with both of hers. He seemed content with her by his bedside. Caleb stood beside her with his protective arm around her shoulder.

"Professor, the doctor said you asked for me before the surgery. You needed to tell me something?" Gabi waited as he struggled to speak.

"Not now." He whispered. "I thought I was going to die and I had to tell you."

"Tell me what?" She pleaded with him. He shook his head and closed his eyes. It was obvious he had nothing else to say on the matter.

She and Caleb ignored the nurse's instructions and sat by his bed for over an hour, watching him doze in and out of sleep. Gabriella kept hoping he would tell her what was so important. In the brief moments he would be coherent, he would only smile and then drift back to sleep. No words were spoken.

The doctor came in briefly and confirmed he was still stable. "It's a miracle. I'm telling you, nothing short of a miracle. This is one for the medical journals." He just shook his head still unable to believe what he had seen with his own eyes. Caleb walked out with the doctor to get a better evaluation of what to expect in the coming days.

Gabriella did not leave the Professor's bedside. She was thinking through all of the years she had known him. He was a remarkable man. Even at the age of seventy-two he was still handsome. His thick, black hair had streaks of gray and his kind face had only a few wrinkles around his eyes. His tall frame, unusually strong for his age, now looked frail and helpless.

She knew they came close to losing him, which reminded her again of the Presence that came into the room just a few hours before. It truly was a miracle he was alive. She knew it was just a silly dream that she had healed him. That was ridiculous! She accepted the fact her subconscious was working overtime in the midst of all the emotional upheaval; however, she had no doubt that something supernatural had happened.

Caleb quietly opened the door and returned to Gabriella's side. He was about to fill her in on the doctor's report when the Professor opened his eyes and motioned to Gabriella.

Gabriella leaned down closer to the Professor as he tried to speak. "I know you don't believe in my God but I saw Him last night." He took a deep breath and labored to speak in spite of his sedation. "I thought He had come for me but He told me I must finish the work. God said He went to the room where the prayers were prayed. Did you pray, Gabi?" His eyes closed briefly and then soon opened again, as he struggled to continue. "After He appeared to me all of the pain left my body. I knew I was going to live." He looked her in the eyes but was too weak to continue.

She turned to Caleb in amazement. "Was that the Presence we felt last night, do you think? Could it be possible?"

Caleb put his arm around her shoulder. "I want to understand this as much as you do, Gabi. I know there was 'something' in that room last night. I don't understand it, not at all."

The Professor's lips turned slightly up and she could tell it was an attempt to smile. He looked at both of them and simply said, "You will." Then he drifted back to sleep.

The nurse opened the door and told them he needed to rest. They walked back to the waiting room hand in hand not saying a word, lost in their individual retrospections.

After the door closed behind them Caleb took her in his arms and whispered. "Don't worry. We'll figure this out together." For a few minutes she just rested in his embrace and let his strength become hers.

"Try to get some sleep." Caleb said seeing the exhaustion in her face. "I'll wake you if they need us." She changed into her jogging suit and cuddled up to Caleb on the couch, waiting for the next time they would be able to spend with the Professor. She looked at Caleb and it was obvious he was exhausted, too.

He kissed her forehead and stretched his long legs that extended beyond the end of the couch. She ran her fingers through his thick, blonde hair as she watched him quickly fall asleep. She wondered how it was possible to love a man so much and why it had taken her so long to admit it.

She laid her head back and as soon as she shut her eyes thoughts of the dream came flooding into her mind. It felt so real! Arcturus knew everything about her, but, of course, that was just a reflection of her self-knowledge manifesting in her dreams. Her thoughts had to be intertwining with the massive amount of information that had flooded her the last few days. Dreaming was a way of filtering through and absorbing it. "Yes, that makes sense," she convinced herself.

Her thoughts were interrupted when Sandee entered the room. She had a rolling suitcase, a small cooler and her laptop. She obviously was moving in.

"I just checked with the nurse and she said the Professor is stable and resting." Sandee set her things down and took charge. "You two go home, get some rest and then get started on the project. There's no time to dilly dally. I am staying here as long as I need to. My work is with him and my place is by his side. That's where I will be. Now go!"

Sandee's commanding voice awakened Caleb and he retorted without even opening his eyes, "Another bossy woman. Don't know if I can tolerate two." He sat up and smiled his captivating smile.

Sandee popped him on the cheek with a fake slap. "Get out of here, boy, before I turn you over my knee." Caleb let out a fake 'ouch' and wrestled her to the couch. They were all laughing and it was a welcome relief from the fear and anxiety.

"Fun times over, kids, now get on home and get to work." Sandee laughingly demanded. "The nurse said they will be moving the Professor to CCU and I'll be able to stay in the room with him 24/7. I'm settling in there and you'll know he's in safe hands. I'll call you if I need you."

Sandee's husband had died before the team came to Haifa University. She had no children so she had devoted her life as a widow to working for the Professor. Caleb and Gabriella both knew she was right where she wanted to be and would take good care of him, while they pressed forward with the project.

Gabriella and Caleb gathered their belongings, gave Sandee a hug and headed for the parking lot. On the way home they stopped at the market for a food supply to last several days. The less the team had to leave her apartment the safer for everyone. The questioning from the Israeli police proved to them the Professor was justified in his safety concerns so they would take extra precautions.

When they arrived at the apartment they smelled fresh brewed coffee and were surprised to find the rest of the team already working. Aaron, Faith and KJ were all sitting around the dining table with laptops ablaze in research. They were chattering away about their findings when Gabriella and Caleb walked in.

"How's the Professor?' They all stopped and asked in unison.

Caleb took Gabriella's bag to her bedroom while she filled them in. "He's still pretty well sedated, but stable. They're moving him to CCU and Sandee has literally moved in with him. She wants us to concentrate on the project."

Faith laughed knowingly. "Sandee is like a mother hen. What would we do without her?"

"One more thing before we get to work." Gabriella said as she sat down at the table. "The Professor said he saw his God last night and God told him he had to finish the work. His God told him he had heard the prayers and that's when his pain totally left!"

"Prayer does change things! Ask and you will receive!" KJ exclaimed, not at all surprised by Gabriella's big announcement. "I knew our Heavenly Father was in our midst last night. We all felt the Presence enter the room!"

Aaron immediately connected to this conversation. He said some words in Hebrew that sounded like thanksgiving and Faith said amen in agreement. Gabriella did not know what to say.

Caleb looked around the table at each of his friends desiring to understand. "You all know I don't understand all this religion stuff, but there's not a doubt in my mind something big happened last night and I know it was real."

KJ's voice was gentle and full of empathy. "I know where you're coming from, brother. I was once there and blind faith is a hard thing. But the written Word of God says we believe by faith and not by sight. It's a heart understanding and not a head knowledge. If you open your spiritual heart, the faith will enter."

Caleb thought for a minute. "That's sounds too simple. You just 'say' you believe and it's done?"

"If you truly believe, it is that simple! No magic, no flashing lights, nothing on the outside changes. The change is all inward, in your spirit man. That is where God's peace and power dwells."

Gabriella was trying to balance what KJ was saying with the words of Arcturus. It sounded to be almost the same. KJ described the power and peace in the 'spirit man' coming from an external, heavenly God. Arcturus said god power and peace was born internally in all humankind and that we just had to learn to release it. Which was it? Or was either really true? The battle of the god truth continued to wage in her mind.

"You're a good man," Aaron told Caleb. "But the Bible says all of our self-righteousness is just filthy rags in God's eyes. It is only when we acknowledge Him as Lord of everything that we truly find peace and discover our purpose for being on this earth."

"But how can I believe something I've never seen?" Caleb wanted desperately to understand how the rest of them were so sure.

"He allowed you to feel His Presence last night, Caleb." KJ spoke with certainty. "You saw Him heal the Professor when the doctors gave no hope and could do nothing more. He has visited you and Gabriella in a special way so you can believe, if you will only choose to."

"How do you know it was a god presence and not the energy of love that was in the room? Love is a powerful force, too." Gabriella was torn inside struggling to know what to believe.

Faith knew Gabriella well and was fully aware of the spiritual battle inside her soul. "Gabi, outside of God there is no true love. He is love! That's why it is so powerful when it flows through each of us."

Gabriella retorted, "I've never known who or what to believe about the gods, but I still love."

"Your love is an earthly love. It depends on relationships and circumstances that can quickly change." Faith was being very careful in how she phrased her next words. "As you know, Gabi, the people we love can be separated from us by death. If you truly believe in the eternal God of heaven, then the love He gives will transcend even death and we can be with them again on the eternal side."

These were almost the same words of Arcturus! He said love was the eternal power and the driving force of the universe and we would see our loved ones again. He also said Yahweh God did not exist and the only true god was the god within us that converges with the powers of the universe.

Gabriella could not speak out loud what was bolting in her mind. "Was her inner god trying to manifest through her dreams? Then she could bring the real truth to their project quest?"

Gabriella could sense Caleb was being drawn to the God of her friends and she had no doubt that a power beyond human ability healed the Professor. Her inner soul silently cried out, "Did the Professor's God heal him or did she heal him through her inner god power of love?"

She walked to the balcony doors and opened them allowing the morning sunlight to filter in. She looked out towards the sea with Mt. Hermon looming in the far distance and whispered, "Where are you, truth? How do I find you?"

Chapter 24

The team knew Gabriella was still struggling to believe in the one Divine God, even after witnessing a miracle. When they would voice their praise to Yahweh, they could see her pull away. It was creating a tension they had not experienced in all their years of working together. KJ, even though he was new to their team, felt the strain and tried to break the tension.

"Okay, guys, let's have breakfast and then get back to work." KJ got up to stretch and walked over to Gabriella. He put his arm around her shoulder with a reassuring squeeze and quietly said, "Just ask to know the truth and the truth will come."

She looked at him with hunger for spiritual understanding in her eyes. "Who do I ask?"

"Just ask Yahweh to reveal if He is the true God. If you truly are seeking, He can be found. The choice is yours." With those words KJ went to the kitchen to help prepare breakfast.

Gabriella followed him. She took the pastries from the shopping bag and arranged them in a basket while KJ made more coffee. She was amazed at the confidence and assurance KJ had in his God. How could he be so sure? There was much more evidence the earth had been visited by extraterrestrial civilizations than there was of a divine creator. Her deepest hope was her father's journal would prove undeniable truth, once and for all.

A sudden wave of exhaustion flooded over Gabriella. She filled a bowl with fresh fruit and set it on the table. As the rest of the team ate, she excused herself to shower and rest.

"Take all the time you need." Caleb said, knowing she needed rest both physically and emotionally. "We'll catch you up." He gave her a hug and gently pushed her towards her bedroom door.

KJ and Aaron were researching the universal database for any matches to the ancient writing found on the cave wall. Faith was reading different articles on recent archeological findings of ancient writings and Caleb sat on the couch next to the black box rereading some of the articles.

Suddenly out of the silence Aaron exclaimed. "Where's the scroll, Caleb? Did anyone mention the Professor's personal items in the car or where they had taken the car?"

"Oh, my lord!" Caleb exclaimed. "I had completely forgotten it! Even Gabriella hasn't thought about it!"

Faith looked from Caleb to Aaron. "What scroll? What are you talking about?"

Caleb explained to Faith and KJ. "The Prophet appeared to Gabriella again and gave her a very old scroll. She opened it just enough to see it was written in an ancient language. The Professor immediately came and took it. Now we have no idea where it is."

KJ looked extremely concerned. "Do you think whoever cut the brake line on his car knew about the scroll?"

Caleb thought a minute. "How could anyone know? We just gave it to him yesterday afternoon. There wasn't much time between him being here and when the accident took place. Sure is suspicious."

"I'm gonna call Sandee and see what she can find out from the Professor." Caleb picked up his phone and called.

"Hi, Caleb." Sandee answered seeing his name on her caller ID.

"Just checking on the Professor."

"He's doing well! His vitals are stable and everything looks good. He's been asleep since I arrived."

"When he wakes up ask him if he has anything in his car we need to get out."

Sandee did not answer right away, as if she knew more than she could say. "Sure, I'll be glad to ask him and let you know. I planned to call you after they moved him anyway. Hope you kids are doing okay."

"Gabi is resting and the rest of us are hard at work. We'll wait to hear from you." Caleb turned his phone off and looked at the team. "She'll call us when she knows something.

Faith looked at Caleb and Aaron. "Was it really just last week we were exploring in Saudi Arabia? It seems a lifetime ago. How could life change so quickly?"

Caleb looked towards Gabriella's bedroom door and said with deep emotion, "Some changes have been wonderful."

"Let's get back to work, Romeo. We've got a lot to do!" Aaron directed and they all agreed. They each concentrated on their individual tasks.

Caleb picked up some of the news articles he had previously read and tried to concentrate, then laid them back down. He was remembering the strange phone calls Gabriella had before he had moved in to protect her. Whoever called knew her name but would not talk. Why had there not been any calls while he was with her? Everything pointed to the fact someone was listening or watching them. Could they possibly know about the black box?

He got up and walked to the balcony doors looking out on the bay. It was a beautiful, sunny day. The marina was busy as boats were sailing out to sea. "Life should be as beautiful as this day is." Caleb said to himself. He wanted desperately to have a normal life with Gabriella experiencing all of the joys of being a husband, and eventually a father. But from all appearances normality was not going to be part of their future. He took a deep breath and slowly exhaled in a physical effort to release the inner pressure of his soul.

He turned around to see Faith and KJ watching him with compassion.

Caleb forced a smile as tears formed in his eyes. The strength of his body could not hold back the turmoil of his soul. It took everything in him to not break down. "I just love her so much and when she finally allows herself to return my love we are dealing with life and death situations. Now should be the best of all times." His voice softened to almost a whisper with the last sentence.

Faith had never seen Caleb shed a single tear. He was always as strong as an ox, both physically and emotionally. Seeing his tears brought tears to her eyes. She had watched Caleb and Gabriella through the years fall in love and neither would admit it. She knew this day would come, but she had no idea that when it arrived there may not be a future for them... maybe not for any of them.

Caleb's cell phone rang. "It's Sandee calling back." He cleared his voice trying to regain his composure. "Hello."

"Caleb, just wanted to let you know they're getting ready now to move the Professor to CCU. He woke up for a few minutes while they were preparing him for the move. I asked him if you needed to get anything out of his car. He just shook his head no. I'll call you back later. They just came in to transport him." Sandee disconnected the call.

"Something's just not right." Caleb told them. "The Professor told Sandee there was nothing to get out of his car. When have you ever known the Professor to be anywhere without his briefcase? Not in the twelve years I have known him! Sandee didn't say it but she knows it, too. I'm sure there was other information in his briefcase, along with the scroll. Apparently someone was willing to kill to get it!"

Caleb immediately thought of Gabriella having been briefly in possession of it. Had she kept it would she have been the immediate target? He shuddered at the thought. He walked to her bedroom door and opened it just enough to make sure she was safe. She was sleeping with the appearance of a peaceful angel, in spite of all the turmoil churning in their lives. A wave of fear uncommon to Caleb consumed him. Not for himself but for her. "I will do anything to protect her. No one will hurt her!" These thoughts were rolling in his mind as fear was immediately turned to anger.

He closed her door quietly and turned to the group. "It's up to us to finish this project and find the truth before someone else gets hurt...or worse. Let's get at it!" A new determination swept over them all as the realization this was a life and death project completely settled in. It was no longer just a possibility. It was now a reality.

Chapter 25

While the team was now working with a new urgency, Gabriella had fallen into a deep sleep and was dreaming again. She was standing at the Professor's bedside with her head bent low to hear him. He was trying to tell her something, but his voice was too weak. She knew in the depth of her soul that it was really important and was desperately trying to understand his whispers.

She put her ear next to the Professor's mouth and she heard the words, "I want to tell you, but it's too dangerous."

"Please tell me! I must know what you mean!" Even though she was dreaming she could feel the tears running down her face and her entire body sobbing.

The scene of the dream changed and Caleb and Arcturus were facing each other in anger. She heard vileness in Arcturus' voice as he told Caleb, "You cannot have her! I will never let her go! She is chosen!"

Caleb was not backing down. "She loves me and she will not go with you!"

Suddenly the Prophet appeared and stood beside Gabriella as she watched Caleb and Arcturus. "I fear for Caleb!" she exclaimed.

The Prophet watched the two men as they prepared for battle and spoke without looking at Gabriella. "I warned you of danger."

"Danger for me or for Caleb?" She pleaded with him. "Or are we both in danger? Please tell me what I need to do!"

The Prophet turned to her with dark eyes that penetrated her to the bone. He did not answer her question but instead asked one. "Where's the scroll?"

Gabriella was confused. "I gave it to the Professor."

He spoke again. "Where's the scroll?"

Gabriella was now both confused and upset. Didn't he understand her? "I gave it to the Professor!"

His piercing eyes narrowed and stayed focused on hers. "Where's the scroll, Gabriella?"

Then she understood. "I don't know." Her voice quivered as a flow of burning tears again washed down her cheeks.

"I know you don't." His voice was now gentle and kind. "*But,* I do. It's in the safe hands of one who loves you dearly." Then he vanished.

She looked for Caleb and Arcturus. They, too, had vanished. Her eyes opened and she was wide awake. She jumped out of bed and hurried in to the living room.

Breathlessly she pleaded with them. "Does anyone know where the scroll is? Was it left in the car after the accident?"

Caleb went straight to Gabriella and put his arms around her. "We're on it, Gabi. Sandee asked the Professor and he said there was nothing in the car."

"Something's not right!" She exclaimed. "We all know he never goes anywhere without his briefcase."

"We'll find it, Gabi." Caleb held her close in reassurance. "I'll go to the hospital and find out from the Professor where he left it. If it wasn't in the car he has to know where it is."

"No, Caleb! It may not be safe. That was the whole point of all of us staying together! Do you think the scroll had something to do with the brake lines being cut?"

Aaron was assimilating the various speculations. "Let's think this through. We know several decades ago someone told the Professor not to reveal the fragmented parts of the prophecy found with the Dead Sea Scrolls. We also know the Professor has financial backers, allowing him to work secretly. He has worked continually in a concentrated effort to find the missing prophetic parts, piece together the ancient manuscripts and come to a conclusion on the 'end of days' timelines. For over a decade we have all worked together with the Professor on this project with no knowledge and no signs of anything dangerous. Why now? What's changed?"

"Good question, Aaron." Caleb replied, musing over his synopsis. "We followed the map that led us to the lava caves. We found writing on the cave wall that matched exactly the clay tablet the Prophet gave to the Professor. The Prophet reappears after all these years with an ancient manuscript matching the Dead Sea Scrolls. There must be a silver thread tying these together somehow."

Gabriella began to relive the lava cave experience. When Caleb and Aaron cut through to the deepest part of the cave she had felt something ominous and terrifying. She remembered the force pulling her against her will deeper in towards the bottomless pit. It was as though something evil had been released.

She had tried to rationalize it as the deep recesses of the cave and lack of oxygen affecting her senses. But she knew something, at that moment, happened and she had no explanation for it! She relived it over and over in her mind. Since that day her life had turned upside down. Emotions totally foreign to her were at war in our soul. It was a constant struggle between darkness and light, truth and lies, joy and sorrow, dreams and reality, sanity and insanity; and most frightening of all...time and untime.

Gabriella realized that was a turning point. Everything changed after that day. Why? How?

"We need to find the scroll." Gabriella stated emphatically, fully aware the visit from the Prophet was an important piece of the puzzle. "Do you think maybe the briefcase was in the car and the Professor just didn't want us to try to get it, because it could be too dangerous?"

The team looked at each other contemplating that possibility. Aaron addressed the question. "I was the last one that talked to him and he had it with him then. He said he was on his way to show it to someone. Maybe whoever he met has it."

Gabriella reflected for a moment before continuing. "The doctor said when they were preparing him for surgery he asked for me. Perhaps when he thought he was dying, he wanted me to know where the scroll was since the Prophet gave it to me originally. Then when he knew he is going to live he decided not to. Could that be the explanation?"

Gabriella thought back to her dream and wanted to tell the team what had been revealed to her. They would think she was losing her grip on reality.

The dream seemed so real she even began to question if she possessed some sort of shaman powers that opened a gateway for her to reach out for truth, during her dream state. Was the Prophet trying to let her know not to worry? If the scroll really was in the safe hands of one that loved her, then the Professor must have it. Other than the people present with her in the apartment, he was the only living person that truly loved her.

Common sense quickly set in. Gabriella admitted to herself the dream was like all of the rest she experienced, merely the events of her life playing out in her subconscious while she was in a deep sleep. Even when she was growing up she would have crazy dreams reliving explorations with her father and imagine spirits trying to talk to her. This was not anything unfamiliar to her. There was just too much happening too quickly, and this was her way of emotionally dealing with it. She knew it was ridiculous to think she had any paranormal ability.

After Gabriella's father died, she was tormented with dreams of him trying to contact her. The dreams were so consuming she sought the help of a holistic psychiatrist, learning how to interpret her dreams and deal naturally with grief and loss. The doctor helped her understand her subconscious mind does not battle with the conscious. The emotional side is not challenged by logic and the subconscious can break through the barriers of loss, fear and confusion through dreaming. He believed dreaming was how she was releasing her true inner feelings and dealing with the fears and tragedies of life, especially the loss of her beloved father. That psychoanalysis at the time of her father's death certainly applied to her situation.

Gabriella was attempting to collocate the information she had stored in her mind. She interpreted her dreams of Arcturus, the Prophet, and her current drama as her mental way of filtering through the myriad of emotions and allowing them to express, as needed through her dreams.

Again, she had rationalized her dreams of the night. "Only a reflection of my daytime reality," she convinced herself. Still, it was a reality that was getting more sinister with each passing day.

Chapter 26

Aaron and Faith had turned back to their computers on the dining table to concentrate. KJ interrupted them. "Before we get back to work, it's important we pray together for our guardian angels to protect all of us involved in this project; and we find the information we need, quickly. I sense we are running out of time."

"Where were those angels when someone tried to kill the Professor?" Gabriella asked with bitterness in her voice. "Furthermore, where were guardian angels when my mother was killed and my father died so young?"

KJ felt her sorrow as he watched the pain and confusion again sweep over Gabriella. Her struggle for truth was so evident that no one could doubt her desire to understand. Obviously, her pain was so deep it clouded her ability to have faith. KJ got up from the table and put his arm around Gabriella's shoulder.

"Those are the questions that plague many people and it keeps them from believing the truth. Many refuse to believe in the Almighty God, because of the suffering they see on the earth. But, Gabi, it wasn't God's plan for man to suffer. He wanted a perfect life for everyone. But suffering came through man's choice. Then they ask why He would allow it."

"And why would He allow it, if He is so almighty?" Gabriella asked, wondering that very thing many times.

KJ patiently answered her. "For those that truly believe in Yahweh, they also believe He gave laws for us to live by. As you know, Gabi, the Bible the Professor keeps with him is God's laws. It's like the laws of our country. They are for the good and protection of its citizens. If laws are broken then there are consequences. It's the same with God's laws. He wants only what is good for us; but if we break His laws, then we suffer."

Gabriella sat down at the table and spoke bluntly. "I know the Professor believed every word in his precious book and look what happened to him. Where was his protection, KJ? He could have died!"

KJ's patient voice continued. "He didn't die, and we all witnessed a miracle of God's power to heal. Even the doctor said it was Divine intervention, and that is the same power that can be with us for protection. We only have to believe and ask."

Instantly Gabriella remembered the words of the Prophet when he gave her the scroll. "The Lord of Spirits will keep you from the evil place, if you will only ask."

But Gabriella kept asking herself, "Who is the Lord of Spirits? Was it KJ's God or was it the god in us, just waiting to be released?" One thing she now knew for sure, there were powers that existed beyond anything she ever imagined.

Gabriella sat silently for a few minutes as the scientist in her was trying to analyze what she saw as facts. "KJ, how do you know for sure these powers come from your Jehovah God or Yahweh as the Professor calls Him? The Professor's miraculous healing shows me there is definitely a power we can't see or touch, but how can you prove it is from this God you believe in? Maybe we all have an inner power and haven't learned how to release it. Or, just maybe, some people are born with paranormal powers that allow them to connect with celestial gods. Your God isn't the only explanation for what we perceive as miracles."

The two opposing forces were battling in her soul. She deeply admired what KJ, Aaron and Faith believed. In contrast, her father had written about the shaman powers of her ancestors and their connection with the extraterrestrial gods. She needed the team to at least look at the possibility they were the ones being deceived. She knew it was time to tell the team about her father's journal.

KJ was about to answer Gabriella when she got up from the table and walked to the sofa. He could see she was on a mission. Caleb knew she was going to allow the whole team to now be part of her father's research.

Gabriella sat down next to the black leather box and put her hands on the top. Her voice was slightly quivering as she tried to explain. "This is what Sandee gave me last Friday. The last landlord my father and I had rented from recently found this box hidden under the floor of that home."

She pulled open the stubborn lid of the box and carefully took the journal from its resting place. "This is one of the most difficult things I've ever done. I am about to share with you the most intimate details of my life. This black box contains information on why and how my parents died. In addition, my father thoroughly researched the very subject we are discussing."

Caleb went to Gabriella and sat down beside her. He began to explain what they had discovered, in an effort to show them he fully supported Gabriella's opinion. "Over the weekend we went through some of her father's journal and research papers. There is compelling evidence our planet has been visited from its beginning by supernatural beings. Everything we have read so far parallels exactly with what the Professor believes."

Caleb took a deep breath knowing how difficult this was for Gabriella. "But Gabi's father seemed to believe it is extraterrestrial visitations. The Professor believes these supernatural occurrences only appear to be of extraterrestrial origin, but are in fact the nephilim spirits manifesting as aliens. It seems we have a battle of the gods going on between her father's and the Professor's opposing opinions."

Gabriella took a pile of articles from the box and placed them on the coffee table in front of her. "We still have the most important research to go through to know what exactly they found out, but apparently it was so important it cost them their lives."

Faith gasped when she heard Gabriella's words. She had been her closest friend and never had there been any indication Gabriella's parents were murdered. Faith finally gained her composure enough to try to understand. "Wasn't your mom killed in an accident, and your father died from a heart attack?"

Caleb knew how difficult the question would be for Gabriella so he answered for her. "That's what Gabi always thought but her father wrote a personal letter to her before he died, revealing things she never knew. He was afraid she would be in danger, too, if she knew the truth. He even indicated something might happen to him, and it wasn't long after that he died unexpectedly."

KJ now understood Gabriella's battle. Her questions and comments made total sense in the midst of the war battling in her mind. If her father believed in extraterrestrial life, naturally she would lean towards his understanding as a scientist. Although he thought it very odd that this research would appear, out of nowhere, just as the project hit momentum.

Aaron leaned forward in his chair, pushed his coffee cup to the side and pulled his laptop in front of him, ready to work. "And what have you found that is so convincing that alien life exists? We will start two columns of notes. One will be 'Nephilim' and the other 'ETs'. We will compare the parallels and see what evidence proves to us."

Gabriella and Caleb spent the afternoon recapping with the team what they had read in her father's journal, and the articles he had saved supporting his hypothesis. The team was amazed at the evidence and research Gabriella's father had acquired. Aaron listed all of the evidence from her father's research in his ET column.

The more Gabriella shared from her father's research, the more a dividing line was being drawn between the beliefs of Aaron, Faith and KJ; and what Gabriella was leaning toward believing. Caleb was standing somewhere in the middle. He was constantly reminded of the Presence he had felt the few times he attended church as a child. He knew it was the same Presence he had felt in the waiting room at the hospital, when KJ prayed to his God. He wanted to understand the source of that power and Presence. However, he was afraid Gabriella would feel he had deserted her if he said so. He could not take the chance of a division in their relationship just when they were beginning their life together.

Gabriella finished the review with a question to the team. "Doesn't it all make sense to you now? It's like I told the Professor in our meeting. If you use the word "extraterrestrials" in the place of the mythical gods, dating all the way back to ancient times, it could explain everything!"

She took a deep breath and finished her explanation: "Perhaps these extraterrestrial beings are watching over us, integrating into our society and planning to enlighten us. They just might be super powers that have the answers to poverty, war and hate."

The team could hear the excitement in her voice as if she had just solved the world's problems.

Tactfully Faith replied to her. "You're right, Gabi. The evidence is pretty overwhelming. But remember the Professor told us that would be the exact description of the deception that's coming? It will be *so* convincing, people will believe the lie."

"Do you think my father was lying?" Gabriella became defensive to the point of anger, which was not like her at all.

Caleb tried to explain to her. "That's not what she's saying, Gabi. We're all sure your father was following what he believed to be evidence."

"Are you siding with them now?" She shot an angry look at Caleb.

It was just as Caleb suspected. If she knew he was leaning toward their beliefs, it would create a major division between them. Maybe one so great it would separate them completely.

"Gabi, I'm not taking sides. I'm just saying we have to look at all the evidence, then come to a conclusion. That's what scientists do. We still have a mound of research papers to go through. Let's hope the answers we need are buried in there somewhere." There was an obvious pleading in Caleb's voice.

"You're right," Gabriella admitted. "But I know my father only followed what he perceived to be the facts."

KJ had quickly become the mediator of the spiritual battle that was beginning to emerge within the team. "I suggest we all get back to work and together find the facts, not only for the Omega Watchers Project, but for our individual truth. Aaron will keep a list of the comparisons of the Nephilim vs. ET's as we continue research. Since the Professor believes this is the crux of the coming deception that information is going to be paramount as we go forward."

"Gabriella and I will continue reading through the research papers." Caleb said as he moved closer to her. He felt her body tense up at his touch. She pulled away from him and took more papers out of the box to begin to read to her self. He knew she felt her father's work had been attacked and she felt betrayed. The divide between them was widening.

"I'm going back to work on translations. Faith can help me document it." KJ said as he and Faith sat side by side with their computers. Aaron did not look up as he was deep in concentration on the Nephilim vs. ETs comparisons.

Gabriella was usually the one giving directions to the team but she was relieved to not have the pressure. She just wanted some answers and hoped against hope she would find them in her father's research.

Just as she opened the journal to begin reading her cell phone rang. "It's Sandee," she told the team as she answered. "Hello".

"Hi, Gabi, I wanted to let you know the Professor said not to worry. His briefcase was in safe hands." Gabriella sighed in relief.

"Did he mention who has it?" Gabriella questioned.

"No, he didn't say." Instantly Gabriella remembered the words from her dream, when the Prophet told her the scroll was in the 'safe hands of one who loved her'. It was ironic the Professor would use the same words. But at least she was sure The Professor had the scroll stored in a safe place.

"Thanks, Sandee. Tell the Professor to rest and not to worry about anything." Gabriella disconnected the call and had a big smile on her face. "All is well! I don't know where the scroll is for sure. The Professor does and he said it's in safe hands."

"That's good enough for me," Caleb said as he gave Gabriella a hug and whispered in her ear. "I love that smiling face, Gabi Girl. It's a face that could launch a thousand caves."

Gabriella relaxed and laughed in spite of her self. "Don't you mean a thousand ships?"

"Nope, we're not in the ship business. Caleb's my name and caving's my game." The team laughed a sigh of relief, as the tense atmosphere lightened with Caleb's jesting.

"Silly guy! But I love you." It was out of her mouth before she realized it. The surprised look on Caleb's face said it all. Just her saying the words was a major breakthrough and to vocalize it in front of their friends was beyond what he expected, especially in her current state of mind. He would not let the battle of the gods come between them. He was determined nothing would.

He wrapped his arms around her in a bear hug and shouted to the top of his voice. "I want everyone to know I love this woman!"

"Don't you think it's time we all got back to work?" Aaron said with his usual voice of disinterest to romance. They just laughed at him and promptly focused on their tasks at hand. But deep inside they each knew there was a division being created as they listed the evidence of Nephilim vs. ET's.

Chapter 27

Caleb took the journal from Gabriella's hand and laid it on the coffee table. He pulled her from the couch and led her out to the balcony, closing the glass doors behind them. "We need to talk, Gabi."

She sat down and looked across the marina toward the sea. Caleb sat beside her, pulling his chair closer to her. "I knew it was too perfect, Caleb", she said without taking her eyes off the distant waves. "Finally I've allowed myself to release the love that's been buried for years, and now, for the first time ever, I feel a division between us. We've always agreed on everything and at the most important time in our relationship, I can feel us pulling in different directions."

Caleb lifted his hand to her face and turned it where she would have to look at him. The misty tears were filling her blue eyes, about to escape to run down her cheeks. Through the tears she discerned the worried look he was trying desperately to veil.

His voice was low and gruff, filled with emotion as he spoke. "We are both searching for truth, Gabi. We can either let this drive us apart or let it bring us closer together. The choice is ours and we have to be totally honest about everything, if we want the latter. Absolutely, I know I do!"

She managed a half-hearted smile as she tried to believe his words. "You know I've studied the mythical gods most of my life. I loved exploring the ancient ruins and piecing together their historical facts, trying to understand why people believed in what I thought were fantasy religions. This past week has changed my thinking on so many levels. All of the evidence declares there is a supernatural power somewhere."

"I agree," Caleb said. "I also believe we'll find the truth. I keep thinking there has to be a common ground somewhere between the God of the Professor and the aliens your father seemed to believe in. Are you ready to get back to work?"

Gabriella nodded. "Bring the box back out here, please." She was hoping the sunshine would dispel the dark shadows that were haunting her.

Caleb leaned over and gave her a quick hug. "I'll be right back."

Gabriella settled deeper into her soft, cushioned chair as she waited for Caleb. She could hear him talking with the others, assuring them she was all right. She did not like the feeling of separation developing in the team. However, the others all believed the same way and she felt like an outsider. Caleb would not come right out and say it, but she was sure he was leaning towards their way of thinking. If only the team had known her father. They would understand he could be totally trusted. They would look at his work more seriously and not jump to the conclusion that he believed a counterfeit truth. She was more convinced all the time he had 'the' truth. She was determined to prove to the rest of the team what was becoming obvious to her.

Caleb brought the box out to the balcony and set it beside Gabriella's chair. "The sea is at peace today," he said. "It's a perfect day for working outside."

She agreed as she opened the box. "I'm ready to dig in."

She took the journal from its resting place and was tempted to jump to the end of his research for the proof to his hypothesis. Since he had asked her in his letter to go page by page and understand each step he took towards his conclusion, she decided she would not. The end was not proof without the research proving his hypothesis. She would reluctantly follow his request. She turned to the marked page and began to read.

March 18, 1983

It is the first day of spring and a beautiful day. The sunrise seems to be smiling upon us as we are anticipating the arrival of our little one any day now. Angelena has everything ready. She placed her favorite rocking chair next to the crib and has been rocking, caressing her stomach, and talking to our baby. She has a glow about her that I can't find words to describe. I am amazed at the love we feel for this child we have yet to meet. We both vowed to be loving, responsible parents who will engender values in our child, ensuring a happy and joyful life.

I am working on some important research I want to complete before my full attention is focused on the baby's arrival. I have narrowed my hypothesis to four major reasons as to why I believe an extraterrestrial society would want access to our planet. Those being:

- *They need our natural resources and will do whatever they need to have partial or full access to our planet.*
- *We were planted here by an alien society and we are being watched, like scientists watching a test tube, to see if we are growing properly. Which of course we are not.*
- *They intend to take over our planet by integrating hybrid beings to pave the way for their coming.*
- *They see we are about to self-destruct and they want to be a friend to our planet, teaching us their ways to a peaceful existence, which our earth has not been able to achieve on its own.*

My research has opened the question to the possibility of many alien societies. Perhaps each of my four plausible reasons for encounters could be true in varying ways, depending upon the needs or intentions of interplanetary visitors. Edgar Cayce was informed in his trance state of the alien societies of "reptilians" and "grays", who had dire purposes planned for earth. However, the Arcturians had come in peace and are protecting us from an adverse alien invasion. It does seem to describe the battles in the heavens that are included in stories of mythical gods.

In my continuing quest for proof, I decided to look again at the Roswell incident of 1947. That appears to be the pivotal point of alien contact in modern times. Immediately after the UFO encounter, the news went around the world an alien crash had taken place at Roswell, New Mexico. Suspiciously, within hours our government explained it through the media as an experimental weather balloon crash. The media reported as they were instructed and then dropped any follow up stories. As a result the incident was almost completely forgotten.

A little over thirty years later in 1978 a UFO researcher interviewed Major Jesse Marcel, who was involved with the original recovery of the debris in 1947. Marcel believed there was a military cover up of an alien spacecraft. As the story spread like wildfire, UFO hunters everywhere jumped on the bandwagon and subsequently the Roswell encounter was reborn. In addition there have been too many other credible encounters to simply explain them all away, as the government has tried to do.

I have just finished reading a book by Charles Berlitz entitled "The Roswell Incident".

Marcel described the debris from the crash as nothing made on this earth. Marcel also managed to get pictures posing with the debris which were included in the book. Needless to say, it was not a weather balloon.

The author claims he interviewed over ninety witnesses, some of which reported intimidation or threat of incarceration (or worse) if they reported what they had seen. A few were willing to speak with the author in spite of the threats. One couple told of seeing inverted saucer shaped crafts flying side by side on July 2, 1947. There were others that reported seeing flying objects around the same time.

Many have thought perhaps the saucers were actually US experimental crafts being tested; but how would you explain a New Mexico resident Barney Barnett that reported on July 3rd he and a group of archaeologists accidently stumbled upon an extraterrestrial craft with alien corpses inside? They were quickly led away by military personnel, who were apparently preparing to transfer the craft. They later heard it was taken to Edwards Air Force Base, but the facts were distorted as to what the object really was. Yet again, the truth was kept from the general public.

The book was very informative and substantiated many other sources of research. I personally believe there have been numerous alien encounters that witnesses reported but were subsequently silenced. It is obvious our leaders do not want us to find out what many hold as truth...that we are not alone in the universe. My question now is why would there be a cover up? What would be the purpose?

My writing and research must be put on hold! Angelena's water just broke! She is laughing and crying at the same time. We are leaving for the hospital. Soon we will experience the greatest gift we could ever receive. The child born from the bond of our love!

Gabriella stared at the book as teardrops relentlessly fell to the pages, staining the words her father had penned. This was the day she was born. How many people were able to get a rear view vision of the true emotions of their parents as they entered the world? Her father's words were solace to her mind and soul.

Caleb reached for her hand and wrapped his strong fingers around hers. She looked into his eyes and with tears streaming down her face, she shared the depth of her soul. "I wish I could talk to him just one more time. I would give anything to feel his arms around me again, assuring me everything will be all right. He was my world, Caleb. The entire time I was growing up we were constantly together."

Caleb got up and pulled Gabriella out of her chair and into his arms. "I know I can't take his place, but I want to be your world now. I'll be with you constantly just as he was. I'll love you with the same depth of love your parents had for each other. Even more, if that's possible. I want us to experience the gift of our own child from the bond of love we share. In the midst of this crazy stuff we're going through, I still believe love can conquer all."

Gabriella relaxed in his arms. This was now her safe place and she feared the looming separation she felt would steal it from her. She definitely still missed her father, but Caleb's love had anchored her again into a place that felt like home. It was a secluded place that shielded her from the harsh realities that encircled her.

"Yes, Caleb. I want to believe love can conquer all. I want more than anything to have a life and a future with you. To have your child would be the greatest gift I could receive in this life."

"The greatest gift for both of us," he said holding her in his arms. All tormenting thoughts vanished into the warm sea breezes, allowing a temporary interlude.

Chapter 28

The emotional escape was only enjoyed briefly. Faith opened the balcony doors and breathlessly called to them. "Come in here...now!"

Faith was not one for giving directions, so they knew it had to be important. "What's going on?" Caleb asked as he and Gabriella rushed inside.

KJ motioned for them to come closer. They could see the excitement on his face. "Look at this!" He said as he turned his laptop where they could get a better view.

"Hmmm," Caleb muttered. "I don't want to seem stupid but what is it?"

Gabriella's eyes widened as she leaned closer for a better view. "Is that what I think it is?" She could hardly breathe as she focused on the images on his computer.

Caleb looked closer and then a smile spread across his face. "Is it really?" He looked at Aaron, knowing he would be able to read his body language.

Aaron was trying to keep his usual composure but he could not hold it back. "Yes, it is! KJ has found identical writing from ancient documents archived in Ethiopia! These documents have just recently been made public. The carbon dating is from approximately 4400 years ago... the time of Noah's flood! We still have a lot of work on translation, but we're either really lucky or divinely blessed to find this!"

KJ looked at each team member with his voice full of expectation and stated as a matter of fact, "I don't believe in luck. I believe in divine guidance!"

KJ pushed back his chair to get a full view of their faces. "Do you have any idea how The Omega Watchers project got started?"

"We don't know all the details," Aaron answered. "When we first joined the project the Professor told us he was researching the language from the time of the great flood, in an effort to understand the antediluvian society. We thought it was just another one of his linguistic projects. I assumed I was asked to join because ancient writing was my field of expertise."

Caleb interjected his reason for being on the team. "The Professor knew studying and exploring caves was my passion. We were to explore caves in the area of ancient Mesopotamia, where Noah's family lived, and try to find cave walls or artifacts with writings that matched the clay tablet. That's what we've done for over a decade."

"As we got further into the project we knew it had a much deeper significance." Gabriella joined in the conversation. "As you know, we've just found out the scope of it. We still don't know the details of how it all began."

"I'm sure the Professor would want you to know, in view of the current events. He told me last weekend he planned to tell you himself very soon." KJ straightened in his chair. "You might want to get comfortable. It'll take a few minutes to give you the back story."

The team sat around the table excited to hear about the birth of the project, which now consumed their lives.

KJ began the story. "As you know my mother and Dr. Brotman have been friends for decades. They had met at a Messianic Conference in Washington, D.C. in 1979. Even though we lived in America they constantly kept in touch, regarding what was going on prophetically in Israel. As a teenager I remember her sharing with me these events, making sure I understood the significance of the prophetic timelines."

"So you've known about the project from the very beginning?" Faith was fascinated with KJ's history of the project.

"Even before the project was formed, Faith, I saw the roots of it. In the late-nineties, the Professor had made a trip to Washington, D.C. My parents met him there. They were joined by an elite group of bible scholars who assembled to hear a private presentation to be given by the Professor. The presentation was based on the Professor's research, and his discoveries were combined with information provided to him by another scientist, who ultimately became one of the founders of the project. Both had been researching for years but it wasn't until they met and compared notes that the entire prophetic picture became perfectly clear."

"And you know what they discovered, KJ?" Aaron was on the edge of his seat in anticipation.

"My mother couldn't tell me all of the details but during their time in Washington, my parents, along with the other meeting attendees, reviewed and discussed the two men's research. Then they compared it to the ancient prophecies. Those in the meeting were all convinced they had reached a new understanding of what the society was in the days of Noah. According to the ancient prophets, that same society would be repeated at the end of days."

"Is it the same as what the Professor told us in the meeting?" Caleb asked.

KJ nodded. "Exactly the same! My mother had studied bible prophecy from the time she was young. Her father also was an avid student of prophecy. But the revelation the Professor presented opened a whole new world of prophetic understanding of the end of days. The conclusion they reached, based on the research they were given, was why the project was started."

"Do you know who the scientist was?" Faith asked.

"No, the Professor wouldn't tell anyone who he was. I do know the anonymous man helped to found the project, working behind the scenes. I also know he is still deeply involved. Even my mother doesn't know who the founders are. She told me when the Professor said it was for safety reasons, she knew he meant it. There's been a lot of mystery around the project to try to keep people safe. After yesterday's accident I wonder how safe any of us are."

"Do you know why the Professor went to Washington and not somewhere else for this meeting? Did someone in Washington have something to do with the project?" Gabriella was intent on understanding all the details about the inception of the project.

"The Professor had invited the Israeli Ambassador to the presentation because he believed it was an international security issue and wanted Israel and America to work together. As you know, the Professor is highly respected in his field of study and he had hoped the Ambassador would be the liaison to speak with other US government officials. He believed if he could present the evidence the two countries could work together in a unified purpose of exposing the coming deception."

"And?" Gabriella pressed him to continue.

KJ smiled at her determination for all of the details. "He came as requested and apparently the Ambassador was extremely interested, although somewhat skeptical. My mother said she never felt comfortable about him being there. Something didn't feel right. The Ambassador wanted a copy of the research for further study but the Professor wouldn't give it to him. He told him he would gladly meet with any credible government official and present the findings, but the research must stay in his possession. Mom said it was obvious to everyone the Ambassador didn't like being rejected, but he told the Professor he would be back in touch with him. He never contacted the Professor again."

"That sounds familiar," Gabriella said bitterly. "It's the same thing my parents were told. Apparently the government isn't interested in the truth."

"I'm not sure it's a lack of interest in truth, Gabi," KJ answered. "It would seem it's more their desire to keep the information silent so they can maintain control. Power and greed are their only motives."

"Why was the Professor so convinced the other scientist had all of his facts right when they compared their research?" Gabriella's scientific mind was questioning.

KJ was ready with answers. "The anonymous scientist, in his explorations, had found some ancient writing that no one could translate. Neither could it be determined as to the dating of the discovered language. He began searching for experts in forensic linguistics and found several articles praising Dr. Brotman and his world renowned reputation for deciphering the Dead Sea Scrolls. He contacted the Professor and they set up a meeting. The Professor had no idea the magnitude of what would develop afterwards."

"And I suppose that began our project." Caleb observed.

"Not immediately," KJ answered. "The two set up a meeting early in 1998. The scientist brought pictures of the ancient writing. After careful review, the Professor confessed he had never seen the language before. When he asked the man where he found the writing, he began to explain the nature of the research he had done. As they combined their research, it became a crystal clear picture of ancient prophecies."

"I wonder why the Professor never told us." Aaron asked.

"It was definitely a safety issue for everyone involved," KJ answered. "Before the scientist contacted the Professor with his findings he had considered publishing his research. He had other articles published and knew the editor well, so he contacted him for a meeting. When he presented his articles, the editor definitely wanted to publish it, even though he knew it would be met with great skepticism. However the research was so thorough, he was willing to publish them regardless."

Before KJ could finish Gabriella interrupted him. "What was the article? Maybe I read it. I read lots of science journals."

"It was never published," KJ told her. "He received a phone call from the editor telling him they had to cancel it. He didn't give him any explanation. The scientist felt so rejected he almost gave up, but there was still an unfinished task. The ancient writing he had found was the only incomplete part of his research. He decided to concentrate on getting it translated to perhaps ascertain further proof of his research. It was that ancient writing that brought him to the Professor."

"What did the scientist know that the Professor didn't?" Gabriella asked. "How was the Professor so sure that the man's research was accurate?"

"That is the amazing part," KJ smiled as he explained. "There was only a hand full of people that knew about the prophecies the Professor was told to keep silent about. So when the scientist explained his hypothesis, based on the evidence he had found, the Professor knew he had been divinely led to his conclusions. The scientist could not have possibly known what was in the prophecies and yet his research proved the prophecies were already beginning to be fulfilled. The major difference was the scientist was looking at it from his intellectual perspective and not from a prophetic viewpoint. This is when the Professor and the scientist began their journey together."

Gabriella was really interested in how science and prophecy could work together. "KJ, how did they manage to merge the two research projects? Had they come to exactly the same conclusions?"

"It's strange how things happen sometimes." KJ was addressing the team but looked directly at Gabriella. "The two men spent hours and hours comparing their research. When the scientist would explicate on one of his hypotheses and conclusions, the Professor would counter with evidence of how it had already been written years ago by the prophets.

The scientist began to realize his research was a counterfeit truth. When he combined all of his findings with the Professor's research, he could no longer deny the obvious."

"Did the scientist already believe in the Professor's God and in the prophetic writings?" Gabriella asked, thinking it would have been easy to accept the fallen angel theory if he was already a religious man.

"No, Gabi, he didn't believe there was a supreme God at all. He had already been sucked into the great deception that we are all working on exposing. Had he not met the Professor, he may never have found the truth. That is what is called a divine encounter."

Gabriella, as a scientist herself, did not know how that could be possible and asked, "Are you saying he just completely changed his beliefs and didn't need proof?"

"He had the proof he needed. He had been gathering his own data of proof for years and didn't know it." KJ said, praying in his heart she would understand. "He realized there was no earthly way that ordinary men, thousands of years ago, could have known what was going to happen in the future. Not unless there was a Creator that knew all things, the end from the beginning, and loved his creation enough to warn them. This is one of the main ways that the true God proves Himself to us."

"Is that when the project started?" Gabriella was feeling the pressure to accept it all as truth and decided to change the subject.

"No, still not yet. The two men composed a dissertation of their combined research for presentation. That's when the Professor set up the meeting my parents attended later that year in Washington, D.C. The Professor believed they had undeniable proof there was a powerful organization setting the stage for the people of earth to accept a friendly encounter with extraterrestrials. These 'beings' would bring peace and harmony to our earth, which is about to self destruct. The Professor was sure he could convince the Israeli Ambassador, being from the epicenter nation of biblical prophecy, this would actually happen; but it would, in reality, be the return of the fallen angels and ultimately God's final judgment."

"I can see why they would be so discouraged," Gabriella said thinking about what her father had written when he was rejected. "Do you think maybe the Israeli Ambassador simply didn't believe him? When you think about demons appearing as extraterrestrial beings and working with the governments of the world, well frankly, most people would think it pretty ridiculous!" As Gabriella spoke the words she knew she was causing a greater division in the team.

"As ridiculous as it sounds, if you believe the prophets were messengers of Jehovah God to earth then you have to believe this, too. It's all or nothing. There are many that say they believe in God but when it comes down to it they want to pick and choose what they believe as truth." KJ stated with consternation.

"When the Professor didn't hear anything I guess he was frustrated just like my father was." Gabriella decided to let the point drop.

"Yes, he was. But, it was then the Prophet visited the Professor and gave him the clay tablets. When the Prophet told him 'as it was in the days of Noah', he knew he had been given a divine encounter and it was a sign to not give up."

"He is a very determined man, that's for sure." Faith commented.

KJ's voice took on a new tone of excitement. "Now here's the most amazing part! The language on the clay tablets, given to him by the Prophet, was exactly the same language in the pictures the scientist had! That birthed the Omega Waters Project and the Professor's ensuing determination for exploration; and to follow the map in search of the unknown language. That's where your team came in. They were determined to connect it all together for what the Professor believes will be a revolutionary message to the world for the end of days. He says he is sure it will be the final proof. There were just too many divine interventions to believe otherwise."

KJ leaned back in his chair as the team allowed the information to soak in. Then he continued: "My mom was so excited when the Professor emailed her and told her about the project and asking my parents to pray for them. He promised to keep her informed as to the progress. It wasn't but a couple of years later Mom began to get emails about this bright research team he had in his university class and his plans to bring the four of you into the project. He told her about you, Gabi, accepting a scholarship and moving to Israel from America. He also told her you had lost your father and he had come to love you, like the daughter he never had."

"I had no idea." Gabriella was overwhelmed with emotion and amazed the Professor would tell his friends about her. He made her feel special right from the beginning but she had no idea how he truly felt.

"Do you all realize now how important this project is?" They could see both the challenge and the excitement that overwhelmed KJ. "I believe it is the most important work of anything on the face of the earth, and we are all part of it!"

Gabriella could see a new purpose and excitement in the faces of Aaron and Faith. Caleb seemed to be mentally weighing the information. Now she had a deeper understanding of what was driving the Professor and why everything had been so mysterious.

"It's time to get back to work, team." KJ directed. "There's a lot to do and little time in which to get it done."

Chapter 29

Gabriella was anxious to resume reading through her father's research and find evidence to prove he was not eccentric in his beliefs of extraterrestrials. More and more she felt alienated from the others, since she could not force herself to embrace the belief all supernatural experiences had to fall in either the category of Jehovah God or evil beings. Watching Caleb being drawn into their convictions was especially hard for her and she hoped against hope that her father's research would bring them all to a final truth.

She looked at Caleb and a flow of emotion rushed through her. What if they could not find a common ground in their beliefs? Would it destroy what had seemed to be a perfect relationship? The very thought felt like a dagger going through her stomach.

As if Caleb had read her mind he got up from the table and pulled out her chair. "Let's go back to the balcony and get to work."

Caleb took Gabriella's hand and stated with determination, "Together we *will* find the truth." Gabriella was certain of it, but would the truth tear them apart?

As they walked toward the open French doors, KJ punctuated their mission. "I'm working on a very interesting program I believe will help break the language code. This could be the turning point for the project. After all of these years, we're on the verge of a breakthrough. You'll get the answers you need, Gabi."

Gabriella again felt like she was being pushed into believing what the others held as truth. Her words were edgy as she walked out the door. "Yes, I will!"

As Caleb and Gabriella settled into their seats, Caleb took her hand. "Gabi, I can feel you pulling away from me. This isn't a matter of taking sides, you know."

"But I seem to be the only one open to the possibility there is extraterrestrial life. How can we be scientists looking for truth if we aren't open to possibilities?"

"The others involved, Gabi, feel they have already found their truth. Now they are trying to find the proof the world will need to believe."

"And what do you believe, Caleb? Until recently you didn't believe anything at all!"

Caleb looked out over the bay and was silent for a few minutes. Then he turned to face Gabriella and chose his words carefully. "I think it was more I didn't know what to believe, so I chose not to believe anything. I have to admit, I can't get away from the Presence that was in the waiting room at the hospital. Gabi, that was real and I know it. We all felt it. I know you did, too."

She remembered how strong the Presence was and the miracle of the Professor's healing. Then suddenly the words of Arcturus rang in her mind. "You did that. You healed him with your shaman power and deep love." Could it be possible? But then her sensible mind took over. She knew it was just a dream mixture of all the emotions raging in her.

"Caleb, I just don't know what to believe. Yes, I felt something but I don't know what it was. Maybe it was just a combination of the intense emotions in the room culminating into a synergy that felt supernatural."

Caleb continued to stare at the blue waters of the Mediterranean Sea considering the possibilities. "Maybe." He admitted. "If so, how do you explain the Professor's healing? Even the doctor said it had to be a higher power."

"But how can you prove what the higher power was? I have realized in the past few days there are powers we can't explain...powers that go beyond human existence, as we know it. Still, to put everything supernatural into one little god box, tie it up and say this answers everything? Well, I just can't accept that!"

Caleb knew to continue the conversation would only bring further division between them and tried to lighten the somber atmosphere. "Aren't you anxious to find out about your own birth? That's where the journal left off, so let's see if you made it into the world."

Caleb made her laugh in spite of the tensions between them. She opened the journal smiling as she remembered reading of her parents' excitement, knowing she was about to enter the world. "You read, Caleb. I want to just listen and savor every word."

March 21, 1983

It has been a glorious three days. Angelena had an easy delivery and was only in labor six hours. We had already decided if it was a girl we would name her Gabriella. It would be a mixture of my middle name and Cinderella. It would mean 'daddy's little princess'.

Gabriella immediately interrupted Caleb's reading. "Now I understand why he called me his little princess even when I was a tomboy climbing rocks and digging in caves. I guess he always wanted me to remember my feminine side." She looked at Caleb. "I lost sight of that for too many years."

"But you've found it now, Cinderella," Caleb said jokingly.

"Oh, how I wish our life could be a fairy tale and you could be Prince Charming, taking me away to Never, Never Land. But it's getting more like a science fiction movie with a horror ending."

"Enough of fiction," he said, as he continued to read.

"This is our first night home and I never realized I could be so frightened by something so small and innocent. What if I drop her? How do I know what she wants when she cries? What if she's hurting and I can't help her? I've only been a father for three days and I have to admit, I am terrified.

Angelena has settled into motherhood as though it was nothing challenging at all. She seems to understand everything Gabi needs. (We have decided this will be her nickname.) It's amazing to me how a mother just instinctively knows what to do. It makes me wonder about the theory of creation. There are just too many things that are unexplained in evolution when it comes to the human soul and spirit.

I plan to put my work aside and take some time to adjust to the new role of father. This is a once in a lifetime event for me and I intend to enjoy every minute with my little princess and her beautiful mother.

Caleb looked up from the journal and waited for Gabriella's reaction. "As precious as these words are to me we have to stay focused. I know I'll read his words many times over in the future, when I have time to cherish each one."

Caleb turned the page. "The next entry is made almost a month later."

April 20, 1983

The first few weeks with our Gabi have been quite an experience. It is amazing how my fears of being a father just melted into unadulterated love. When I hold her and look into her big blue eyes there is a supernatural connection I can't explain. When she smiles at me, my heart melts like hot butter. I would do anything for her. I would even gladly give my life to protect her. The love of a parent is beyond comprehension of the human mind and definitely beyond explanation by mere words.

I have taken this time to focus on fatherhood but I must now refocus on work. I am working from home to be able to give Angelena a break when she needs it and I can be close to Gabi.

When I took a hiatus from research I had determined at that point to delve further into why the government would keep the extraterrestrial visits a secret from the citizens. ETs would obviously have a tremendous amount of technology to offer our planet. This is where I will focus my time and energy until I have found a viable answer or exhausted every avenue of possibility.

Realizing her father's journal had changed from personal back to research, Gabriella interrupted Caleb. "I'll read now." She reached for the journal. "It helps me to feel more connected when he's writing about his work."

June 25, 1983

It was a year ago this month we left our sabbatical in Israel and returned home. I have learned so much in my research. And the more I find out, the more concerned I get for the future of our nation and for the world. I want my daughter to grow up in a safe place, never experiencing the fear of uncertainty. What I do is for her and not for my own self- satisfaction of discovering truth.

In a thorough study of the Roswell incident and combining that information with my additional research, I have assimilated information that points to the possibility our government has collaborated with alien visitors, taken advantage of their technological genius; and due to the selfishness of our leaders, have used the information for their individual power not allowing the citizens to know the existence of our extraterrestrial superiors.

Their plan has worked for several decades, but if my research is correct there is a reckoning day coming soon. The superior race that has tried to be a friend to our planet, will not be used for greedy purposes. In a desire for power, many nations have developed weapons that could completely destroy the earth. Those who are guardians of our planet will soon come. This superior race will bring harmony and peace to our world; and the greedy, selfish leaders will be forced to submit to a supreme authority. Edgar Cayce knew this long before WWII. It's commonly thought that Cayce was not taken seriously by the world in his clairvoyant knowledge. I beg to differ! I believe the government knew very well he was correct and did all they could to destroy his credibility!

Gabriella laid the journal on the table and stared at the words her father had written thirty years ago. These were the very words from her dream! Arcturus told her about the greed of the earth leaders and a day was coming when the Arcturians would bring peace to the earth. Arcturus also said her father had discovered this truth and the government did not want it known. That was the reason her mother was killed and they intended to kill her father, too. How could she have dreamed this, before reading it in her father's journal?

"What is it, Gabi?" Caleb asked, as he watched the expression on her face. "Do you think your father was actually able to prove this?"

How she wished she could tell him about her dreams but she could not, at least not yet. She had to determine for herself what was really happening.

She continued to reason and question in her mind: "Have I inherited some type of supernatural, extrasensory powers that are beginning to manifest? Shamans in a dream state would connect to their spirit guides. Is this happening to me? What other explanation could there be?"

"Think about it Caleb! If my father was able to prove this, it would explain why they wanted my parents dead. If he did prove it, then we are back to believing in extraterrestrial superpowers instead of just one god controlling everything."

Confusion was evident in Caleb's face. His beliefs were like a pendulum swinging back and forth as he tried to settle into what was undeniable truth. Gabriella could feel him being torn between the two. Just maybe they would end up on the same side after all and their love would not be challenged.

As if Arcturus was there in the room reading her mind, she heard his words: "There would be no limit as to what you can do for the good of others, but only if you separate yourself from unbelievers who will dilute your vibrational frequencies. You are chosen, Gabriella!"

Gabriella battled against the very idea she would ever have to make that choice!

Chapter 30

Gabriella was fighting the agonizing thoughts of making a choice between Caleb and her shaman powers when Faith slung the balcony doors open. "Hey, guys! You've got to see this!"

Caleb and Gabriella quickly joined the others. There was an energy you could cut with a knife flowing through the room.

KJ turned from his computer for Caleb and Gabriella to see. "This just hit the information highway. A language called Dahlaki recently was discovered. It's still spoken and written by a small tribe of secluded mountain people in Eritrea, which borders Ethiopia in the south and across the Red Sea from Saudi Arabia. These people have stayed secluded and the language has been used exclusively by this unknown small tribe for thousands of years. Remember this is the area settled by Noah's grandson Cush. I've compared the writing to the clay fragment and the pictures you guys took in the cave. Look how close it is!"

It was obvious to all of them that KJ was getting close to a breakthrough. "There's more!" KJ continued barely taking a breath. "Apparently the Dahlaki language is a dialect of the Tabadawi language, which is now being considered the mother of all languages. It originated before the flood. In a recent archeological dig in southwestern Ethiopia, a clay fragment was found with this ancient writing. It is Tabadawi. Take a look at the picture!"

Gabriella caught her breath. She looked back and forth comparing the two languages. "I have little knowledge of ancient writings, but even I can tell it is exactly the same as what we found in the cave...and the clay tablets!"

"Yes, it is!" KJ could no longer contain his excitement. "Most importantly, the clay fragments were given to the Professor by the old man *before* this was discovered!"

"What do you think that means?" Caleb asked.

Aaron answered his question. "It's obvious to me the Professor had a divine encounter, just as he has always believed. God sent him a sign to continue the work when he was ready to give up. The language was unknown by forensic linguists at the time the Prophet visited him and many years later, the language is rediscovered. It's been proven through archeology the language is antediluvian."

Caleb eyes narrowed as the words sunk in. "Are you saying the Prophet was an angel or some sort of supernatural being?"

Aaron looked his usual serious self and asked Caleb: "Do you have a better explanation? In fact, could there be another explanation?"

"And how amazing is the timing?" Faith asked. "It's like Yahweh had kept this hidden until now. The timing of this discovery can't be just coincidence after thousands of years."

The group all laughed simultaneously and chimed together, quoting the Professor, "The word 'coincidence' is not in the original Hebrew language."

Gabriella was thinking here we go again and spoke her aggravation. "Why does it have to be someone sent from your God? Why couldn't we, for one moment, consider it could be an inter-dimensional being from another world that has all knowledge? My father wrote in his journal he has evidence such beings have been visiting the planet since the beginning of man, living on the earth and interacting with the people."

Gabriella truly thought she would get them to see there were other possibilities to explain supernatural occurrences. She waited for the slightest affirmation but none came.

Gabi's anger was growing and she quickly retorted, "Whoever this so called Prophet is, I have looked him straight in the eyes and he doesn't look all that different from any other Hasidic Jew. He certainly didn't look like an angel!"

KJ pulled the team back to the mission at hand. "What we've got to do now is take what we know and try to translate what we have. Hopefully, the pieces will start to all fall into place."

Faith's face showed her confusion. "How can you translate a language that has been lost? Where do you even start?"

KJ smiled at her. "There is currently software available that can translate texts from known world languages. The problem is the current translators cannot generate meaningful texts from unknown languages. It will take a specialized program to process all of the algorithms containing the combinations and permutations necessary to factor in the differences between grammatical and conjugational rules. There are morphology programs that can assist and this would create assurance of the greatest probability of the correct translation."

Caleb voiced what the rest of the team was thinking. "I have no idea what you're talking about. Bottom line, KJ. Are you sure it will work?"

"Let me put it this way," KJ tried to explain. "There's been a progression of dialects and changes through the years which is normal for developing civilizations. To regress through the languages and achieve the ability to translate this ancient language, we need three components: a powerful and fast processor, a highly refined algorithm and two complete language databases."

"Clear as mud," Caleb said scratching his head in confusion.

KJ just laughed at him and continued. "The first database would contain a complete dictionary of the language to be translated to, in this case Ge'ez, with all of its known morphology. The second database would contain all of the unknown language characters found on written two-dimensional text and antiquities containing three-dimensional text, symbols or drawings."

Aaron seemed to be the only one of the team that could follow KJ's explanation. It was obvious the others were totally confused. KJ continued. "I know this is not easy to understand but I believe Aaron and I can begin with the Professor's Ge'ez translations and work backwards through the languages as they evolved watching how the letters changed. I am also going to use a third translation database of all known world languages. This might assist with further translations of the unknown language to a modern language. The two primary databases can be created by entering the unknown language characters and Ge'ez characters into the computer utilizing a XRCE Xerox 3D optical code reader."

"I get the jest of what you're saying in spite of all the technical mumbo jumbo, but don't we need the Professor to guide us through this?" Gabriella asked. "We have to be sure this is correct to the precise detail."

"Yes, we do," KJ agreed. "While we're waiting for him to get out of the hospital, we will get this as far as we can. Then he will be the final authority."

"This is our plan of action," Aaron said. "Hopefully it will get us to the place where the Professor can verify the translation. In order for the program to generate all possible translations of unknown text, it will be necessary to process each individual unknown character against the Ge'ez characters found in the two language databases. At that juncture, we will factor in text phrases of both languages by employing some simple strategies."

"That makes sense, but it still sounds extremely difficult. I'm glad that's not my job." Caleb sat down on the couch, crossed his legs and put his arms behind his head, in a comical effort to show he would have no part in it. They all laughed at him and it brought a brief recess to the intense atmosphere.

Aaron was soon refocusing on the business at hand. "This is where it will require the knowledge of the Professor. It's possible to have many resulting translation texts with different subjects. It's imperative to choose the context of the known text, and its associated characters; then have the processor program select the translation in direct relation with that context. If it's not found, an indirect relation with it will need to be stored in a 'completed translation file', which is formatted to print out the comparative results in Ge'ez. From that file, the Professor will do the final translation."

Caleb looked at Aaron and KJ in total perplexity. "I guess I'll just stick with caving. That I understand. The only thing that matters to me is getting the accurate translation and we'll leave you computer geeks to working on that. I have no doubt you know exactly what to do. In the meantime, Gabi and I will get back to what we understand...or at least what we're trying to understand."

KJ laughed at Caleb's response. "The truth is the final destination for all of us." KJ turned back to the computer in immediate concentration.

Gabriella had tears in her eyes as she softly spoke. "I can't wait for the Professor to hear all of this. After all of his years of research, discouragement and frustration, he is finally going to get some answers. Hopefully, we all will. I just wish my father could have seen his personal research come to fruition."

KJ looked up from the computer and spoke with kindness. "I don't think we are as far apart in what we believe as you may think, Gabi. I believe we are holding the key to understanding the truth in these ancient writings. We know there is a power beyond our human ability. It's just who you designate as the power source that makes the difference."

Chapter 31

The team was hard at work, knowing they were pushing against the enemy of time. Well into the night, KJ and Aaron worked on translations of the ancient language while Faith documented their research.

Caleb and Gabriella read through more of the articles and information her father had collected in his research. It all substantiated his belief that encounters with extraterrestrials had been greatly on the increase since WWII ended and the encounters started mainly with the Roswell incident.

It was after midnight when Aaron was the first to admit his exhaustion. "It's been a long day for all of us. Let's get some rest and get a fresh start in the morning."

The team quickly agreed. Gabriella and Faith adjourned to Gabriella's bedroom, while the guys settled in for the night.

Faith sat down in the chaise lounge by the window, looking out at the late summer skies, while Gabriella was changing and getting ready for bed. She whispered a prayer through the silence in the room: "Lord, reveal Your truth to Gabi. Help her to see You are the Living God and Your love for her is everlasting. I don't know how to reach her, but You do."

Tears of love were running down Faith's face when Gabriella came out of the bathroom. "What's the matter, Faith? Are you okay?"

"I'm fine. Just thinking about how close we've become through the years. We have so many wonderful memories of our university years and all the explorations we've been on. You're like a sister to me. I don't want our search for truth to cause division. I know you well, Gabi, and you feel like you're being pressured to accept our beliefs. All I ask is you be open-minded and not pre-judge. Let truth reveal itself to you."

Gabriella gave Faith a hug. "Your friendship means the world to me. I don't know how I could've gotten through those years after my father died without you. I didn't have anyone and then, almost like magic, you appeared in my life. I feel so lucky we were roommates."

"Maybe it wasn't luck. Maybe an unseen force put us together." Then Faith quickly changed the subject. "They're wonderful memories that can never be taken away from us."

Gabriella was thinking about the twisting and turning of events that had brought her to Haifa University. It truly was as though an unseen force guiding her when she was lost in the sadness of life.

Gabriella sounded more like her normal self when she replied to Faith. "Then we met the Professor, Aaron and Caleb, and I found a new family. Nothing will come between us, Faith. We may not always agree; but we will do as we promised when we all started working together, agree to disagree, agreeably. I promise, we'll always be like sisters."

Gabriella was musing over the series of events of the last few days as she brushed her long, curly hair. "Do you think it's possible for my parents to still be watching me and guiding my life in some way? Can they see me from the other dimension they've moved into?"

In all the years Faith had known Gabriella, she had never talked about her parents still existing in any form. When she spoke of their having passed away, it was always in the context of they had ceased to exist.

"Gabi, you know I believe in the afterlife. Maybe they can see us. I know God does. He is always watching over us. He's always listening."

Gabriella wanted desperately to confide in Faith about her dreams. Faith's God and Arcturus were so much alike. At least in her dreams she could talk to Arcturus, ask questions and get answers. Faith's God had never appeared to her in dreams or otherwise. If she had any degree of shaman powers, it was suppose to help her connect to a higher spirit for wisdom and knowledge. That she desperately needed. She so wanted to talk to Faith and get help in balancing her sanity. Sadly she admitted, Faith would not understand. No one would.

"It's going to be a long day again tomorrow. Let's get some sleep." Gabriella said, climbing into bed. Faith went into the bathroom to brush her teeth. When she came back out Gabriella was already sound asleep.

She looked at her dear friend as she got into the other side of the bed, praying again Gabriella would find the truth that her soul so desperately longed for.

Gabriella had barely closed her eyes when sleep overshadowed her. Almost immediately the feeling of falling engulfed her. Deeper and deeper she was descending into the bottomless pit. Complete darkness surrounded her as her screams echoed, "Arcturus!!!"

As she called his name, light immediately appeared at the end of the long, black tunnel and she could see Arcturus waiting for her. The fear quickly faded as he caught her hand. "I'm here," he whispered. "I will always be here watching over you. All you have to do is call my name."

Gabriella relaxed as peace saturated her. She looked around her and the scenery was very familiar. "Where are we, Arcturus?"

"Don't you recognize it? This is the place you lived until your mother was killed by the evil ones that want to destroy the truth. This is your bedroom. You wanted to see your parents again and there is important information you're about to hear. In earth time this is June of 1988."

Gabriella vaguely remembered her bedroom. She was only five years old when they left the home they lived in when her mother was killed, but she definitely remembered her furniture that went with her through numerous moves from university to university.

"That's my bed! I loved that fluffy pink and red Strawberry Shortcake bedspread! I remember getting up in the mornings and dragging the entire bedspread off my bed, down the hall, through the living room and into my father's study. I would crawl up in his lap and cover us both with it, while he would hold me. I wouldn't let my father replace it until it was completely worn out and even then I cried myself to sleep missing the comfort it gave me. Before he threw it away, he cut a piece off the edge and it's always been with me, tucked into my pillowcase, wherever I'm sleeping. It's a piece of my past I still hold on to." She turned and looked at Arcturus. "You know, I've never told anyone that."

His penetrating eyes looked deep into her eyes, as though gazing at her soul. "I already know. I have watched you from the time you were born."

As she was reminiscing, her mother walked through the bedroom door. "Come on, Gabi, it's time for bed!"

Gabriella caught her breath. "Momma!" She cried out and tried to move towards her.

"She can't hear you." Arcturus instructed. "You're in a time warp. It allows you to visit the past, but you are in an alternate dimension. You can see her, but she cannot see or hear you."

Gabriella saw herself, as a five year old, come running into the room with her long, blonde hair bouncing around her face. "Sing to me, Mommy."

Her mother pulled the bedspread and sheets back as Gabriella climbed in. She tucked her in as Gabriella pulled the bedspread up around her face. Her mother sat down on the side of the bed and Gabriella snuggled up next to her. Her mother's voice was like liquid love filling the room as she began to sing. She sang until her cherished daughter fell asleep.

"I miss her so much it hurts!" Gabriella's voice was cracking from sorrow. "I was cheated, losing her so young. It just wasn't fair! Why are you showing me this? It only makes it hurt more!"

Arcturus' dark eyes looked into Gabriella's. "This isn't to hurt you. This is to reveal truth. Come with me." Arcturus pulled her away from the heart-breaking scene and they were immediately transported to her father's study.

"There's my dad!" Her father was sitting at his over-sized wooden desk, concentrating on the papers in front of him. Gabriella tried to move towards him, but Arcturus held her back. She knew she could only watch. Oh, how she longed to crawl up in his lap and have his strong arms wrap around her, just one more time.

Her mother entered the room, walked behind his chair and put her arms around his neck. "What are we going to do?" She asked with an expression of complete confusion.

"I don't know. I just don't know." His face was full of bewilderment as he reached up to put his hands over hers. "It's obvious the government is keeping the encounters with extraterrestrials secret, and it's apparently because of greed and power. It's more than coincidence that there was an explosion of knowledge after the Roswell incident, especially in the areas of gravitational propulsion, beam weaponry and mind control. It all fits together perfectly and it just doesn't make any sense they wouldn't talk to us. We have compelling information."

"Do you think the MJ-12 already know about the implants? If they do, and it's classified information, they would be extremely concerned about anyone outside their secret group knowing."

Gabriella's father pulled his wife around the chair and into his lap. He wrapped his arms around her as if protecting her from the danger he sensed was coming. "That's my concern, Angelena. Since we haven't heard from them, I can only assume it's one of two things. They don't believe us and consider it totally ridiculous, *or* they already know. If they do know, we could be in serious trouble just having access to this information."

She laid her head on his shoulder and was silent as the possibilities of why there was no contact swirled in her head. "Do we just sit and wait?"

Her father hesitated before he answered. "This information is too serious to just sit on. Seems we're forced to try to make other contacts. We have to do something with the information we have." He took a long breath and then slowly released the air in an effort to relieve his frustration. "But tomorrow is Saturday and we'll have our weekly family outing. We'll enjoy our time together and not even think about this extraterrestrial web we're caught in. Tomorrow it will just be the three of us. No ET's, no government, nothing but our family."

Angelena kissed his cheek and got up to head for the kitchen. "That reminds me, I need to get things ready tonight so we can get an early start. I have to make a quick trip to the grocery first thing in the morning. I'll leave Gabi with you so I can hurry."

Gabriella looked at Arcturus with tears streaming down her face. "Is this the night before my mother was killed?"

"Yes," he said without emotion.

"I wish I could warn them and change what happened."

"Once destiny has been fulfilled it cannot be reversed," he replied. "There is a purpose in you seeing this. You will soon read about the implants in his journal. Then you will understand the importance of his discovery. You have been chosen to help prepare the world, Gabriella."

"Prepare the world for what? What are implants? What are you talking about?"

Arcturus' dark eyes penetrated hers. "You will soon understand. His discovery will change the world."

Chapter 32

Gabriella awakened to sunlight streaming through the window. Her first thoughts were of her parents. She lay still for a while savoring the dream. Seeing her parents again was bittersweet. She still missed them so desperately. It was without question that they truly loved each other and loved her. Her soul ached with desire to feel the comfort of their arms, just one more time.

Her longing for her parents was quickly replaced with the memory of the implants. What were they? How could they be so vital to national security? She did not remember anything being mentioned about implants in all of their team discussions that could have caused thoughts to bleed into her dreams.

Faith was already up and she could hear the team talking in the living room. Gabriella jumped out of bed. She was anxious to read more of her father's journal and see if there were any entries that would explain these devices.

As she was getting dressed, her mind was rehearsing all of her previous dreams of Arcturus. They started after she returned from Saudi Arabia and after receiving her father's journal. She would read his entries and then dream about what she had read. Now it had reversed. She was dreaming about information from his research before reading it. If there was information about implants in his entries, she would know it was not just her obsession with the project mixing into her night dreams. Something much deeper was going on and she was not sure if she was prepared to accept the possible reality.

She went out to join the team already hard at work. Caleb pulled out a chair for her to join them at the table. "Morning, Gabi Girl," he said as she sat down. "Sleep well?"

Faith answered for her: "She sure did! She was sound asleep from the time her head hit the pillow and she didn't move all night. I was the one tossing and turning. A couple of times it felt as thought someone was in the room with us. Weird, huh?"

"Any news about the Professor this morning?" Gabriella asked wanting to change the subject.

"Sandee called earlier with an update," Faith answered. "He slept well last night and is regaining his strength. Of course he's anxious to get out of the hospital but the doctor wants to keep him until the end of the week, just to make sure there are no unexpected complications."

"Where will he go when he's released? Is Sandee going to stay with him? He shouldn't be alone, you know. He needs someone to take care of him until he's completely recovered." The concern in Gabriella's voice reflected her obvious love and devotion to the Professor. "And most important, whoever cut his brake line will probably try something else, since their mission failed!"

"We've been working on a plan." Caleb sat down beside her and put his arm around her shoulder as he explained. "We've been talking about the mountain lodge where we go for work retreats. It's secluded from view, has a gated entry and surrounded by impregnable fencing. If we could all stay there when the Professor is released, we would have a relatively safe place to work."

"Sounds like a great plan to me. But what if we're followed?" Gabriella wanted to make sure all details had been thought through.

"We've thought of that, too. Detective Richards called this morning and was asking a lot more questions. He thinks this goes much deeper than some sort of personal vendetta against the Professor. He was very curious about the Dead Sea Scroll Project and was extremely informed on how involved the Professor was with the project. He even asked if we knew of anything connected with the scroll translations that were controversial. Seemed to me he already had some information and was fishing for more to build a case on."

"You didn't tell him about the project!" Gabriella exclaimed.

"Of course not. If anyone tells him, it'll have to be the Professor. The detective is coming by this afternoon with more questions. We're going to try to coordinate a plan with him to get the Professor released from the hospital and get all of us to the mountain lodge without anyone knowing."

Gabriella was trying to process how it would work. "It sounds like a good solution, to continue working together and have the Professor join us, too. We're so close to a breakthrough, we can't stop now. I suppose we need to tell Detective Richards something that will explain why we all need to go into hiding with the Professor."

Aaron joined in the conversation. "We've discussed that, too. We don't want anyone to know about the project. Not until it's complete and the Professor decides how to proceed. So we came up with another possible explanation."

Gabriella could tell no one really wanted to explain to her what the 'other' explanation was. "Well? I'm waiting!"

Faith spoke up. "It was my idea, Gabi, and if you don't want to do it, we all totally understand."

"Do what?" Gabriella was getting the deep sense this had everything to do with her.

Faith continued cautiously. "What if you told the detective your suspicion that both your mother and father were killed because of scientific research they had done and you had just recently received his research journal, with information that you feel could put you in danger, too. If it looked as though your getting this information caused someone to be after you or anyone close to you, it could possibly take Detective Richards in a different area of investigation. Hopefully in the meantime we can finish the project, while he would be on a totally different rabbit trail."

The color drained from Gabriella's face. "Use my parent's death as a decoy? Then they would want to know all of the intimate details of my father's journal and the work he did!"

"Isn't that what your father wanted, Gabi? Wasn't that what he was trying to do when he spent years in research? He wanted people to know. You wouldn't be betraying him at all. The detective may think all the UFO stuff is strange, but you have to admit, it could be a distraction to give us time to get the project finished."

"But how about the Professor's accident? How would that tie in?" Gabriella was not convinced this idea would work.

Faith continued to explain. "He had possession of the box before Sandee gave it to you. Maybe someone found out and went after him first, not knowing it was already in your possession."

Caleb's arm was still around Gabriella's shoulder. "If you're not okay with this, just say so. None of us are pushing you. We just need to come up with a plan to protect the project and Dr. Brotman."

When Caleb said protect the Professor she knew what she had to do. Knowing that he loved her like a daughter brought her to an entirely different level of commitment to him. She would not lose another father from her life. Not if she could do anything to stop it.

"All right," she finally agreed. "It's not what I want to do, but I'm willing to for the Professor. In fact, all I have to do is tell the truth about what I believe happened to my parents. If the journal coming at this juncture can buy us some time, then so be it."

Faith looked deep into Gabriella's troubled, blue eyes and quoted from her favorite Bible story about Esther: "*Who knows but that you have come to your royal position for such a time as this?*"

A sigh of relief could be felt in the room. None of the team wanted to put Gabriella in the position of taking the brunt of the questions from the detective, but there did not seem to be any other way. The team just needed enough time to break the language code and assimilate all the information. They had no idea what the detective would think of all of the extraterrestrial research, but they were not worried about that. He probably would not believe a word of it.

Gabriella, however, believed every word to be true.

Chapter 33

Gabriella and Caleb spent the morning reviewing the research they had previously gone through. Gabriella was mentally preparing for the questions she expected when Detective Richards arrived. She had mixed feelings about using her parents as decoys, however, she was certain if her father could reach into her reality and give his blessing, he would without hesitation.

KJ and Aaron were hard at work morphing each letter to the ancient original. It was a slow and tedious process. From the expressions on their faces, progress was being made.

Shortly after lunch came the knock on the door. Caleb showed the detective into the living room where the team gathered to answer his questions. Gabriella appeared to be her usual confident self, but inside a battle of conflicting emotions raged relentlessly.

"Please have a seat, detective." Gabriella pointed to the chair next to her. "Can we offer you something to drink?"

"No, thanks." Detective Richards walked over to the balcony doors and looked out. "Nice view." The team knew he was not interested in the view but was making sure the area was secure. He walked back and sat down next to Gabriella. He had a countenance she could not explain. It was almost like he already knew the answers before he asked any questions and just wanted to give them the opportunity of verifying the truth.

"What questions do you have, sir?" Caleb asked in an effort to jump-start the conversation.

The detective got out his notepad and pen. He sat perched on the edge of his chair. His dark eyes were stern as he responded to Caleb. He ran his fingers across his head in a gesture to express confusion, although Gabriella was not buying it.

Finally he spoke. "I've been to visit Dr. Brotman and he's doing well. Anxious to get out, as you probably know. They say it will be a few more days." He paused for a response.

"Yes, Sandee gave us an update this morning." Caleb replied. "Naturally, we're all pretty concerned about his safety when he's released. You were able to post a guard at the hospital, but what happens when he goes home?"

"That is one of the reasons I'm here. But first I need a little more information. Seems every time I get an answer to a question, more questions pop up." The detective looked from one member to the next. It was obvious he was watching their body language.

"We're more than willing to help any way we can," KJ interjected in his cool, composed way. "What is it you want to know?"

"First, let me put you at ease. I'm convinced none of you had anything to do with the accident, but is there anything you've not told me that might shed some light on the case?"

Gabriella slightly leaned toward the detective, quickly formulating her words. The rest of the team sat silently praying for her to have the wisdom she needed to express herself without confusion or fear.

"We've all talked a lot about this, detective, and I am going to tell you some recent events that we think might possibly be linked to what's happened. We really didn't make the possible connection until just this morning."

It was obvious she had his full attention. His eyes portrayed a hint of expectation as she continued. "My father was an American archaeologist, as I am. He passed away twelve years ago and that's when I came to the University of Haifa and met Dr. Brotman."

"I'm sorry about your father. But to be honest I already knew that from your background check. What could this have to do with the accident?"

Gabriella took a deep breath and continued. "You probably already know the exploration team had been out of the country for six months. While we were gone a box was delivered to the Professor's office. Sandee said it arrived about four months ago and she had stored it until I got back." She gave the detective the letter to read from her former landlord. "This will explain the box."

He read the letter and passed it back to Gabriella. "Was there something in the box that connected to the Professor?"

"No, the information is all about my father's research, however, the box *was* in the Professor's possession for four months. The contents of this box resulted in the murder of my mother and possibly even my father."

The detective sat straight up and his eyes were piercing as Gabriella explained the events detailed in her father's journal. "There is so much we don't know or understand, but it's obvious that my parents discovered information that someone wanted silenced. There is the box. You can read it all for yourself. We've only had a few days to go through it and there's a lot we haven't read yet and even more we don't understand."

Detective Richards skimmed through several pages of the journal and reviewed several articles making notes as he went. All eyes were on him as the team waited. Was he going to buy it? Every word Gabriella had said was the absolute truth, but was it strong enough to get the focus off the project?

He laid the journal down and neatly stacked the articles he had reviewed. Gabriella could not wait any longer to ask. "What do you think, detective? Could this be the missing link?"

The detective leaned back in his chair. "I will take something to drink now, if you don't mind. Coffee if you have it." Then he reviewed the notes he made. He showed no emotion. None at all. The tension in the room was so thick, the team felt sure the detective would sense it.

Faith made a fresh pot of coffee and brought a cup to the detective. He thanked her and then looked at Gabriella. "This could be an important link. There has to be a motive and this is a good place to start looking. What are the chances of all of this happening right after the box arrives? I'm not sold on all of the extraterrestrial stuff, but this certainly is suspicious."

Each team member struggled to not show their obvious relief. They impatiently waited to see what the next move would be on the detective's part.

The detective's Israeli accent dominated his English as he expressed his professional thoughts. "If this is the connection, then my great concern is now for you, Gabriella, and for the rest of the team that are so closely connected to you. Maybe the Professor's accident was a warning for you to stay silent about the contents of the research. There's no doubt, if someone wants to destroy this information, they'll destroy anyone that has had access to it. What I will have to do first is contact your former landlord and see if he has any additional information. I'll find out if anyone was asking him questions and if he told anyone about the box. I'll see where that might lead. Odd that there was silence for twelve years then all hell breaks loose."

"Exactly my thoughts, too. Will this put Mr. Donald in danger?" Gabriella was thinking of the sweet man that had been so kind to her when her father passed. "I don't want him to be in any danger."

"I'll be very discreet. He won't even know why I'm asking and no one will know that I've contacted him. Now it's your danger we have to address and decide on a protection plan, at least until I can get a better handle on this."

"Can I offer a suggestion, detective?" Caleb had sat quietly much longer than Gabriella imagined he could.

"Sure, if you have any ideas I would love to hear them."

"The Professor will be getting out of the hospital the end of the week, if all goes as planned. He has a friend who has a secluded lodge in the mountains out of Tel Aviv, close to the ski resort. We've often stayed there and it's really isolated. There is only one narrow, winding access road to the lodge and the entry is gated. There's a fence around the entire property and no one can enter without permission. It's almost like a fortress and I honestly believe the place was originally built for that purpose, although I have no idea why. If we could manage to get out of the city without anyone knowing it, I believe we would be safe there."

"Give me the address and I'll look into the location. Getting you out of the city won't be a problem, but I've got to make sure the lodge would be secure. I have to run it by the chief, of course. Do you know who owns the lodge?"

"Sandee would have all the information. She always took care of travel details for us." Caleb informed him.

"Okay, I'll get right on it. Might be a good short term solution," the detective said, making notes before he left.

Gabriella had the uncanny feeling the detective knew more than he was telling them. She also knew he would not admit it, even if she asked. Nevertheless, she was greatly relieved she only had to tell the truth about her father's work. It bought them some time.

The detective received a call and went into the kitchen to talk privately.

Gabriella needed to clear her mind and walked to the balcony doors that were standing open, allowing the breezes to move through the room. The curtains caught in the winds and swirled around her as she spoke silently from the depths of her soul. "Dad, if you can hear me from the other side, I know you understand the motives of my heart. Maybe karma balance will finally allow your research to be known and we can prove you are right."

At that moment a dark cloud began to form over the waters and move towards the bay. Within minutes the winds started strengthening, as a storm was brewing out to sea. "Could this be an omen"? She whispered, not knowing it paralleled the storm on the horizon of her life.

Chapter 34

The detective left the apartment assuring them he would be in touch. As soon as the team heard the elevator doors close in the hallway, there was a concert sigh of relief. They had bought some time to finish the project. Gabriella remained on the balcony where the approaching storm was mimicking her mood.

Caleb pulled her inside and closed the French doors. Collapsing on the couch in emotional exhaustion, Caleb sat down beside her and took her hand. She laid her head on his shoulder as tears began to trickle down her cheeks. The others came to join them.

"I'm so sorry, Gabi," Faith whispered, as tears of compassion swelled in her eyes. "I guess we didn't realize just how difficult this would be for you."

KJ and Aaron pulled chairs into a circle around her in a gesture of protection. Their caring attitudes made her cry even more. Aaron, who seldom displayed emotion, was not used to this softer side of Gabriella and tears were even welling in his eyes. He took her other hand and squeezed in reassurance he was there for her.

"I don't mean to be a baby about this," Gabriella said in a quivering voice. "I just feel like I'm going to explode from all these emotions pent up inside."

The dream of her parents the previous night was still so real she felt she could reach out and touch them. Seeing them in her dream made the longing for them hurt even more. How could she explain that to her dear friends? She would just have to let them believe it was all due to the meeting with the detective.

Caleb pulled her closer to him. "Believe me you're no baby! It took a real woman that's strong and confident to do what you just did."

"Really, Caleb? All I did was tell the truth. In fact, the more I talked, I began to believe it myself. What if someone was trying to get a message to me, warning me to keep my mouth shut?"

The silence was deafening as the team allowed that unexpected possibility to sink in.

"The accident happened right after the Prophet brought the scroll...*to me*! He warned *me* of danger. Maybe the scroll is going to reveal my father discovered the real truth!" Gabriella's blue eyes were widening in fear. "Is it possible we've been wrong about the motive in the Professor's accident? Maybe wrong, too, about what and who these people were really trying to silence?"

The very possibility brought a new foreboding to the team and no one said a word. Finally KJ replied. "We don't know anything to be certain. We have to be open to all possibilities. Regardless of who, what, when and where possibilities, we must continue with the project. Once we have the required sequencing to use for translation, hopefully, we'll be able to start getting some answers instead of just more questions."

Caleb had not said a word. Gabriella knew the very idea of her being the target had overwhelmed him. She turned her face toward his and the color had drained from his beautiful, tan skin. She found herself this time assuring him it would be all right.

"We'll get through this, Caleb. The detective will get us to a safe place and then it'll all get sorted out."

He was trying with everything in him to regain his composure. He wrapped both arms around her so she could not see the anxiety in his face. "Yes, we will." He said sternly trying to convince himself. "Yes, we will." Again he was thinking about the anonymous calls. Who was it? Were they trying to find out if she was back in Israel? Was someone trying to find the box? Are they watching their every move?

Gabriella pulled away and jumped to her feet motioning for Caleb to follow her. "We've got to get our mind off this. Let's get back to the journal. The answers have to be there somewhere. I can't just sit here wondering." Gabriella's determination was evident, but even her strong spirit could not dispel the shadows of fear surrounding her.

"Take it to my bedroom, Caleb. The rain is pouring outside. We can work there without disturbing their translations."

Caleb picked up the black box and carried it to her bedroom. He placed it in the middle of her bed. Gabriella jumped on the bed, propped up pillows and leaned back against the headboard ready to read. Caleb pulled the side chair to the edge of the bed, despairingly trying to push the ominous thoughts from his mind.

Gabriella sensed his trepidation. Reading would help them to get their mind off the foreboding that had gripped their souls. She opened the journal and turned it to where they had left off.

April 1, 1984

Gabriella celebrated her first birthday last week. This has been a magnificent year of watching her grow and develop her own personality. I already know she is going to be stubborn like her mother. However, that can also be to her advantage in life when used with wisdom. She took her first steps today and you would have thought Angelena won the jackpot with her screaming in excitement.

I have become consumed with my work and feel guilty that I am not spending more time with my wife and daughter. But the information flow has been continuous and I am trying to assimilate all I am learning and bring these facts to a conclusion.

If my research is correct, extraterrestrial encounters take place all around us daily and the population at large has no inkling. Most people are like blind sheep going through a maze day after day seeing and hearing nothing except the dull details of their mundane existence.

While the masses are sleep-walking through their cookie cutter lives, the leaders of the nations are ushering in the destruction of our planet through greed and hunger for supreme power. This selfishness and self-centeredness is causing the earth to be set up for a celestial super power to save us from our own destruction.

My research has become extensive and I am trying to leave a paper trail of evidence which I will keep locked away in my black box until time for the revelation. Everything centers around one very critical detail that continually comes to the forefront of my research. Of those that have been abducted by these extraterrestrial beings the majority have one thing in common. They have a small device implanted under their skin. It is made of a material not known to this planet and no one can explain the purpose.

I question if it is some sort of alien tracking device? Is it a medical device of some sort? The possibilities are endless but I have no clue at this time as to the purpose. I am aggressively pursuing to understand the meaning. I truly believe it is the link between the two worlds.

Gabriella caught her breath as she read the words. This was what her parents had been discussing in the dream just the night before. Caleb saw the color drain from her face. It was obvious she knew something she had not told him.

"Okay, Gabi! You know something or this wouldn't upset you. What are you keeping from me? What are these devices?"

She felt his frustration and understood totally why he would be upset. "I honestly don't know, Caleb!" Then she began to tell him only half the truth. She assured herself she was not going to lie. She just would not give all the details.

"There is something I've been keeping from you." Her voice was soft as she tried to formulate the right words.

He leaned back, put his hands behind his head and stared her straight in the eyes. "Finally," he said. Then he waited.

She took a long, deep breath and exhaled slowly giving herself time to determine how she would start. Arcturus would not be mentioned. That much she was sure of.

She got off the bed and walked to the window. Rain was beating against the glass. The winds were howling around the corners of the building. She turned back to Caleb and sat down on the side of the bed to look him directly in the eyes. She would only tell him the parts that were essential to her father's research.

"The very first night after we returned from our exploration I began to have dreams. They were crazy and mixed up and at first didn't make a lot of sense. It was as though everything that was happening was getting wrapped up in my mind and becoming center stage to my dreams."

"What were the dreams about?" Caleb leaned forward and took her hand giving her support to continue.

"All sorts of stuff. I dreamed about my parents, about aliens, and even dreamed I was a Cherokee Shaman."

"A what?" Caleb looked confused.

"It's someone with Cherokee blood that can contact the spirit world and tap into supernatural powers. Isn't that crazy?" She watched his eyes to see if he thought she was losing it. All she saw was love and concern. No judgment whatsoever.

"No, not crazy. With the emotional turmoil you've been in, it's a wonder you're not having horrible nightmares." His voice was soft as he squeezed her hand as a sign to continue.

"This is what's really weird. For the first several nights I would dream about things we read in the journal. Then my dreams took a sinister turn and I am now dreaming about the things in the journal before we read them. Last night I dreamed about the evening before my mother was killed. She and my father were in his office and they were talking about the information they had presented to the government. You remember, don't you, us reading they had the meeting and were never contacted again? Caleb, they were talking about alien implants. That's what their presentation to the government was about!"

She watched his eyes turn from soft and caring to confused and questioning. "Gabi, we didn't read anything about implants until today." He was trying his best to keep his voice steady.

"Exactly! That's my point! It's not just the implants. I also dreamed about the government knowing about the aliens and using their knowledge for their own selfish purposes, while keeping it secret from the people. There are other things, too. How could I, Caleb? How could I possibly know those things before we read them?"

The tears were starting to cascade down her cheeks again. As hard as she tried to fight them back the emotions were just too strong. Caleb reached up and pulled her into his lap and she laid her head on his shoulder. She felt protected from the whole world in his arms but she knew reality was waiting as soon as he released her.

Caleb's mind was quickly searching for some response to assure her there was an explanation. There was nothing to cling to. He could not explain how she could have these prescient dreams. He had to admit there was something strange occurring. Good or bad, it was facing them head on and there was no averting the collision.

He desperately wanted to know more about the details of the dreams but he could not put her through the anxiety of reliving them.

"Gabi, in all the years you and your father were exploring together, did he ever talk to you about his research? Do you think it's possible your dad told you about this when you were young and it's been hidden in your subconscious? Maybe reading the journal is resurrecting subconscious information from years ago and it's manifesting in your dreams."

"Dad never talked to me about his research. Never! When I would ask him he would just say he would tell me when I was older. When I was older he wasn't here to tell me. His journal always stayed locked in this black box. There's no way I could have known what was in it."

"There has to be some explanation. Maybe you overheard your mom and dad talking when you were young. There has to be someway this has been stored in your memory and the journal causing it to resurface."

Gabriella leaned forward and Caleb released his embrace. She got up and walked back to the window. She could hear thunder rolling in the distance, echoing sinister warnings.

"I don't know. Maybe. I hadn't really thought of that possibility, but I don't remember ever hearing or reading anything about any of it."

"The mind is like a computer. You know that, Gabi. It sorts and stores information and, unless we have reason to access the information, it stays filed away. We don't even know what's in our subconscious until something happens, the file opens and the information is accessed. I believe your dreams are doing just that."

"Maybe you're right. At least I can deal with that possibility better than having some type of shaman powers. That really is going off the deep end."

Caleb hoped he was right but he could not fully convince even himself. He felt engulfed in consternation, realizing maybe the Professor's accident was not to stop the Omega Watchers Project but instead was intended to be a deadly warning to Gabriella?

In an effort to sidetrack Detective Richards had they actually opened a doorway to the real truth?

Chapter 35

Caleb's mind was filtering through all of the events of the past week. He knew Gabriella had changed drastically after returning from Saudi Arabia. She had always been emotionally strong, almost fearless. He knew the emotional roller coaster was taking a tempestuous toll on her mind.

He watched her standing at the window. She looked so vulnerable, so fragile. He wanted desperately to protect her, but how could he? How could he reach into her subconscious soul and battle the strongholds of her mind?

She turned to him with a pleading voice. "Please don't tell the others about my dreams. They will think I've gone off the deep end."

"Whatever you want, Gabi, but I do believe there's an explanation. We'll find the answers and we'll do it together. I'm with you to the end, no matter when that is."

She crossed the floor and sat down on the side of the bed and took his hand. "I know you are. You're the only sanity in my life and that keeps me going right now. Let's get back to the journal. I've got to make some sense of all of this."

"You read, Caleb." She laid her head back on her pillow and listened to her father's penned words.

September 12, 1984

I have just come from a meeting with a scientist who specializes in metal alloys. He read my article regarding possible alien existence and contacted me. He has in his possession an implant that was surgically removed from a young woman in her early twenties who is referred to as 'Jane Doe.'

Jane Doe states she began to have dreams about being visited by an extraterrestrial approximately two years ago. She was very sick with diabetes and was insulin dependent. It was so serious it had become life threatening. The alien visitor told her his planet had found the cure to all diseases and could completely heal her with a small injection under her skin. She was taken to a spaceship that had a surgical type room and received what she described as a simple incision to insert a device in her hand. When she awoke the next morning there was no evidence of any injection and she dismissed it as only a dream. Subsequently the dreams stopped.

The amazing thing is immediately after the surgical dream her pancreas started producing insulin and she had no further health problems. Her doctors have no explanation as to how this could have happened. However after a series of tests, they determined there had been a mutation of her DNA, which was astounding as that is medically impossible.

Three months ago Jane Doe had X-rays for a potentially broken wrist and it revealed an unexplained object in her right hand. The object was removed and sent to a medical laboratory for evaluation. Her doctor told them there was no sign of entry for the implant. No scar, no incision, nothing.

The metal analysis showed meteoric iron (containing non-earthly isotopes) with cobalt and significant amounts of iridium. These isotopic ratios do not occur on Earth. One was of a class of nickel-iron meteorites called hexahedrites.

Further examination revealed the object (implant) was covered with an oily shell coating that prevented body rejection, therefore it produced no immune response. Further, biological tissue was growing from the metal and when analyzed with an EDX Electron Microscope it revealed it had begun making changes in the body cells that cannot be scientifically explained.

The lead scientist at the laboratory stated, that in his professional opinion, this device wasn't of earthly origin, at least nothing the scientific world had knowledge of.

Even after the device was removed the diabetes did not return and it appears her DNA had been permanently altered keeping her pancreas in perfect working condition. It appears the implant is some type of device for genetic improvement. It's beyond comprehension the kind of power this would give to those on earth that could control it.

What is the ET's long term agenda? I believe it is to gradually and methodically enter our civilization to save us from sickness, disease and our own self-destruction. After WWI and WWII it became obvious man was on a path where no one would survive.

My search for truth has brought me to the conclusion these implanted devices will bring an evolution to our earth. The extraterrestrials coming to our planet will not be as movies portray of an invasion of alien spaceships coming in hostility to take the earth hostage. They will be our salvation!

Evidence shows it began at Roswell and since then there has been a slow, methodic introduction of far advanced technology from a highly developed extraterrestrial civilization. These ETs consist of multiple factions that can exist in alternate dimensions and locations of space and time. Through the overseer of an Ascended Master they will be saviors to the human race that now has the capability of totally destroying the planet.

Caleb looked up in total amazement and waited for Gabriella's response. He already expected what it would be. Instead of the awaited retort that her father was right and the Professor was wrong, she was staring into the air as though lost in another world.

"Gabi, are you with me here? Did you hear what I just read?"

"I heard every word. I'm beginning to truly understand the depth of his work now. This is far beyond anything I could have imagined. These implants must be real and there's no way of knowing how many people already have them. Do we tell the team about this?"

Caleb needed a minute to let the information process. He got up, stretched and paced the floor a couple of times before responding.

"We can't hold anything back, Gabi. If we're going to come to a joint conclusion, we have to have all the pieces and just see where they fit. I would say this is a very important piece!"

"Of course you're right," she reluctantly admitted. "Apparently the government didn't want these implants known about and are planning to use them for their own selfish powers. I wonder why they're still not known, after all these decades."

Gabriella could not contain herself any longer and Caleb could see what was coming next. "Don't you see that my dad was right?" She picked up the journal and held it in front of him in a defiant stand. "This perfectly explains there is other life that exists in this vast universe. It explains so many things."

Caleb saw the excitement in her eyes and he could not deny the mountain of evidence that was building. "I've got to admit, it's pretty convincing."

She knew he was leaning further into her camp of belief. "Before we say anything to the team I want to find out how all this leads to when my mother was murdered. The more information we have, the clearer the picture will be for all of us."

Late into the evening they read from the journal, also reviewing the supporting research papers and articles her father had clearly labeled, making them easy to follow. He apparently knew there might be a time he would not be there to explain his findings and the information would have to speak for itself with clarity and supported proof.

The more Caleb read the more his pendulum of uncertainty was swinging towards the evidence of extraterrestrial life. It seemed almost undeniable. Gabriella could see the multitude of information was overwhelmingly convincing. She was sure Caleb would be on her side when the 'Nephilim vs. ETs' subject was once again reviewed.

The final entry before her mother's death was on June 12, 1988. Gabriella wanted to digest every word in an effort to come to grips with why she was murdered. After all, this was the essence of her father's work and the reason she lost her parents. This would be the driving factor of her passion as she fought for his work to be determined as truth. With emotion swelling up inside, she turned the page and read with a quivering voice.

June 12, 1988

After numerous efforts, this past fall we finally were able to present our research and evidence on the ET implants to a high security level of the government. We were informed to not disclose our information to anyone else and they would be in contact. We have waited for months expecting every day to hear from someone. It finally became evident they do not intend to contact us. We have decided to take steps in a new direction.

This evening Angelena asked if I thought the MJ-12 already knew about the implants. My educated guess is they do and that puts us both at great risk. It takes my breath away when I think of my little princess facing a world without us. For safety purposes, I am making plans to move my family to a secure location as soon as possible.

Caleb heard the pain in her voice as she read those words. She forced herself to focus on the information more than the sorrow.

"Caleb, in my dream last night my mother was asking my dad about this MJ-12 group. To my knowledge, I've never even heard of them. Who are they? How could I have known about them unless there is something paranormal happening?"

He took her hand and squeezed. "I still think you heard them talking about this at some point and it was stored in your subconscious. There's usually an explanation, if you look hard enough."

She just shook her head desperately wanting to tell him the whole truth about Arcturus. Instead she changed the subject.

"I wonder what my dad was planning to do next, before my mother died the next morning and everything in our lives changed."

"Perhaps he was going to release it through some big scientific journal. Then the government would have had no other choice but to get involved."

Gabriella just rolled her big, blue eyes. "Really? Don't you know the government would deny it and make my dad look like a scientific quack? People believe what they're told by the government and don't even question it. My dad was right. Most people are just blind sheep following wherever they're led. They don't want to believe anything will ever change and if it frightens them the least little bit, they sure don't want to know about it! We live in a world of ostriches. They stick their heads in the sand so they don't have to deal with reality. They believe because it has never happened before, it never will. There's even a word to describe that witless attitude...'normalcy bias'. What will it take to wake people up?"

Caleb was aware she did not expect an answer and he sure did not dare argue with her. When her mind was made up the only thing that would change it was cold, hard facts to the contrary.

There was still one undeniable fact that plagued Caleb. "I agree that people don't want to hear anything that rocks their world, but there's something I need to understand. All this research on aliens still doesn't explain the miracle healing. Neither does it explain the Presence we felt at the hospital, when they had given up all hope for the Professor."

Gabriella could not tell him, according to Arcturus, *she* had healed the Professor with her inner powers releasing universal love but even if that were true, it did not explain the mysterious Presence.

She had no answer for him.

Chapter 36

The storm had finally passed over. Twilight unveiled the lights of the harbor, blinking in the misty haze now cloaking the marina. Gabriella went to the bedroom window and watched the fog as it slowly crept around the harbor slowly erasing the twinkling lights. She felt much like the harbor looked. She was living in a fog of darkness that had settled around her, slowly engulfing her life.

Caleb had been watching her, not knowing whether to give her solitude in her thoughts or wrap his arms around her in an effort to ease her mental agony. Finally, he walked over to the window and just stood beside her. It was his way of saying without words, "I'm here if you need me." She reached out and took his hand. Neither spoke. The misty fog grew thicker and thicker until the lights of the harbor disappeared.

Gabriella broke the silence with a quivering voice. "I'm afraid to sleep, Caleb. I know the next event to take place in my dreams is the murder of my mother. I don't remember seeing the car explode. My father said I blocked it out of my mind and I don't want to see it...not even in my dreams."

"Are you dreaming every night? Is there a sequence to your dreams?" Caleb asked with tenderness in his voice.

"Yes, every night. It seems to start as soon as I fall asleep and lasts until I wake up. I don't know how to stop them. The last few dreams started with the sensation of falling into a deep hole and then I scream for help. Then..." She stopped short of telling him Arcturus is always there to catch her.

"Then what?" Caleb noticed her obvious hesitation. He knew she was still holding something back.

After an uncomfortable delay, she continued. "Then I find myself leaving my body and traveling either through the universe or back in time. I have no idea where..." She hesitated again, almost saying where Arcturus would take her. Carefully she reformed her words and started over. "I have no idea where my dreams will take me."

She was totally aware he was reading her like a book and he knew she was hiding pages of truth. She loved him even more when he did not push or probe her for more information. There would be a time she would open to him, but not yet.

"Gabi, do you think if I hold you while you sleep it would make any difference? If you feel safe it might lessen the intensity of your subconscious thoughts. It would be worth a try. Wouldn't it?"

Her mind was spinning with thoughts of what Arcturus would say. Then she realized how foolish she was. Arcturus was not real. It was her mental anxiety she was dealing with, not some supernatural being.

Caleb was watching her face intently. She had an expression he could not read. He was about to argue his case when she gave in. "Okay, but I have no idea what to expect."

"If you show any signs of sleep walking, talking or anything else I'll wake you up, unless you're talking about me, of course." Caleb smiled trying to lighten her somber mood.

She forced a smile and motioned towards the door. "Let's see how they're doing."

They walked back into the dining room and the team was still hard at it. They looked up, briefly mumbled something about morphing and went back to work. It was obvious everyone was feeling the exhaustion stemming from the unknowns and the time pressures. It was enough to bend steel nerves.

"I'm going to finish dinner," Faith said, as she got up from her computer and left for the kitchen.

"Thanks, Faith." KJ responded. He looked up from his computer and took off his glasses to briefly rest his eyes. "We'll work until dinner is ready and then call it a night."

"How's it going?" Caleb asked.

"We're managing to morph the words, but we have no idea what they will translate to. Only the Professor can help us there. This is a very slow, tedious process. I just pray we're getting it right." He turned back to his computer, put his glasses back on and was quickly lost in concentration.

Gabriella sat down to review KJ's notes. It was beyond her comprehension, but it sure looked impressive. All kinds of signs and symbols were printed out and arranged on the table in what appeared to be a distinct sequence.

"I know it looks confusing." Aaron said. "However, it's coming together extremely well. The Professor is going to be shocked at the progress we've made. He should be able to translate the scroll pretty quickly after breaking through all the transitions of what we have here. By the end of the week, I think we'll be ready to let the Professor put all the pieces in the puzzle."

"I can't wait to see the look on his face when he sees this," Gabriella commented trying to make heads or tails out of the pile of documents.

A strong knock on the door broke their concentration. Caleb cautiously approached the door and asked, "Who's there?" Immediately Detective Richards identified himself.

Relieved, Caleb opened the door and let the detective in. He took off his hat and held it in his hand as he addressed the young team. He wasted no time in letting them know why he was there. "I thought it best to do all communication in person. I wanted to let you know I got the information from Sandee and we have the location secured for you to move to on Friday. That's when Dr. Brotman will be released. Of course, that's assuming he'll have no complications. I'll work out the details for transportation and everything you'll need. Be ready early Friday morning for the relocation."

The entire team sighed simultaneously with relief. Caleb shook his hand and thanked him. "That's great news. We'll all be packed and ready."

"Can we go back to our apartments for things we'll need? How long will we be there? Rosh Hashanah is next week. I'm always with my family for the celebration." Faith was thinking on the practical side.

"Too risky to go back home," the detective responded quickly. "Take what you have here and we'll supply whatever else you need. At this point your stay will be indefinite. Safety is our number one concern." His voice was matter of fact and had an overtone of finality. No one questioned his decisions.

The detective moved towards the door and then stopped. "I'm still working on the lead you gave me and I'll be in touch." He put on his hat and left the apartment.

After the door closed behind the detective, KJ gave instructions. "We have a lot to do in the next few days, team. Let's have dinner and then call it a night. We'll get a fresh start in the morning. We can do this!"

Faith had tears in her eyes...fear and sorrow mixed. "But I always celebrate the Jewish New Year with my family."

"We will celebrate together!" Aaron assured her. "We will eat apples, dipped in honey and wish each other a prosperous, sweet new year!"

"I don't think I would count on that," Gabriella muttered under her breath. She believed their Jewish Feast days were a bunch of nonsensical traditions, but she knew they were important to their culture and their celebrations did not make any difference to her one way or the other.

KJ again took control. "We are instructed in the Torah to keep these appointed days with God forever. It doesn't matter if we are Jew or Christian we are to observe his "moadim', holy convocations. We will do as instructed, no matter where we are!"

Gabriella was accepting the fact that somewhere in all the craziness of the last week, she had allowed KJ to take the lead of the team, which had always been her position. Strangely she did not care. She could focus more on the proof she needed to convince the Professor the fallen angel theory, which he held as truth, was simply explained by extraterrestrial life. It was so plain to her she could not understand why the rest of the team refused to look at the facts.

Her mind was set and she knew what she had to do. Dig, dig, and dig! This time not in caves and dirt but in the valuable research her father had left.

Chapter 37

After dinner the team lingered around the table for some lively discussion about the direction of the project.

Caleb was fully aware Gabriella was waiting for the opportunity to interject her father's research.

She kept wondering what the response would be. Would they consider him to be a scientific laughingstock? The evidence was overwhelming, but it had to be received by open minds, and she was not sure she would find even a sliver of openness to his hypothesis.

Faith looked at Gabriella. "You've been really quiet, Gabi. Anything you're ready to share?"

She took a deep breath and looked at each one. "I just ask you keep an open mind. I've been really surprised by the depth of my father's research and the extent of what he discovered. I can clearly see now why the 'powers that be' would want to silence him."

All eyes were focused on Gabriella. No one said a word waiting for her to continue. She got up from the table and went to her bedroom to get the journal. She would read word for word about the implants. How would they be able to deny the truth? She sat back down, opened the leather journal to the marked page, and began to read what she and Caleb had read earlier that afternoon. When she finished she looked up and held her breath. What would be their verdict?

The silence was deafening. Every eye was on her as if waiting for her to make the next move.

"Well? Don't you see what's been going on for decades? This explains so much!" Her eyes were pleading with them to just think about it.

Caleb reached over and took her hand. A squeeze of assurance told her he was proud of her. She looked at him and he could see the questioning in her eyes. Why no response? She was about to break into tears when KJ's strong voice exploded into the silence with two words.

"Genetic engineering!"

"What?" Gabriella was stunned. She had no idea how genetic engineering could apply to the implants.

KJ's eyes were lighting up like a Christmas tree. "This makes perfect sense!" He declared in a voice filled with revelation. Gabriella was not the only one confused. All the team looked at him in bewilderment as he stated, "I think your father may have found the answer we've been searching for."

Gabriella could not believe it! Had KJ finally seen the truth? If he realized her father was right after all, it would change the entire direction of the project. She was beyond ecstatic.

"You see it, don't you, KJ? You finally understand!" Gabriella was waiting for the Aaron and Faith to accept the truth, too.

KJ nodded his head in excitement. "I see it with crystal clear vision! This could be the link we've been missing!"

Caleb was as confused as the rest. "Explains what? What in the world are you talking about?"

KJ tried to calm himself down enough to explain. "One of the biggest obstacles we've faced in researching 'as it was in the days of Noah' has been explaining how the hybrid beings would return at the end of days."

"True." Aaron interjected. "What are you thinking, KJ?"

"Nowhere in the ancient prophetic writings does it say that more angels would choose to leave their heavenly estate to take wives of the woman of earth. BUT! If the society at the end of the age is going to be just as it was in the days of Noah, there has to be a repeat of Genesis 6... giants in the land, men of renown, hybrids or to put it in modern terms, super humans!"

Faith narrowed her dark eyes in confusion. "Would you please put this in terms I can understand?"

"Just think about it, team, for decades the stage was being set for people to believe there are extraterrestrial civilizations. It's obvious to me now, it's been the master plan for the end of days. If demonic spirits are transforming themselves to appear as extraterrestrial beings and using these implants to alter the human DNA, we have hybrid beings! A genetic return to the days of Noah! These 'super beings' would be just like the giants, or more accurately translated, the nephilim in the Old Testament."

Aaron jumped from his seat in a rare display of emotion. "I get it! You're right, KJ. That explains how it could happen! I can't wait for the Professor to hear this!"

Gabriella could not believe it. She was absolutely furious. KJ had taken the alien proof her father had discovered and in an instant turned it around to being the fulfillment of biblical prophecy. She felt her father's work had been totally violated.

KJ was fully aware Gabriella did not grasp the meaning of it all. "Gabi, think about it! Your father was searching for truth and he found it. He just didn't realize the depth of the meaning or fully understand what he had discovered. This is a major breakthrough. Once we do all the translations I truly believe the entire prophetic picture will now be perfectly clear."

Aaron started pacing the floor in excitement. "I can't believe it! Now we know!"

Gabriella got up from the table, took the journal and ran to her bedroom. She closed the door with a slam, letting the rest of the team know how upset she was.

"Give her some time," Caleb said. "Anything you say that discredits her father's hypothesis is going to upset her. She just needs some processing time." They all hoped he was right.

"Understood," KJ replied. "However, I have to ask a question. Does anyone besides me see divine guidance in what's going on here? What's the chance this information would surface right when we need it? Her father did the research decades ago and the Professor has built his project on the fact the word 'coincidence' does not exist in the Hebrew language. That can't be just a coincidence. God's divine hand had to guide this information to us at this appointed time."

"I agree." Aaron said, allowing the revelation to settle in his mind. "This is getting stranger by the minute."

"Why do you suppose there hasn't been any media coverage on these implants in all these years? You would think that would be big news." Faith's dark eyes were filled with perplexity and edged with doubt.

Caleb tried to explain additional information from the journal. "In some of her father's writings he said the government was keeping all ET encounters under top security. After the Roswell incident they formed a group called the MJ-12 to make sure anything to do with alien activity was kept secret. It was so secret this group of elite men could not even share the information with one another. If any alien incidents leaked to the public, they immediately explained them away scientifically; or the people experiencing encounters were made to look like kooks. Seems they would silence them one way or another, if you know what I mean. The U.S. Government has tried to debunk the entire extraterrestrial scenario."

KJ laughed out loud. "So explains the movie 'Men in Black'. That was based on the MJ-12. It's obvious it was to make them look ridiculous, so no one would take the group seriously."

"But why would they?" Faith pressed to understand. "This is all so confusing to me."

Caleb's eyes reflected his own confusion about the entire ET matter. "The best I can tell, her father believed the US Government, and possibly even other world governments, were not only covering up the implants, but also concealing other technology they were gleaning from an intergalactic society. Apparently, the government intends to use it for their own selfish reasons and not for the good of the world as her father thinks is the purpose of extraterrestrial visitations."

Now Faith was beginning to perfectly comprehend where Gabi was coming from emotionally. "I know how close she was to her father and I totally understand she wants to protect his image and reputation. He was highly respected in the scientific field and I'm sure his research is very convincing to her. You guys just totally insulted her and her father. She truly thinks he's right."

"I realize that and I truly am sorry", KJ spoke with grave concern. "However, we have to follow the trail of facts."

Aaron had been piecing the new information into his mind, connecting it with all the other prophetic details. "Let's recap, team. According to the Book of Enoch, the fallen angels brought all types of knowledge to the people on earth. Things humans could never have known. By transforming themselves into the form of a man they pro-created with the women of earth and giants were born, which were superhuman. Could it be, the demonic spirits of the air are again transforming themselves into a physical form and appearing now as friendly extraterrestrials, wanting to bring knowledge to the earth, just as it was in the days of Noah? Could these 'angels of light', in fact, be setting the world up for the rise of the Anti-Christ and the mark of the beast?"

Caleb was beginning to follow KJ's thinking. "Isn't that the number 666? I've seen that in apocalyptic movies."

"Yes, the media has presented it to the world as a sci-fi scenario, but it will be very real."

Aaron sat down at his computer and began researching alien implants, while still listening to the conversation. After a few minutes he informed them without looking up, "I'm finding plenty of information on alien implants but most of what's out there is made to look pretty idiotic. There is a link for a Dr. Roger K. Leir. He's considered to be the foremost authority on alien implanted devices and seems highly respected in his field. He says he's even removed numerous implants himself."

After a few more minutes, Aaron looked up in frustration. "I'm sure any truly credible information the government doesn't want known would be censored though."

"Of course it would be." KJ said emphatically. "Had it not been for Gabi's father we would never have linked together what apparently has been going on for decades."

"And you really think these implants could be used by the Anti-Christ?" Caleb asked. "This all still seems like science fiction to me."

KJ sat down at the head of the table next to Caleb as he answered. "No one can say definitively, but God's Word tells us to watch the prophetic signs He has given us. By doing this, we will be able to 'discern the times'. When Israel was reborn as a nation in 1948, the countdown to the end started. The powers of darkness knew their time was almost up and it seems they may have chosen the deception of extraterrestrials to make their appearance again on earth. Their purpose is to deceive the nations into believing a lie."

The team continued to discuss the various scenarios that could develop until finally Faith admitted her exhaustion. "I've had it for today. Let's get some rest. I'm just not sure where I'm supposed to sleep tonight," she admitted looking at Gabi's closed bedroom door, which appeared to be a 'stay out' sign.

"Let me talk to her, Faith." Caleb walked to the closed door and softly knocked.

"Come in," she said in a barely audible voice.

He pushed the door open and quietly entered the room, saying nothing. She was sitting in the middle of the bed holding the journal to her chest. He sat on the side of the bed and waited for her lead.

Her blue eyes were filled with pain and it broke Caleb's heart. He understood where KJ was coming from and it was exciting to see how the two worlds could be merging into one. If only Gabi could realize it was not an insult to her father's research, but a potential breakthrough. This was not the time to try to reason with her. Instead, he reached for her hand.

"You need to get some rest, Gabi. Everyone's ready to call it a day."

"I'm afraid to sleep." Gabriella looked down at the bed avoiding eye contact. Caleb still could not get accustomed to this strong, independent woman openly expressing fear.

He covered her small hand with his. Words escaped him. How could he promise to protect her from the tormenting dreams? That was a secluded place he could not reach. If the enemy were in the real world, he would fight to his dying breath. There was no possible way to physically fight the images of the mind.

"Come with me." Caleb gave her no room for argument. "You can sleep on the couch. If you show any signs of troubled sleep I'll wake you up." His voice was soft and tender and his concern melted her heart. She did not know what the night would hold but she knew he would be there when she awakened.

"Faith!" Gabriella called out.

"Coming!" Faith entered the bedroom while Caleb and Gabriella were getting ready to exit.

"The bedroom's all yours. I'm going to sleep on the couch."

Faith did not ask any questions, knowing with Gabriella's state of mind, Caleb needed to be with her. Faith closed the door as they exited. Aaron and KJ had already gone to their bedroom. Caleb and Gabriella were alone.

Caleb sat on the couch and propped his feet on the footstool. Gabriella stretched out nestling her head into Caleb's strong shoulder. She felt safe from the world around her, but it was not this world that concerned her. It was the world of her dreams. What started out to be a beautiful escape into fantasylands, now was revealing darkness from the past. She had no control in any part of her dream travels.

She was too mentally exhausted and upset for even small talk. She quickly succumbed to the wave of sleepiness that engulfed her. Caleb held her close and could feel her finally relax. He watched her face for signs of restlessness. She appeared to be at perfect rest. He hoped against hope her being in his arms would give the subconscious security she needed to escape the dreams. Little did he know the torments were already raging in an alternate dimension...another dimension of time and space, where Caleb could not reach.

The moment Gabriella had entered into a deep sleep, the sensation of falling began again. This time she was in the cave in Saudi Arabia and had fallen into the bottomless pit, filled with horrible smells and the sounds of screaming in the distance. She instantly knew she was descending into Tartarus.

"Arcturus! " Her screams echoed through the darkness. The sounds of torment were growing louder. "Arcturus! Where are you?" Fear saturated every fiber of her being as she plummeted deeper and deeper into the excruciating heat. She was descending into the abyss.

"Arcturus! Help me!"

Gabriella felt a strong hand grab her and pull her upwards. She held onto the hand with a grip of death. The heat began to subside and she opened her clenched eyes, knowing she was now safe. Relief flooded through her as Arcturus' face came into view.

"I thought you weren't coming! I was so afraid!" A strange smile spread across his face, but he did not say a word. The scene transformed into one of serene beauty. They were traveling through the starry night with celestial winds blowing around them. With the touch of Archturus' hand, everything had changed. Mystifying sounds encircled her and peace flowed through her as they descended upon a mountaintop looking over the earth.

Finally Arcturus spoke. "You can't survive without me, Gabriella! I've warned you not to try. You must be with me to travel into alternate dimensions."

"I can't help it. I can't control the soul travel. What do I do, Arcturus?"

"Before you sleep call my name and I will be waiting for you. There is power in my name. It's the same powers I can release into your inner spirit. You must open yourself, body soul, and spirit, to receive them. Separate yourself from unbelievers to enter into the higher truth. You are chosen to teach the people of earth how to find their inner peace, how to prepare for the appearing of the Ascended Master."

"Why, Arcturus? Why am I chosen to reveal this truth? Why me?"

"The shaman calling has been passed to you. Your father has revealed the truth you are to proclaim to the world. The Ascended Master is coming! He will bring love and unity. He will save the planet from destruction."

"No one would listen to me, even if I tried." Doubt was evident in Gabriella's voice.

His voice was commanding. "Oh, yes they would! You have the power within to do anything you desire. You only have to release your inner powers and believe. The truth will set you free! Remember, you brought healing to the Professor. You did that! Don't let anyone make you doubt it. Help prepare the way!"

Gabriella struggled between the two worlds. "I want to help others. I truly do! But I love Caleb and he doesn't truly believe."

The face of Arcturus grew dark and ominous when she spoke of her love. She could feel his hand tighten on hers until it became painful. When she tried to pull away his countenance totally changed. "I have someone that wants to talk to you, Gabriella, someone very special to you."

"Who?" She asked in confusion.

"Look behind you."

She turned around to see her mother smiling behind her. "Momma!" Gabriella held her arms out.

She felt the arms of her mother encircle her, pulling her close. Memories of their short time together turned and twisted in her mind, as though she was watching a kaleidoscope of childhood pictures all at one time.

"What a beautiful young lady you are, my Gabriella. I have been watching you through the years and I am so proud of you."

"How can that be, Momma? Can you see me from the spirit world?"

"Yes, my little princess, and many times I have been there to protect you and you were not even aware."

Gabriella held on to her mother not wanting to ever let her go. "How about daddy? Can I see him, too? Is he watching me?"

"Gabriella, you must return now." The words of Arcturus were cold. "No more time."

"No! I want to talk to my mother. I want more time!"

"If you want to communicate with her spirit, you must converge with the universe. Communication with the spirits that have crossed over is one of the hidden powers you have deep within you."

Arcturus pulled Gabriella away. The last words of her mother would continue to echo in her ears for days to come. "It's up to you, my little princess, if you see me again."

"Momma! Momma, don't leave. Momma!" She cried out as her mother faded into the night skies.

"Gabi! Wake up, Gabi! Gabi, can you hear me?"

She forced her eyes open to the sound of Caleb's voice. "Gabi, Are you alright? Gabi!" His eyes were filled with a mixture of fear and concern.

She struggled to speak and finally forced the words in a faint whisper, "I'm okay."

"You were crying out 'Momma' over and over." He took her in his arms and held her until she stopped shaking. "Tell me, Gabi. What were you dreaming about?"

She shook her head and buried her face deep into his comforting shoulder. How could she tell him that to see her mother again she could not be with him? Not unless he believed! He must truly believe with all of his heart, spirit and soul there are god powers within each person, just waiting to be released.

Gabriella held on to Caleb for dear life, battling the desire to tell him everything. How could she tell him she was beginning to believe her dreams were, in truth, revelations from the spirit world? He would never believe she was chosen to help prepare the planet for the coming Ascended Master. Just thinking about it sounded absolutely ridiculous, even to her.

Her sanity slowly began to return. Of course she was only dreaming. Reading the journal had awakened memories she had no idea were even buried in the painful recesses of her subconscious. This could not possibly be a prophetic reality.

Gabriella could not go back to sleep. The feel her mother's arms around her, lingered in her mind. Even at her age she longed for that embrace. The tormenting words of her mother continued to ring in her ears, "It's up to you, my little princess, if you see me again."

She looked up at Caleb who had dozed from the sheer exhaustion. He had forced himself to stay awake to protect her while she slept. How could she sacrifice such love? Even in his sleep she could still see concern etched in his face. She snuggled against him and repeated over and over, "It was only a dream. It was only a dream."

Chapter 38

The light of morning slowly filtered through the windows dispelling the night's ominous darkness. The balcony door curtains were dancing in the morning breezes. Gabriella silently moved to not awaken Caleb. She slipped outside onto the balcony and settled into her favorite chair. She needed the solitude of the sunshine and sea breezes to clear and refresh her mind.

She was not one given to talking to herself. But she found herself speaking questions of the soul out loud.

"Do I truly have inner powers? Chosen? What does all this mean? Give up Caleb? I could never give up Caleb!"

The words of Arcturus were repeating in her mind over and over: "To continue to grow in your powers you must separate yourself from unbelievers. The Ascended Master is coming to bring peace on earth. Prepare the way."

To stop the repetitive thoughts she got up and moved to the edge of the balcony for a panoramic view of the marina. Everything appeared normal. The mariners were preparing for their day at sea. The sea gulls were flying around the bay, ascending and descending, in what seemed perfect rhythm. Fishing boats blowing their horns, sounding their departure, could be heard echoing across the crystal blue waters. All appeared to be well with the world.

She slipped back inside, quietly passing Caleb. She slowly pushed open her bedroom door. Faith was still asleep. Retrieving the journal from the chair by the bed, she closed the door behind her, returning to the balcony. For the first time, she would be reading and researching all alone.

She opened the journal back to the September 12, 1984 entry. Took a deep breath and read again.

My search for truth has brought me to this conclusion: An evolution has been taking place for many decades as non-human forces, far superior to us, were populating our planet through genetic changes. They consist of multiple factions that can exist in alternate dimensions and locations of space and time. Through the overseer of an Ascended Master their goal is to assimilate into our society using the implanted devices. This creates a civilization that is part human and part superior, extraterrestrial beings. They will be saviors to the human race that now has the capability of totally destroying the planet.

Could it be possible her father was referring to the Ascended Master that Arcturus spoke of? Could they be one and the same?

After rereading the paragraph she understood KJ's opinion of genetic altering, especially if you were looking from his biblical point of reasoning. Maybe she was overreacting and she could reason with them.

She turned the page to the entry from June 12, 1988 and reread the information on the MJ-12. She decided to research for herself and see if she could find current supporting information on this group.

She opened her computer and began to filter through several websites until one in particular caught her attention: *"MJ 12 Operations manual from 1954 leaked and published in 1996 on how ET recovery operations should be carried out."*

Instantly the thought came to her mind how odd that this article had been published not long before the Omega Project was formed. "Must be a coincidence," she whispered to herself. Then she giggled, in spite of herself, remembering the Professor did not believe in 'coincidence'. He reminded them over and over it was not in God's Hebrew language.

Reading through the article it was apparent her father knew this information over a decade prior. This could be proof the government was behind the cover-up her parents worked so hard to reveal. It also explained why they would want her parents silenced.

There were numerous articles in the manual that supported her suspicions. One in particular jumped out:

"Mission Assessment of Recovered Lenticular Aerodyne Objects – 19 September 1947

No one without express permission from the President may disseminate the information contained in this report or communicate it to any unauthorized person not in possession of a MAJIC SECURITY CLEARANCE."

"That's the MJ-12!" She exclaimed to herself.

Could this be the organization behind silencing her father? According to his journal, this was the same period of time when major sightings and encounters started. The Professor had also stated they began in mass numbers around the time of the Statehood of Israel being declared in 1948. There were just too many related occurrences, and subsequent questions, that kept accumulating. So far, there were very few answers.

Gabriella continued reading the article from the government documents and her belief in extraterrestrial life deepened with each sentence:

"Studied by classified teams of experts, many interesting and provocative details were recorded in this report of unidentifiable crash remains. The document is broken down into various sections that address concerns specifically: Preliminary Intelligence Estimate, Technical Evaluation, Scientific Probabilities, Political Considerations, and National Security Structure."

As she continued to read, word-by-word and sentence-by-sentence, the government was verifying the very words written by her father. It seemed infallible truth to her.

She heard voices inside her apartment and knew the team was up, preparing to start the day. Did she dare bring up the article she found? Would they even listen? She felt totally alone...lost in an isolated, bizarre truth. If unbelievers diluted her ability to release the powers within, she certainly was surrounded by a group that not only did not believe, but would not even consider the possibility.

She picked up the journal and held it close to her before going back inside. "Dad, if you can hear me please show me what to do. Mom said she protects me and I am asking you to guide me. If I really have inner powers I want to release them and carry on the work you began. I will try to listen to my inner voice. Speak to me there."

A phone ringing interrupted her plea to her father. She heard Caleb talking inside and knew it was time to leave her solitude to rejoin the others.

"Yes, I understand. We'll be ready. Thank you, detective."

"What did he say?" Faith asked before Caleb could even turn the phone off.

"He told us to be ready to leave Friday morning at 8:00 am. They'll send someone to pick us up. We will leave through the private parking garage beneath this building, where we can't be seen from the street."

"How about the Professor?" Gabriella asked.

"They will bring him and Sandee by separate transport. We'll meet at the lodge."

The time pressure showed on KJ's face. "We've got a lot to do and we best get at it."

After a quick breakfast KJ, Aaron and Faith were back at their computers morphing words. Caleb and Gabriella separated from the others and went out on the balcony to work. She knew she had to tell him about the website she had found and the importance of the MJ-12.

Settling into their chairs, she opened the journal to the last article they had read. "I want to read this one more time, Caleb, and then I have something to show you."

After reading her father's entry about the government secret group, she turned her computer towards Caleb showing him the website that leaked the secret documents in 1996. As he skimmed through the article, Gabriella was trying to read his expression. She could not tell if he thought it was a grand hoax or the truth they had been seeking.

When he finished, he turned the computer back to her without saying a word.

"Well? Tell me what you think! Does this not prove that my parents were right and the government wanted to shut them up?"

His face displayed total confusion. "I feel like I'm on a swinging pendulum. I listen to the rest of the team and it makes so much sense. Then we read these articles, Gabi, and that makes sense, too. I just swing back and forth and I don't know what to believe!"

"You've got to believe me, Caleb! You've just got to!"

The pleading in her voice caught him totally off guard. "What do you mean? I've 'got' to? Tell me what's going on? I know when you're keeping something from me, Gabi Girl." His voice was soft as he urged her to open her heart to him.

She stood up and walked to the edge of the balcony struggling with the intense desire to tell him everything.

She turned to face him. "Please don't think I'm a total idiot. What I'm going to tell you, I'm not ready to share with the others." She took a deep breath and the words poured out of her soul. She told him about her dream, about seeing her mother, and about the powers she supposedly had within. She still could not call Arcturus by name, but she finally admitted she had a spirit guide.

"What kind of guide?" Caleb asked, totally amazed.

"A spirit guide! He takes me on these night journeys and teaches me about universal knowledge. He tells me things I couldn't possibly know. He says I'm chosen, Caleb, just like the Prophet told me. If all of this is true, then you have to believe with me." She cried in a pleading voice. "If you don't believe, I have to decide between you and the chosen calling I have. That is, *IF* my dreams are real and not my crazy emotions playing tricks. I stay so confused that I don't know what to believe. Sometimes I can't tell the difference between reality and dreams."

He got up and wrapped his reassuring arms around her. "I told you we'll figure it out. I'll stand beside you no matter what, you know that." He would not voice what was questioning in his mind. Was she teetering on the edge of an emotional collapse?

She had no idea behind Caleb's comforting words were concerns for her mental stability. Instead, his words breathed a new strength into her very soul. The confusion and fears of the last few days began to fade away. She was ready to delve into whatever was waiting for her...whatever her destiny was.

If the others chose to believe something different there was nothing she could do about that. If she was wrong her father himself would have to come to her and show her a different truth. Since he had crossed over to the spirit world she could only contact him through her inner powers... powers that she was beginning to feel releasing from within. She could imagine her mother smiling in approval.

She gave Caleb a big hug. "That's all I needed to know. If you're with me, nothing can stop us from proving my parents were right. Perhaps we'll be the ones to bring truth to the Professor and the rest of the team. Let's get to work!" He could see the confident, self-assured woman he had known all of these years suddenly and instantly re-emerge like a phoenix from the ashes. He had to admit, something far beyond what he understood was happening. He was convinced it meant danger for Gabriella.

Gabriella turned her eyes back toward the bay. "I don't think we need to say anything to the others just yet. I'm doing a test run on these inner powers, just to see if there's something real happening or if I am totally delusional. If these powers are real, the team's unbelief could affect my abilities to connect with my inner godhood. At least that is what my spirit guide told me." She turned and looked Caleb straight in the yes. "I have to know the truth, before I lose my sanity."

Caleb gave a nervous laugh. "I won't say a word to anyone." He honestly did not know what to say and certainly did not know what to believe.

Chapter 39

As soon as Gabriella entered the room it was obvious there had been a transformation. The emotional highs and lows of the previous week had transformed back into a confidence the team was familiar with, but yet was different. They were amazed at the sudden metamorphosis.

KJ had not seen this side of Gabriella. Something did not feel right, but he sat silently as she began to give orders.

"We have two days left to get everything in order and ready to present to the Professor. Although we may have varying views, we'll present the evidence we have and hope the final translations of ancient writings bring us to a conclusion we can all agree upon."

Faith and Aaron just stared at her. This did not sound like Gabriella, not at all. She had been a great leader, not a demanding one. Her countenance had changed, too. Caleb just watched. He would not dare say a word.

She read their body language and realized she needed to tone it down. "Okay, guys, I know I've been on an emotional roller coaster for several days now. Reading through my father's journal has been extremely difficult for me, but it has also enlightened me to so many areas of understanding. He had a wisdom and knowledge far beyond what we've tapped into so far. I know you don't agree so we'll just pursue both sides until, hopefully, we can find a common ground to stand on."

"Gabi, what's happened?" Faith watched her intently over the rim of her glasses.

"Faith, don't worry about me. I just realized that I had to get a grip and put my emotions aside for the sake of the project. Let's get cracking and see how much we can get done before Friday morning! Caleb, ready to get back to work?"

"Yes, ma'am." He said with an army type hand salute. "Lead the way."

As they exited back out to the balcony the other three just looked at each other. "What just happened?" Aaron asked.

"I have no idea," Faith replied totally confused. "Probably another one of her mood swings we've being seeing since we got home. She may break out in tears any time and be right back where she was."

KJ did not even venture a comment. Since he barely knew her, he did not feel qualified to make a judgment either way but something was not right. He was sure of it.

"She hasn't been the same person since Saudi Arabia. Surely she'll get back to normal." Faith said trying to believe her own words. "Let's get back to work."

Caleb and Gabriella settled back into their balcony chairs where they would spend the day in an effort to finish reading the journal. That would allow one more day to review all the supporting articles they had not yet read and still have time to prepare a presentation for the Professor.

They took turns reading out loud and discussing the various entries in his journal. In her opinion every entry was another nail in the coffin of the fallen angel/nephilim theory. The proof of extraterrestrials was undeniable. Gabriella was amazed that all through her years of exploring with her father she had no idea he was really searching for any clues to alien existence. Now as she read his comments, she could connect the dots and realized it was all undercover exploration. He had documented everything but never released it. She was sure it was for her protection.

She wished her father and the Professor could have met. They would have had so much in common. She giggled as she imagined the heated debate they would have had.

"What's so funny?"

She looked up at Caleb and giggled again. "Can you imagine what it would have been like to put my father and the Professor in the same room and let them present their research, then battle to the finish on whom was right?"

"That's one debate I would've enjoyed watching." Caleb laughed at the match that would have been. "Oh, I forgot to tell you. I checked on the

Professor this morning. Sandee said he is doing great and anxious to get back to work. She told me the doctors are documenting it as a miracle."

She just smiled. "I'm sure it is beyond what the human mind can conceive. There are powers beyond us, Caleb, powers that we haven't even begun to understand. I just wonder what my parents could have accomplished if they had more time. Would they have been able to bring the knowledge of healing to the world, using the implants? More miracles like the Professor experienced?"

Caleb hesitated before asking, "What do you think happened with the Professor? We know it wasn't an implant that healed him. What do you really think the Presence was in the room, Gabi?"

She turned and looked him straight in the eyes, ready to reveal the truth. "Okay, Caleb, here it is. If I'm to know if I truly have supernatural powers, I have to give it everything I have and see what happens."

She took a deep breath. "My spirit guide told me I healed the Professor through my perfect, unconditional love for him. The Presence was pure love! Through my love I unknowingly released the powers within me that connected with the powers of the universe and brought healing to his earthly body." She leaned back and watched the expression on his face. She could read him like a book. "You asked, so there it is!"

Caleb tried to not show his complete shock. For a moment he could not speak a word. He never expected this.

"Shocked, aren't you? I knew you would be. If we're going to go forward in unity of belief then you have to know what I believe to be the truth. How else can we be in one accord?" Her voice was certain and unwavering. She had moved to a whole new level of self-belief and he was not sure how to respond to it. He certainly was not comfortable with it.

She reached over and took his hand. Her voice softened. "You know I love you, Caleb. This is all new to me, too, and all I know to do is go with it. Please don't prejudge! Let's see where this leads us." Her crystal blue eyes were pleading and his heart melted.

"I would follow you anywhere, Gabi."

But where would it lead, he wondered? He had no earthly idea and there was a gnawing sensation deep within him that he may not want to know.

Chapter 40

The sun was going down and the night shadows were creeping across the misty bay. This was Gabriella's favorite time of the day. She loved watching the harbor lights begin to flicker as darkness slowly veiled the marina. She closed her eyes and listened to the foghorns of incoming fishermen. The muted sounds of laughter and music were streaming in the distance, coming from the various restaurants and pubs along the boardwalk. These were the sights and sounds that made this her home.

She was heartbroken, knowing she would be leaving soon for refuge and safety at the mountain lodge. She had no idea how long she would be there and when it would be safe to return, or even if it ever would be. Her entire life was uncertain and the looming danger cast a menacing cloak over everything pleasant.

If ever there was a time she needed inner powers and guidance it was now. She no longer feared her night travels but actually was looking forward to it, now that she was beginning to understand the meaningful purpose and the mission she was to accomplish. She had nothing to fear, Arcturus would protect her.

All the people she truly loved were in danger and if she could protect them in any way she was more than willing. No, they did not believe what she held to be ultimate truth, but that did not matter. She was certain she could lead them into the enlightenment. Her spirit guide would tell her what to do.

"It's been a long day, Caleb. Let's join the others for some dinner. I plan to go to bed early. We have to finish tomorrow and get ready to leave for the lodge."

She took another long look at the bay and took a deep breath. She sure was going to miss this little peace of heaven. Caleb read her thoughts. He put his arm around her shoulders and gave a comforting hug. Words were not necessary.

Dinner consisted of salad, sandwiches and plans for departure. "I think we can complete our part of the work tomorrow and it will be just in time." KJ said with certainty. "When we get access to the scroll it should be a breeze to reverse translate it, now that we have the morphing sequences."

Gabi swallowed her last bite and offered her own work update. "We only lack a few more journal entries, which we'll finish first thing in the morning. There are more articles to read and we can coordinate our presentations to the Professor during our travel time." She seemed more like herself and less pretentious, which put everyone more at ease.

Caleb leaned back and stretched his legs. There was a sense of satisfaction in his words. "Over a decade and we are finally seeing the end."

"The project may be ending," Aaron said with an edge of concern. "My great concern is we're about to see THE end of life as we know it. If all of the prophecies that were written are true, we are about to see the biggest events to ever take place on this planet. I for one believe every word of the prophets."

"I'm with you on that," KJ confirmed. "There have already been too many biblical prophecies fulfilled verbatim to deny what's happening. If only people would just open their eyes, they would see the signs all around them. This earth just can't go on the way it is. Man is literally destroying everything."

Gabriella could not hold back any longer. "You are exactly right, KJ. If the earth is going to continue, there has to be a cleansing and a higher power to give enlightenment and direction for a new earth. This is what I have been trying to tell all of you. He is coming soon!"

Faith's dark eyes peered over her glasses at Gabriella. "Who is coming?"

"My father's journal explains it and gives supporting evidence from scientific articles. That is the very crux of his research. Some information even comes from government documents. I've tried to tell you all, but you wouldn't listen." She stopped short of telling them about her dreams.

Aaron's piercing eyes looked straight into Gabriella's. "Do you remember what the Prophet told you?"

"Which part? He told me many things." Her voice was sharp as she glared back at him.

"He said you had been chosen to reveal the ancient truths. Didn't he say a great deception was coming and you were in danger?"

"What's your point, Aaron?" She asked, with impatience evident.

"I have all respect for your father's work and he did follow a trail of truth discovering what, I believe, will be a major part of our project. Listen to me, Gabi, the truth he perceived was an alien theory...a deception to counterfeit the truth. It's all designed to deceive people into believing a lie. The words of Yeshua said 'even the elect would be deceived if it were possible'. The Anti-Christ's false religion will be a counterfeit to the truth of the Living God. Extraterrestrials are a deceiving counterfeit. Just be willing to look at the possibility." Aaron's voice was pleading with her. He knew she was totally captured in that deception.

"What if yours is the counterfeit truth?" She retorted as she could feel her inner strength rising up.

"Okay, guys. Let's end it here. We've been down this road already." Caleb took charge. He did not want Gabriella upset again and this was getting them nowhere.

Aaron's face was not hostile, but filled with concern. "I worry about you, Gabi. I pray the truth will be revealed inside your spirit and you will be set free."

She was taken aback by his words. They were almost identical to the words of Arcturus. "The truth will set her free."

"I have found the truth!" Yet very deep inside, there was a still small voice whispering into her spirit, "Really?"

She pushed her chair back, got up and spoke with blatant anger. "I'm going to bed!" She left the room and slammed the door.

Caleb just shook his head, staring at her closed bedroom door. Whatever inner strength she had found was altering the person he loved. He already missed the Gabi that needed him for protection and his love for solace. Was that person gone forever as this new stronger, more independent woman emerged from a preternatural metamorphosis?

Faith pulled her dark rimmed glasses off and laid them on the table. She leaned back in her chair and took a deep breath. "Who was that? It's like a stranger has stepped into her body."

Caleb made a feeble effort to defend her. "This journal stuff is really working on her. You know, reliving the death of her parents and then feeling like all of her father's work isn't taken seriously. We gotta cut her some slack. She'll come around when things settle down." At least he hoped she would. He was not even certain himself she would ever be the same.

Faith got up to start clearing the table. "I miss my best friend," she muttered under her breath.

"I'll help you clean up," KJ offered and began to carry dishes to the kitchen. He felt like an outsider to this team that had worked together for so many years, however, his spiritual discernment warned something evil was trying to find entry into the project, with the purpose of destroying the work. He was fully aware a war was raging and prayer would be the only way to win. Arguing and debating would only fuel the battle.

Within an hour everyone was in bed. There was restlessness among the team. At the most crucial time of the project, the divide that had been created after their Saudi Arabia exploration was widening. Their hope was the Professor could bc the bridge to unite them again.

All the team was restless, except Gabriella. She immediately fell into a deep sleep where time, space and dimensions had no barriers...where her deceptive truth was unfolding in absolute clarity.

Chapter 41

This night was different for Gabriella. As she began to doze there was no sense of falling. She felt no fear whatsoever. She called Arcturus' name and as she descended into a deep sleep, he was waiting for her with his hand extended. The journey began.

He held her hand tightly as they began their flight. "Now that you totally believe, I can show you great and mighty things. Are you ready?"

She nodded her head and he whisked her into the night. "You are not dreaming, Gabriella. Dreaming and soul traveling are totally different. You will soon have complete control of where you go and what you allow to be part of your journey. Dreaming is only your subconscious thoughts over which you have no control."

"I need to know what is about to happen on our earth. How can I convince others, especially my own friends, if I don't understand?"

"Your wish is the command of the universe. There's only one more step you must take to release your powers." He pulled her closer as they began their ascension upwards.

There was no way to describe with human words the tranquility that pervaded her as she experienced oneness with the universe. It was an ecstasy that permeated her body, soul, mind and spirit.

She could see Mt. Hermon in the distance. She was very familiar now with the stargate that would teleport them into their journey. "Where are we going?" She whispered breathlessly.

Arcturus gave a graphic description of their destination. "We are going to the constellation Bootes which the planet Arcturus suspends in the center. It is twenty four times larger than the earth's sun and thirty six light years away."

She watched as they flew closer and closer to the giant red planet. She had no fears...only inner peace and tranquility. "I feel the very essence of this place, Arcturus, it is consuming my soul."

"Our planet is known as the herder of the Divine Will. It is a bridge between Virgo the Virgin, which is the nourisher of the divine consciousness within every being, and all other planets. This, Gabriella, is the center of all universal knowledge. It is from here the Ascended Master has watched the humans of earth slowly destroy the planet. For many years he has been preparing the way to reveal himself and usher in the dawning of a new age."

"Can I access the universal knowledge? How would I?"

"It's simple now," Arcturus replied in a strange voice. "You have already recognized your inner powers. As you converge with the enlightment you will cleanse your body, soul and spirit from the negative influences that have surrounded you. Your godhood within will begin to release. That in turn will intensify your vibrational frequencies and allow you to hear with your inner being."

Arcturus' voice became melancholy. "The human mind is consumed with the daily concerns of life, totally unaware of the supernatural powers within. Their lack of awareness hinders the stream of universal knowledge that openly flows to all who will listen. You have listened, Gabriella, and soon nothing will be impossible to you."

Drawing closer to the planet, she saw magnificent colors of rainbows crisscrossing the mountaintops. The mesmerizing sounds of cascading waterfalls filled the air as it created the same melodic music of Arcturus beautiful voice. They began to descend into a valley filled with translucent flowers that vibrated with colors unknown to earth.

"We've been here, Arcturus. This is Summerland!"

"Yes, you are correct." Arcturus' voice was hypnotic, pulling her upwards toward the top of the mountain and to what appeared to be an altar of worship. "I could not tell you before where we were. You were not prepared then for the convergence."

"Convergence?"

"Convergence is the power of your inner being coming into total unity with the power of the universe. It will allow you access to the Akashic

Knowledge, which can then be used for the good of others. It is the cosmic law. Convergence must take place before you begin. You have been chosen and now you are ready to enter in."

A brilliant light illuminated the altar at the mountain's apex. She was drawn to the light, ascending through the falling mists of the cascading waters and towards the beckoning translucence. It was the same impregnable force she felt in the lava cave, pulling her towards the bottomless pit; but this was beautiful and peaceful, not like the darkness of the abyss. Melodic music, vibrating from the waterfalls, surrounded her as the beckoning light drew her higher and higher. An electrical energy began to pulsate through her being. She was becoming one with the light. The convergence had begun. Her body began to shake uncontrollably.

"Wake up, Gabi! Wake up!" The shaking became more violent. "WAKE UP!" Her eyes opened to see Caleb's eyes filled with fear. He was shaking her shoulders, trying to wake her up. The entire team surrounded her. She could hear them praying.

Caleb pulled her into his arms. "Oh, my God! We thought we'd lost you, Gabi. We've all been in a panic. You'd stopped breathing!"

She felt anger vibrating through her. She was so close to entering her destiny.

She wanted to push Caleb away so she could go back to Summerland. She wanted to complete the convergence.

She had no strength, no control over her body and lay limp in Caleb's arms. She wanted to scream to them to get out of her room. The words would not come. She was briefly suspended between time on this earth and untime in the universe, being pulled back to earth against her will.

She could hear Faith crying. "I'm calling for help. Something is terribly wrong!"

"No," Gabriella managed to whisper. "Just leave me alone. All of you. I'm fine."

"Me, too? Do you want me to leave, too?" Caleb asked as he slowly leaned her back to her pillow.

"Yes," she replied.

"Gabi, you weren't breathing! There's something wrong." Faith's dark eyes were filled with fear.

"I told you I'm fine! Just leave me alone." Her friends reluctantly left the room and closed the door behind them. Caleb was determined to stay by her bedside but she turned her face from him. "Please go, Caleb."

The sting of rejection penetrated like a knife thrust into his heart. He backed away from her and slowly left the room, closing the door behind him.

She laid her head back and closed her eyes, hoping to magically step back into untime and complete the convergence. It was too late. The planet Arcturus was thirty six million light years away.

But there was always another night and another soul trip. She would complete her calling. She would become one with the universe.

Chapter 42

The team left Gabriella's bedroom at her insistence. Caleb pulled a chair close to her door and sat silently, having no idea what to do. KJ motioned for Aaron and Faith to join him on the terrace where they would not be overheard.

The morning sun was streaming down and the sounds of the bay echoed in the background. They stood against the iron railing looking out over the sparkling waters. The serenity of the tranquil September morning in no way reflected the spiritual war that was now raging.

Faith's face was full of fear. "Did Gabi almost die? She wasn't breathing. I know she wasn't."

Aaron echoed the same fears. "There is something really weird going on. I've read about things like this, when people connect with paranormal activity."

KJ was silent for a minute, trying to get an emotional and spiritual hold on the situation. "We must be on the verge of a major breakthrough with the project. Gabi doesn't understand the powers of darkness. Evil spirits are trying to use her as an entry portal for destroying the truth about to be revealed. Since she isn't a believer, she's an open target."

Faith nodded her head in agreement. "But you know, if she heard you say that it would only make things worse."

"I'm fully aware of that." KJ looked off into the distance, not really seeing the peaceful bay. He was looking towards heaven, searching for wisdom and guidance.

Aaron was formulating just the right words before he spoke. "Caleb is hanging in the balances, you know. He doesn't know what to believe.

When he listens to Gabi he's convinced she's right. When he listens to our biblical argument he's convinced we're right. Poor guy sure is a mess right now."

"The Word tells us where two or three agree, according to the will of the Father, it shall be done. We know His will is that all would be saved," explained KJ. "We're going to agree together in prayer for their protection and that the Holy Spirit of Jehovah God would lead them both into His understanding. NOT the understanding of the counterfeit spirit."

They joined hands and KJ led them in prayer: "Holy Father, in the precious name of your son Yeshua Jesus who gave his life on the cross that all might be saved, we agree together a hedge of protection will be around both Gabi and Caleb. We ask for angels to protect them from the powers of darkness that come to kill, steal and destroy. Lead them into your truth, Father. We ask that the blood that was shed on the cross cover them, keep them and guide them. It is through the death, the blood and the resurrection of our Lord and Savior that we know you have heard our prayer. Amen."

Immediately, the same Presence experienced in the surgery waiting room descended upon them again. Peace filled their minds and encouragement entered their hearts. As if a sign from heaven had appeared, a white dove came and perched on the terrace railing at the end of the balcony. They knew God had heard their prayer.

For a few minutes they stood together in the Presence of the Lord, looking out over the beauty of the Mediterranean Sea, thanking Him for answered prayer. They had faith, in spite of what they were seeing in the natural, their God was moving in the spirit realm to answer the petitions of their heart.

Faith did not doubt God had heard their prayer, but expressed her deep concern. "God gave us all a free will to believe in Him or deny him. He won't *force* Gabi to believe." Faith knew how head-strong and stubborn Gabi was and how dedicated she was to her father and everything he believed. "I know with certainty God will reveal Him self to her. I'm praying she makes the right decision."

Caleb stayed beside Gabriella's bedroom door sitting on the edge of his chair. He was full of fear and had no idea how to deal with it. Something beyond the normal was definitely happening and all of his physical strength was totally useless.

He closed his eyes and began to whisper under his breath. "If there is a God in heaven I need you. God, I need your help. I need wisdom. I need strength beyond my human strength." At that same moment the curtains that stood perfectly still on the French balcony doors began to gently dance as a soft breeze entered the room. Caleb felt it move through the open doorway, across the floor and saturate the entire atmosphere. It was the same Presence he had experienced at the hospital. He closed his eyes and allowed it to cover him with peace.

He felt tears fill his eyes and said to himself, "God, if you are real, please help me." Gabriella's pain had touched a place deep in his soul he did not even know existed.

KJ was standing by the balcony doors and felt the Presence enter the room. He watched the emotional scene as Caleb released the agonies of his heart to God.

KJ crossed the room and put his hand on Caleb's shoulder. "It's perfectly all right to be human, Caleb. Sometimes we need to express what we feel. It makes things a lot easier to deal with inside when we allow our emotions to flow out. We've all been pushed to the limit this week. I hang on to the fact that the Lord is my strength and my salvation. I have nothing to fear."

"How can you be so sure, KJ? I thought we had lost Gabi! What's going on that would make her stop breathing? She's done this before and then she just acts like it's nothing. There's something really weird happening and she won't open up to me."

KJ pulled up a chair next to Caleb. "There is a real phenomenon called spiritual warfare, Caleb. That's what this team is experiencing. There are opposing sides of the spirit world, the battle of good against evil. These are the angelic spirits of the one true God constantly warring against the demonic spirits that try to destroy the plans and purposes of Yahweh. All of us working on the project, except for you and Gabi, are committed to the Spirit of Yahweh God. You are drawn toward that Spirit, Caleb, I can feel it. Gabi, however, is going deeper and deeper into the dark side. As a result, we have spiritual warfare in our project. The powers of darkness do not want the truth to be revealed."

Caleb looked totally exhausted. "I am so tired of battling back and forth and not knowing what to believe! I want to be strong for Gabi and support her, but I'm just not sure what I'm supporting. Honestly, it's a little scary this stuff she's been talking about but she tells me I have to believe it or we won't be together. Plus, she would disown me right now, if she knew I was breathing a word of this to you."

"I totally understand, man. I won't say a word to her. It's not like we're ganging up against her. We're joining together to try to help her. She's being sucked into the very deception we are trying to expose. That's the way the evil spirits work. A house divided against its self cannot stand and in this case it's our team. If we can be divided, the enemy can conquer."

"KJ, just a few minutes ago I talked to God and I felt that same Presence that was at the hospital. Weird, huh?"

"Just a few minutes ago we were praying on the balcony and asking His Presence to surround and protect you and Gabi. That's the Spirit of God drawing you to Himself and His truth."

"I've fought this as long as I can. I've swung back and forth between the two opinions until I feel so weak I can't help anyone...especially the woman I love."

"There's only one way you can help her. It's through the power of the Holy Spirit of God that will dwell in you, if you only ask. It is the only power stronger than the powers of darkness and the only way the enemy can be defeated."

"What do I do? How do I find God?"

"Do you believe, Caleb? Really believe?"

"I have no doubt this Presence I have felt is more real than anything I've ever known in my life. If that is the Presence of God then I want it. Not just today, but everyday. I need help in reaching Gabi and I can see she's getting way out on a limb, a limb that could break at anytime."

"If you really believe you just tell Him. Faith is the key that unlocks the door to a relationship with our Heavenly Father. You can instantly become part of His eternal family, Caleb." KJ made it sound almost too easy.

"That's it?"

"It's just that simple. I can lead you in the prayer that will change your life forever."

"I'm ready. I know I can't go on like this." Caleb dropped his head and covered his face with his hands in an effort to hide the tears that were freely flowing.

"Repeat after me." KJ led Caleb in the sinner's prayer.

"Heavenly Father, I believe in the death and resurrection of your Son, Yeshua Jesus. I believe He died on the cross and His blood was shed for my sins. I believe He was resurrected and through Him I have everlasting life. I accept your forgiveness today and will live according to your Word and depend upon the guidance of your Holy Spirit. Amen."

Caleb repeated the prayer. The words seemed almost too simplistic. How could just a few simple words change everything? Yet with those words, a peace flooded through him like he had never known. The Presence he had felt around him now saturated through him. Joy like a fountain began to bubble up inside and the confusion washed away. A smile spread across his face, reflecting the internal transformation.

Aaron and Faith stepped in from the balcony. Faith was chattering away and then became totally silent. They both felt the Presence in the room. One look at Caleb's face and there was no need to question what just happened.

Aaron came over and slapped him on the shoulder and said with a hearty laugh, "Welcome to the family, you're now my brother in the Lord."

Faith threw her arms around his chest and shouted. "This is wonderful! I've prayed for this day for years!" Then she became silent and dropped her arms. "Are you ready for the battle you'll have with Gabi?"

Concern spread across his face but the joy was still shining through. "I'm new at this but if prayer changes things, like you say, then things are about to change, big time."

"We're with you all the way." Aaron encouraged him. "You're now a child of the Living God. That's big stuff, Caleb, the most important decision you'll ever make in your life."

Gabriella opened the bedroom door. "What's all the celebrating about?" And with one look at Caleb she knew something was different. Something from deep within her rose up in uncontrollable anger.

"What have you done?" She screamed the words.

KJ laid his hand on Caleb's shoulder in support. No one said a word.

A voice inside her screeched out. It did not at all sound like Gabriella. "Traitor! How could you desert me, Caleb? You were going to believe with me so we could be together. Now, it's too late!" She ran back into her bedroom and slammed the door. Then immediately the door reopened and she threw her engagement ring at him. "Sure didn't take you very long to side with the enemy!" She slammed the door again.

"That went well," Aaron said dryly.

"Pretty much what I expected." Faith admitted, as the color drained from her face. "I didn't expect to be called her enemy, though."

KJ's voice was certain. "The battle is raging, but we will win the war. Let's get back to work and give Gabi time to settle down. Caleb needs some time to himself."

Caleb only knew one thing to do. "I guess now is when the praying begins. I just don't know how."

Aaron went to his briefcase and pulled out a copy of the Book of Psalms, which he kept with him constantly for encouragement and strength.

"Here, my friend. Read this and find comfort in the Word of God. When you find a promise in His Holy Word that you need in your life, claim it for yourself. All of his promises are 'yes and amen' for those that will believe."

Caleb took the book and went out on the balcony, closeing the French doors behind him. He realized the decision he made was not going to take him down a road of ease, especially with Gabriella. He might even lose her because of it. He knew in his heart of hearts that he had made the right decision.

As he opened the Book of Psalms, Caleb remembered this was the last day before leaving for the lodge and they needed to finish their work. There were only a few more chapters in the journal they had not had time to read. The project had to wait. Finding a way to reach Gabi was the most important thing in his life.

Caleb looked towards the crystal blue sky above. It was the same color as her eyes. He was sure those eyes were crying right now and he could not comfort her.

He prayed his first prayer after becoming part of the family of God. "I know you hear me and I need wisdom and guidance, Lord. How do I reach her? I have no idea where to start or what to do. Help me, please."

He opened the book and the pages fell to Psalms 23. He began to read.

The LORD is my shepherd.
I will always have everything I need.
[2] He gives me green pastures to lie in.
He leads me by calm pools of water.

[3] He restores my strength.
He leads me on right paths to show that He is good.
[4] Even if I walk through a valley as dark as the grave,
I will not be afraid of any danger, because You are with me.
Your rod and staff comfort me.
[5] You prepared a meal for me in front of my enemies.
You welcomed me as an honored guest.
My cup is full and spilling over.
[6] Your goodness and mercy will be with me all of my life,
and I will live in the LORD's house a long, long time.

The words were like medicine to his tormented mind. He had found the peace he had been searching for in the midst of the greatest storm of his life. He had no answers, but he was sure the God of the Universe had all the answers he needed.

Chapter 43

It was afternoon before Gabriella came out of her bedroom. Her eyes were red and glared with anger. Caleb spent the entire morning on the balcony praying for her and reading through Psalms of encouragement. The more he read, the more at peace he felt. He had just come back inside when she exited her bedroom.

Gabriella did not say a word to anyone. She went to the kitchen and made a fresh cup of coffee. Starting back to her bedroom, she picked up her father's journal, looked Caleb in the eyes and stated emphatically, "I'll be working on my own today." Her bedroom door closed with a thump.

Tears began to run down Faith's cheeks. "In all these years of our friendship there's never been anger between us. Many times we didn't agree but we would laugh about it and say 'we agree, to disagree, agreeably'. I feel like I'm losing my best friend and there's nothing I can do to stop it. Most of all, I'm really afraid for her."

Caleb laid his hand on her shoulder and spoke with a certainty that gave her comfort. "We have to trust God, Faith. We've put it in His hands." Coming from someone that was only beginning a spiritual walk, it made Faith realize her weakness.

She knew Caleb was right, but it still hurt. She could deal with Gabriella's stubbornness and strong personality. She was that way from the time they met but she was different now. It was not the friend she knew. "God help her," Faith whispered, trying to concentrate on her work. Focusing was a struggle and she found herself more in prayer than in work.

In the solitude of her bedroom Gabriella tried to concentrate on the journal. She was just too angry. She kept asking herself how Caleb could betray her so quickly. She had never felt more alone in her life. A few days ago, life was a dream come true. She would have a family again and a husband totally dedicated to her. Now, in an instant, it was all stripped away. She did not know how she could go to the lodge and be confined indefinitely with unbelievers.

She laid the journal down. "Dad, what am I suppose to do?" She whispered to the silent room. "I need guidance." She closed her eyes and waited for inspiration. None came. She tried to find inner strength and tap into the powers she was supposedly possessed. There was only emptiness.

The tears continued to stream down her face until she dozed from emotional exhaustion. As she fell asleep, she was surrounded by a misty fog that gradually began to clear revealing a crystal clear river. Arcturus was on the other side, watching her with eyes filled with anger.

"Is something wrong, Arcturus? Are we going to travel?"

"I can't come to you. You must choose to come to me." He was motioning for her to cross, but her feet would not move.

"I don't understand. What's happened?"

Arcturus simply pointed to the river.

The river created a transfixing sound as the waters rushed between them. It was a mixture of many voices, blended together in perfect harmony. She tried to distinguish individual voices. She thought she heard the voice of her father in concert with the other familiar voices. In unison, it made it impossible to hear just one. She could not understand the language but the words obviously created a barrier between her and Arcturus. The voices became louder and louder in beautiful melody, until she could no longer hear Arcturus' voice. He was fading deeper and deeper into the recesses of darkness, as he kept motioning for her to come to him.

She was awakened by the sound of voices in the living room, growing increasingly louder. She could hear Detective Richard's voice above the rest.

She closed her eyes hoping to see the river again. The blended voices were mesmerizing like nothing she had ever heard. It was even more beautiful that the melodic music of the waterfalls in Summerland, but why did the waters separate her from Arcturus?

Her thoughts were interrupted by a knock on the door. She hesitated wanting to be left alone, but finally spoke. "What do you want?" Gabriella's voice was still edged with anger.

Faith peeped through the door, not knowing what to expect. "Detective Richards is here and he needs to talk to you."

"Okay. I'll be out in a minute." Gabriella washed her face and ran a brush through her curly hair. The mirror was not kind to her. Her eyes were red and her face flushed. For a moment, she regressed to her childhood when she would stand in front of the mirror, imaging herself a princess, and ask, "Who's the fairest of them all?" Well, she knew it was not her, not today. "Oh, who cares?" She asked herself and went out to join the others.

The detective motioned for her to take a seat by the couch. The others sat down at the dining table and did not say a word.

"What is it, detective?" Gabriella finally asked.

He paused for a minute trying to decide how to begin. He knew his next words would be a shock to her. "I told you I'd try to get in touch with your former landlord, Mr. Donald, and try to make some connections. You know, find out if he might have talked to someone about the box he sent you, if anyone was asking questions about you or your father. I wanted to see if anything felt suspicious to him."

"And what did he say? Was he able to help at all?" The next words he spoke sent a shock through her soul.

"He didn't say anything. He died five years ago."

Gabriella gasped for breath. "What!" Her eyes filled with confusion. "Then who sent the box? Who forged the letter to make it seem so real?"

"I have no idea," the detective admitted. "I spoke with Mr. Donald's widow and she obviously had no idea what I was talking about, although she did remember when your father passed away and how sad she felt for you. I even talked with each of his three children and they knew nothing. They didn't remember your father at all, sorry to say. I asked Caleb if you still have the shipping box it came in. He said he had taken it to the dumpster over the weekend."

She finished his sentence for him. "And they pick all the garbage up on Monday, so it would be long gone. I never dreamed I would need to keep a shipping box."

"Of course you wouldn't. I had just hoped maybe. It might have helped. I'd like to take the letter and have it analyzed for fingerprints. It might give us some leads. Can you remember anything about the handwriting, the return address, anything that might help?"

Gabriella closed her eyes and tried to visualize the box. "I remember the return address was where Mr. Donald's funeral home was when I moved to Israel. The handwriting wasn't familiar. Nothing that I recall looked unusual. It was postmarked Cherokee, North Carolina. From the town we used to live in."

"Someone went to a lot of trouble to make you believe the box came from Mr. Donald. What I want to know is why? Is there anything strange in the box? Anything you wouldn't expect that was your father's?"

"No, nothing. We showed you the contents. It was his personal journal and his research papers, nothing else. Who could have had those all these years and why would they send them to me now?" The fears that had been dancing through the shadows of her mind were now taking center stage.

Gabriella thought back to her conversation with Sandee when she gave her the box. "I remember Sandee told me Mr. Donald had called while we were on exploration and asked if she had a forwarding address for me. Whoever called knew that I had left the states when my father died, to go the University of Haifa. She told the person I was working there but out of the country indefinitely. She said she wouldn't give them any personal details and just instructed him to send the box to Dr. Brotman's office. She would make sure I got it. Who would impersonate him and why?"

"It really makes no sense to me," the detective admitted, scratching his head. "If the information in that box was so important that the U.S. Government would want to silence anyone that knew about it, why would someone send it to you? You would think they would have realized the value and sold it to the highest bidder."

"I have no idea, but I would love to know. I tried to find this black box when my father passed. I looked through everything when I was liquidating before I moved. I thought the mystery was solved with the letter I received. I thought it really was from our landlord, but apparently not."

Caleb was watching her intently. He longed to go to her and be the solace she had come to depend on. She showed no signs of wanting him anywhere near her. She would not even make eye contact with him and it sent emotional daggers through his heart.

The detective got up to leave. "I'm not through with this. Not by a long shot. If you think of anything at all, give me a call. Otherwise I'll see you at 8:00 sharp in the morning. You'll all be ready?" It was not really a question but more a demand.

Then he was gone, leaving Gabriella in total confusion. She could not discuss it with the team now. She had alienated herself from the others and had no one that cared anymore. She had no one at all...again.

She knew her disbelief and sharp tongue pushed them away. Why would they even care what happened to her? Her inner voice kept whispering, "No one cares, but you don't need them anyway. They don't believe in anything the journal says, so what difference does it make to them?"

She made eye contact with no one. She went back into her bedroom, firmly shut the door and sat down by the window. A big part of the day was gone and she had not read any more of her father's journal.

"It will just have to wait," she told herself. "There'll be time at the lodge to complete the work and then I'll have the Professor. Surely he won't betray me, too."

Her mind was swirling with the uncertainty of the box. Who had it all of these years? Who sent it and why would they want her to believe it came from Mr. Donald? Why now?

Could she tap into her inner powers to find answers? Could Arcturus take her back to her father's death and allow her to see what happened to the journal? Now she was even separated from him by the anomalous river.

"The Professor will help me make sense of this. I will have one friend left." Gabriella lay across her bed and returned to her solitude of tears.

Over the last week she had gone from being independent, with no family, to the joy of having a family again. She had allowed herself to love. She had opened her heart in trust. She even envisioned a life with Caleb, a home, children. In a moment, she lost it all. She would never allow herself to be hurt again.

Chapter 44

Caleb wanted desperately to go to Gabriella, to hold her and comfort her. He knew she was behind her bedroom door in agony of uncertainty.

He no longer tried to hold his emotions back from the rest of the team. "I know she needs me…I know she does! She's feeling like everyone's betrayed her." He began to slowly pace back and forth in an effort to release his anguish.

"She'll calm down, Caleb. Give her some time." Faith hoped her words would prove to be true, but no one really knew what to expect.

Caleb stopped pacing and turned to the team. "Gabi and I desperately need to read the last entries in the journal and try to make some sense of this tangled mess. She made it perfectly clear to me to stay away from her." He felt helpless. It was not an emotion he easily dealt with. She was so close, but totally unreachable.

They just listened and allowed Caleb to vent. "I know you guys are close to finishing your part but there's no way Gabi and I will be ready. We still had several pages to read and research to go through. I don't know if she'll let me anywhere near her to finish. She might just finish it on her own and I'll hear when you guys do, *if* she will tell us anything now."

Faith walked over to Caleb and put her hand on his shoulder. "Caleb, we have to believe God is somewhere in the midst of all this chaos."

"I'm trying, Faith." Caleb left the room and walked out to the balcony to be alone. "I really am trying."

The sun was going down on the last evening they would spend in Haifa. No one knew how long before they could come home again. The team, all but Gabriella, went out on the balcony to join Caleb and watch the breathtaking sunset. Jointly, they prayed for guidance in the coming days. Uncertainty filled their minds. Had it not been for the comfort of the Holy Spirit, their hearts would have been full of fear. They felt a peace that passed all understanding.

Gabriella, all alone, watched the sunset from her bedroom window. "Was this the way her life would be now?" She angrily questioned. She wished they had never found the lava cave or the writing. She wished she had never seen Arcturus or been visited by the Prophet. If she could erase the past weeks she would do it in a heartbeat, especially allowing herself to love Caleb, who so quickly deserted her.

Most of all, she did not want to be chosen for anything.

Tears continued to stream uncontrollably. She made no attempt to be strong. Her moment of taking control earlier in the day quickly was surpassed by the subsequent events. She just did not care.

She packed what she would take with her to the lodge, asking herself why she was even going. She found what the Professor needed. He had his ancient writings. He did not need her anymore. It was KJ and Aaron he needed now for the translations.

There was only one thing that pushed her and it was not her safety. She did not even care about that. She had to know who had her father's journal all of these years and why did they choose now to send it to her? This was her only motivation to continue.

She finished packing, showered and crawled into bed leaving room for Faith, but Faith never came. She cried herself to sleep and for the first time since she returned home she did not dream. When she needed answers from the spirit world there was no spirit to guide her.

Her alarm went off at 6:00 AM. She pushed the covers back and stretched, watching her bedroom curtains dance in the morning breezes while the sun peeped between the circles of movement. It took a minute for all the clouds of despair from the previous day to settle back around her.

"I can do this," she spoke to the flowing curtains. "I'm strong and don't need anyone. I will find out where the journal has been and why it came now. Then I'm leaving Israel. I'm finished, the spirits can choose someone else because it won't be me!"

She carefully dressed wanting to look her best. Not for Caleb, she tried to convince herself, but because she needed confidence and self-certainty to ooze from her. The team would not see her defeated. She would not be the emotional wreck she had struggled with for days on end. She had a mission and she would stay focused for her father's sake. As far as the project was concerned she was finished with that, too.

She zipped her roll bag and was ready to go. She had her father's journal and research papers carefully stored back in his black box, ready for transport. She took a moment to run her hands across the rough leather binding. "Where have you been these past twelve years? I will find out, you know. Whatever it takes and whatever I have to do, I *will* find out."

She rolled her luggage into the living room and left the box for one of the men to carry. She realized Faith had slept on the couch, and a pillow on the floor told her where Caleb slept. It seemed he was always taking care of everyone else and not concerned about his own comfort. Waves of emotion hit her and she struggled to not let them show.

Caleb walked out of the kitchen with his blonde hair slightly ruffled and exhaustion in his eyes. Something about his face was different, like a peaceful glow, in spite of all the turmoil. She resented it and yet hungered to experience it.

He had a cup of coffee and handed it to her. "I thought you would need this."

She took the coffee never making eye contact and whispered, "Thanks."

She longed to have him wrap his arms around her. She longed for that place of refuge. But she knew it would not be the same now. She could never trust him again. If only he had talked to her first and explained why, but it was too late now. She would learn to live with the pain. She managed when she lost her mother and then when she lost her father. She could lose Caleb and everyone else and still survive. Mentally she was rebuilding the walls of emotional protection around her heart.

She took her coffee onto the balcony to seclude herself and waited for the transport to arrive. She was determined to enjoy her last morning views of the peaceful bay. This could be her final time to experience the serenity of the Mediterranean Sea, which had become a soul soothing part of her life. When the mystery of the box was solved, she would move to some secluded location to wait for the Ascended Master to come and deliver the earth. "If there is such a thing," she whispered.

Promptly at eight o'clock there was a knock on the door. Gabriella went inside, closed the balcony doors, made sure they were locked and pulled the curtains closed.

"I cleaned out the fridge last night, Gabi."

"Thanks, Faith." No other words were said.

Two men came with Detective Richards and were waiting with a roll cart to take their luggage to the underground garage. Caleb went to her bedroom and carried out the box without being asked, the box that had brought her to the place where she finally released her love for him, only to feel betrayed almost immediately. He did not speak a word as he carried it to the door.

All the lights were turned off and one by one they exited the apartment. Gabriella refused to look back.

In the garage they loaded the luggage in the back of a large, black Suburban. The two men kept watching in every direction the entire time. When they were ready to leave, Caleb sat in front with Detective Richards, while the others settled in the back seats. The two other men both had cargo vans they drove. One was in front of them and one was in back. They departed the dark garage into the light of a beautiful September morning.

"What time will the Professor be released?" Caleb asked the detective.

"It should be any time. He and Sandee will be joining us by separate transport soon after we arrive."

Gabriella sat silently as they drove along the familiar streets past her favorite coffee shop and towards the freeway. They passed the city park that bordered the seaside. She reflected on the numerous times she had walked along the water's edge and enjoyed the serenity that surrounded her there. Would it ever be again?

Everyone in the vehicle seemed to be lost in their own retrospective thoughts, wondering if life would ever be normal again. They exited the city and drove through the enchanting Hula Valley surrounded by orchards growing numerous seasonal produce. The beauty of the lush foliage and colorful fruits and vegetables was breathtaking. It was almost harvest time, which would be followed by the annual Sukkot celebration. It was a joyous time in Israel when the Feast of Tabernacles was celebrated. Gabriella always looked forward to the fall festival even though she had no spiritual connection to the meaning.

She refocused on their journey. She had wonderful memories of the drive through the lush valley in past years. The team would continually be discussing their explorations and research while they traveled to the mountain lodge for a work retreat.

She continued to watch the scenery along the road that led to the Sea of Galilee, where they would begin their ascent into the mountains towards the region of Mt. Hermon Ski Resort, the area her mother and father were exploring when she was conceived. There, they would be isolated indefinitely in a lodge built like a fortress and everyone there would be against her and her father's work.

The unity they had at one time did not exist any more. Even the detective noticed something very different about the attitude of the team. He marked it off to uncertainty, fear and the mental affects of being cooped up together for a week.

It would take approximately three and a half hours to reach their destination. Gabriella decided to make good use of the time and make it clear to the others she was not going to be part of any conversation. She unbuckled her seat belt and turned around in the back seat of the SUV where she could reach the black box. She pulled the stubborn latch open and removed the journal that lay on the top. She promptly shut the lid with an obvious thump and turned back around and snapped her seatbelt back in place. No one made a comment as she opened the book to where she and Caleb had left off.

June 25, 1989

It has been a year since I lost my soul mate and my little princess lost her mother. It has been the hardest year of my life. The only thing that has kept me going is Gabriella, and my determination to finish my work in spite of the dangers. We have moved to Utah where I am teaching at a small, private college. I have tried to disappear from the scientific scene and look as though I am not continuing my research on extraterrestrial life, for the safety of my daughter. Here, in a remote area of this western state, Gabi and I will explore caves and canyons as weekend outings. She will have no idea I have a two-fold purpose, to spend every minute possible with her and to continue the pursuit for ancient signs of intergalactic visits.

'Nine Mile Canyon' in eastern Utah is actually 40 miles long and is referred to as 'the world's longest art galley'. Some of the most spectacular rock

art in the world is found here. Most of the art was created by the Fremont Indians over 1000 years ago. But some of the art dates back millenniums. These ancient petroglyphs display thousands of etchings of ancient aliens and are amazingly similar to the cave drawings we found at Mt. Hermon.

There is still so much to learn, but I have no doubt our planet has been visited over the ages by alien civilizations. Many of the encounters are preserved on the rock walls of time. How anyone can deny this, I do not know!

I continue to be secretly in touch with the scientist that is working on the ET implants. He has been researching additional findings of these devices and the affects they are having on humans receiving them. What he has discovered could literally change the world.

The implants seemingly have varying affects when injected into the body. It appears not only can the device heal incurable diseases, but also reverse aging, control addictions, open the mind to extrasensory perception, and be used as a human tracking device. In every case, it has altered the DNA to create physical and mental changes.

The scientist and I speculate the implants are being done as experimentation by our government to determine their effectiveness in preparation for the day of their revealing, using the technology gleaned from extraterrestrial resources.

Anyone that controls these implants can rule the world!

"Of course." Gabriella thought. "This makes perfect sense and goes along with everything the Professor has been saying about the return of what he thinks will be the fallen angels. This is what Arcturus was promising to bring to earth. We would finally reach the apex of universal understanding, the Akashic Knowledge. These implants are experiments preparing for the enlightenment."

She wanted desperately to shout it to the team. If they would only look at her father's evidence, they could resolve the entire matter. She allowed herself to briefly glance at each team member. Faith was staring out the window, Aaron and KJ working on their computers, and Caleb was in the front occasionally making conversation with Detective Richards. Not one of them realized or even seemed to care about the earth changing information contained in the journal she held in her hands. With a deep ache in her stomach she knew they did not really care about her either. She had become an enemy to the project.

In an effort to forget the agony of her soul, she continued reading.

Our apartment was broken into a few days ago. Someone had methodically gone through every nook and cranny but nothing was missing. I am sure the culprit was looking for my research, which is being kept in hiding. It looks as though Gabi and I will be constantly on the move, although I am sure they will follow us wherever we go. They will take whatever measures necessary to make sure the implant information is never released to the public.

I applied for and have recently been offered a temporary professorship in the area of Pyramid Lake, Nevada. We will be moving before the beginning of the fall semester. This area is home to the oldest petroglyphs in North America, dating back almost 15,000 years. The exploring will continue for Gabi and me, although I may never be able to reveal my discoveries. No discovery is worth risking the life of Gabriella .

Gabriella turned the book over face down in her lap and stared out the window. She was only six when they lived in Utah and she barely remembered any details. She did remember their apartment being broken into. That unsettling event had been branded into her memory permanently. Her precious Strawberry Shortcake bedspread had been stripped from the bed and lay crumbled on the floor. The mattresses were turned upside down and every drawer had been pulled out and dumped upside down. She never felt safe in that room again.

Her mind went back to Nine Mile Canyon. She had vague memories of exploring along the giant walls that displayed carvings that seemed to never end. Her father had taken lots of pictures. He mused over them for years to come as he added more and more research from the subsequent explorations.

Gabriella's mind was drawn back to the present as they started the ascent into the Golan Heights where the views became spectacular. She thought about the year her parents spent exploring the caves in these mountains. This is where her parents' belief in extraterrestrial life began and, apparently, what would ultimately end their lives.

Somewhere in a cabin in these mountains she was conceived by loving parents. She so desperately missed them and wished they were present to guide her. "Daddy would know what to do," she whispered to herself.

Her mind was in turmoil as they ascended the mountain. A battle was raging inside of her. Should she choose to travel one more time before she rejected the powers within, and then live in seclusion until the day of reckoning?

Chapter 45

It was almost noon as they rounded the last curve that would lead to the gated entry of the private lodge. They were now 6000 feet above sea level. The views were spectacular and any other time Gabriella would have enjoyed every moment of the turning and twisting drive up the majestic mountain. All she could think about was Caleb's betrayal and how her friends had turned against her. There was no end in sight to the pain.

She continued to stare out the window, dreading the days to follow, as the lead van turned into the private entry and stopped at the huge iron gates. The driver's arm reached out and entered the code that would open the gateway. Slowly, the barriers parted allowing entry. The three vehicles passed through and the gates closed behind them. A tall metal fence encircled the property with barbed wire along the top.

"I am officially in prison," Gabriella thought. She had always loved the retreats in the past and it was home to some of her favorite memories. This trip, however, promised no rest for her weary mind and soul.

They slowly climbed the winding driveway through the trees, around another steep curve, and up the final incline. She listened to the foreboding sound of the gravel crackling beneath their vehicle as they approached the main entrance. With a breathtaking backdrop of blue skies and the apex of Mt. Hermon resplendently framing the background, the palatial stone lodge appeared.

Cedar railing lined the rustic front porch that wrapped around the massive structure. Large, cushioned chairs were strategically placed against the stone walls of the porch facing the majestic mountain views.

Wood shutters, closed when the lodge was not in use, were open on all the windows saying 'welcome' to the arriving guests.

The trio of vehicles pulled to the front of the lodge and stopped beneath the covered main entrance. As the men exited the vehicles, the sound of a natural creek flowing and cascading over rock formations welcomed them. The streaming waters were caught in a crystal clear pond near the edge of the porch. It was truly a piece of heaven on earth.

Detective Richards stood in amazement at the majestic beauty. "Who owns this place?"

"We have no idea," Caleb responded. "The Professor would just say a personal friend of his was allowing us to use it."

"I could use a friend like that." The detective joked and then directed the two other officers to take the luggage inside. Aaron and KJ assisted while Caleb took possession of the black box.

Gabriella could see the expression on Caleb's face change when he saw her holding her father's journal in her lap. She quickly looked away. She knew he felt left out, but that was his problem. He chose to be. Any eye contact would surely reveal the agony of her soul, so she immediately began to gather her personal items and exit the vehicle. She was determined to not show him any signs of weakness.

Gabriella and Faith followed the men in while Detective Richards came in last with his eyes constantly watching the surrounding area. "Where do we take the luggage?" He asked.

Faith directed them to the upstairs. "I'll show you. We always stay in the same rooms when we're here." She started up the steps and the men followed with their bags.

"We'll unload the supplies right after I check the house out." The detective went from room to room, making sure everything was secure.

Gabriella was waiting for the luggage to be put in the rooms and everyone out of her way before she went upstairs to unpack the few belongings she brought with her.

"Do you want the box in your room?" Caleb asked trying to make eye contact.

Gabriella just turned and started up the steps. "Please."

The weight of the heavy box was no challenge for Caleb as he followed her up the stairs. She pushed the bedroom door open for him to enter first.

Immediately catching both of their attention was a vase of fresh cut yellow roses sitting on the nightstand.

She looked at Caleb. "I didn't do it." Although he wished he had.

"Maybe they're not for me specifically." Gabriella mused as she bent over to enjoy their wonderful aroma. "Odd though. Yellow roses have always been my favorite."

Caleb looked in the other bedrooms and reported back. "No flowers anywhere else that I can see. Maybe the Professor or Sandee will know something. They should be here pretty soon."

Caleb lingered by the door hoping she would ask him to stay but no invitation would be forthcoming. She just turned her back and started unpacking. "Thanks," she said without emotion. He left the room and closed the door behind him.

When she heard the door securely latch she collapsed on the bed in full flow of emotional release. She buried her face in the fluffy brown comforter and beat her fists against the side of the bed. "I can do this, I can get through this. I won't feel anything!"

Trying to regain self-control she forced herself up and walked to the window that looked out toward Mt. Hermon. She unlatched and pushed it open, taking a deep breath of mountain air. The cool air flowed into her bedroom and she realized she would need to dress accordingly before she went back downstairs.

She started to close the window when she saw someone move towards the guesthouse in the back. She did not have a clear view of the person walking beneath the trees, but it looked like...yes, it was!

She could not breathe as the realization fully dawned on her. It was the Prophet! She grabbed her sweater and ran down the steps and out the back door from the kitchen, following the path that led to the guesthouse. She was out of breath as she beat on the door. No one came. She beat harder. She had seen him. She knew it.

The shutters were closed and locked, indicating no one was residing there. She knocked a third time but heard no sounds of movement inside. She darted from window to window all around the structure hoping for a peek inside, but the shutters completely blocked any possible view to the interior.

"I must be losing my mind!" She said as she turned hesitantly back towards the lodge. She kept glancing back, hoping the Prophet would reappear.

Caleb ran to meet her. "I saw you run out like the place was on fire. What's going on, Gabi?"

Her first instinct was to fall into his arms. He would understand. He knew all about the Prophet and the messages he had given her. Instead, in her stubborn determination to not show any emotion, she walked past him not even looking in his direction. "It was nothing."

After she went back into the house he walked around the guest house. There were no signs of life anywhere. Normally, he would not discount it too quickly but Gabriella was not herself, overreacting to almost everything. Still he would keep watch, just to be sure.

"What's going on?" Faith asked when Caleb came back into the lodge. "Gabi just came through here like a steak of lightening."

"I don't think it's anything. With her mood swings it's hard to read her and that's a first for me." Caleb longed for the days when he sensed her every mood and was always a step ahead of what she would say or do. No more. He felt the woman he loved slipping away and out of reach.

They heard a car horn blow outside. "The Professor's here!" Faith cried out jumping up and running to the door. She pulled the heavy wooden door open and ran to meet him. The rest of the team, minus Gabriella, followed Faith to welcome him to what would be their indefinite home.

"My team!" He exclaimed with a smile that lit up his face. He opened his arms to embrace each one of them.

"Don't over-excite yourself," Sandee warned him as she pulled her briefcase from the car. "You know what the doctor said." Then she smiled and stretched out her arms for her team hugs, too.

"Where's Gabi?" The Professor looked around and she was nowhere in sight. All the team was silent.

"Isn't she here? Where is she?" His voice was demanding and edged with fear.

"She's here but only in body. Not in spirit." Faith narrowed her eyes not wanting to even say the words. She knew this would hurt him deeply. He had no idea how much Gabriella had changed in the short time he had been in the hospital.

"What are you talking about, Faith? What's happened?" The Professor looked at Caleb knowing he, above all the rest, could explain, or was Caleb the problem? "Has there been a lover's spat?"

"More like a war of the worlds," Caleb mumbled as he helped carry in their luggage.

Sandee's first concern was for the Professor. "Let's get you inside and settled in. Then we'll find out what's going on."

"You would never know you were close to death just a week ago, Professor. You look great." KJ gently slapped him on the back as they crossed the stone walkway towards the porch.

"I feel great. The doctors are calling it a miracle, you know."

"So I've heard, there is nothing too big for our God! Still got work to do, don't we?" KJ opened the door for the Professor to enter first. "We've done a lot of that while you were recuperating."

"I'm ready to get back to work. So much to do and so little time." He crossed the hardwood floor to the recliner by the stone fireplace. He sat down by the fire one of the officers had built to take the chill off the room. "Now, go get Gabi. Tell her I'm waiting for her."

Just as he said the words he could see her standing at the top of the stairs. Even from a distance he observed the distress in her face. He stood back up and opened his arms.

She ran down the steps, across the room and into his arms. Tears were flowing like a river and it totally took the Professor off guard. He had always known, beneath the exterior of this independent woman, was a little girl, needing love. The tragedies of life had buried those emotions deep inside her.

He wrapped his arms around her as a comforting father would. He did not push for conversation but wanted his affection for her to be her solace. No one wanted to interrupt their private moment. They went to the kitchen to start putting away the supplies brought in from the vans.

As Faith stocked the refrigerator, she voiced her hopes. "Do you think the Professor can bring Gabi back?"

Caleb's heart flooded with that very hope but he did not say a word. He knew it was really a comment, not a question. He just kept unpacking the boxes while Faith organized the food and supplies.

Sandee came into the kitchen after she had unpacked the Professor's personal items in his bedroom. She could not wait any longer. "What's going on?"

They all looked at Caleb to give any explanation. A big smile spread across his face in spite of the circumstances. Sandee watched his expression and then looked at the others. Faith nodded and smiled.

Sandee knew Caleb had finally found the truth. "This is wonderful, Caleb! You have no idea how many prayers I've prayed for you and Gabi through the years. When? How? Give me the details!"

"It's not all good news," Caleb confessed. "It's wonderful, finally knowing the truth, but not when the woman you love is on the opposite side of the belief."

"And that's what's bothering her?"

"A lot more than that," Faith interjected. "Caleb's decision to believe in God and become part of the family of Yahweh was just the icing on the cake of what she thought was betrayal. Her father's journal is what has totally torn the team apart."

"Really?" Sandee looked totally confused. "Did she finish reading it? All of it?"

"I guess I threw a wrench into finishing it." Caleb tried to explain to Sandee how the events played out. "The journal kept leading Gabi into all kinds of supernatural beliefs. I think something has taken control of her, Sandee, and I can't reach her. She thinks I've abandoned her. I'm the enemy now."

"Oh, this is not good. I dread to tell the Professor. How deep is she into the paranormal?"

Caleb tried to remember the different phrases Gabriella had used and details of the dreams she had shared. "She said she had a spirit guide and she had been chosen because she had some kind of inner powers. I think she called it shaman powers. She even thinks she's the one that healed the Professor, through her deep love for him connecting with the universe, or some sort of nonsense like that. The part that concerns me most, Sandee, is she has been talking to her dead mother. This all happens in dreams."

KJ, Aaron and Faith were shocked. They had no idea how deeply she had moved into the world of demonic activity.

"Do you think believing in extraterrestrials opened the door for all the rest of the stuff?" Caleb was desperately trying to understand. "His journal was full of all kinds of articles he considered facts. It convinced her, too."

He knew personally how easy it would have been to believe. Had the others not shared with him the real truth, he could have blindly followed her and almost did.

"Is it too late to reach her, Sandee?" Caleb asked in a pleading voice.

Sandee did not hesitate to answer. "Believing in any type of the paranormal can open all the other doorways into the occult. Deceiving spirits come in many forms but all come from the same evil source. It's always beautiful at first and then the powers of darkness take over the mind, the soul and the body. If she's already been visited by a spirit guide and a familiar spirit, then she's in way too deep."

"The Professor was telling Gabi about these spirits when we were with him at the hospital. He was trying to warn her and she wouldn't listen," Caleb realized.

Sandee sat down on a stool at the kitchen island and motioned for Caleb to sit beside her. She realized how important it was for him to understand what Gabriella was battling and how far- reaching the consequences could be.

The expression on her face told him this was very serious. "Every person has spirit beings that are with them all through their life. That's what the bible refers to as 'the watchers'. They are also called angels. There are both good and evil watchers. A battle for the soul is continually waging in the spirit world, between these two forces. We decide who wins by what we choose to give in to. These spirits know everything about you, see everything you do and hear every word you speak. They know your weaknesses and your strengths. You've heard of guardian angels?"

Caleb nodded his head. "They're real?"

"Very real! They're the forces of good. But the watching evil forces are constantly looking for an opportunity to enter the mind and control the person. They use our weaknesses as an entryway. We have to know how to get the thoughts out of our heads. If the mind opens itself to the thoughts planted there, they eventually become our reality. Every action has a reaction...good or bad. It all begins in the mind."

Sandee reached over and put her hand over Caleb's. She did not want to frighten him but he had to understand just how serious the situation with Gabi was. "Opening the mind to the paranormal is the greatest way these spirits can deceive and trick people into believing a lie. They know what a person wants and that's what they offer them. Gabi wanted her mother and father back. She always felt cheated. So that is what the evil watcher offered her. But it's a lie, a trick, and the end is always the same... total destruction."

It was becoming clear now to Caleb. "That's what Gabi's fallen for! How does the familiar spirit thing fit with this?"

"When a person dies their evil watcher can take on that person's form and appear as if it was the ghost of the departed. Without spiritual discernment, you would be deceived into believing it was actually your loved one. The spirit can answer any question you ask them about the person they are appearing to be. Even intimate details no one else could possibly know. The familiar spirit was with that person all through their life. It's easy to see how people can be deceived."

"Is that what Gabi thought was her mother? A familiar spirit?" Caleb was beginning to understand how her mind was working and his concern was growing deeper with each detail.

"It couldn't be anything else. The soul of the departed dead only has two destinations. To return to their loved one is not one of them."

The fear was plainly written on Sandee's face. "She'll sink even deeper into the supernatural abyss if we don't move quickly. The farther she goes, the harder it will be to bring her back. Sometimes, Caleb, they go into a dream trance and can't wake up."

The blood drained from Caleb's face and Sandee could see the unadulterated fear.

"What is it?" Sandee demanded. "There's something you're not telling me!"

He struggled for words. "There have been several times I thought she wouldn't wake up. She would almost stop breathing. When she would come to, she was perfectly fine. None of it made any sense, until now. My God! What do we do, Sandee?"

She jumped up from the stool. "There's no time to waste, I've got to talk to the Professor!"

She went back to the gathering room and immediately noticed concern on the Professor's face. Gabi was sitting in the chair beside him, totally silent.

Had Gabriella already told the Professor? Had the Professor finally told Gabriella the secrets of the past?

"Oh, God, help us!" Sandee whispered in a desperate prayer.

Chapter 46

Detective Richards and his officers came in from their final outside security check at the same time Sandee came rushing from the kitchen.

"Is everyone all settled in? Do you need anything?" The detective was making sure all needs were met before his departure. I'm leaving Officer Chris Harris here for security. He'll be reporting to me. Just let him know if you need anything. Detective Harold and I have got to get back to Haifa."

"We're just fine." The Professor assured him. "Thank you for all you've done. We'll make sure Officer Harris is treated as part of our family here."

"Appreciate that," Officer Harris replied and promptly went outside to patrol the grounds.

Detective Richards shook hands with Dr. Brotman and headed towards the door. He addressed them one more time before leaving. "Everything is secure. All the alarms are set and no one can get in or out of the main gate without the code. I'm still working on that mystery box. I'll let you know if anything turns up."

"What mystery?" The Professor asked. "What are you talking about?"

"I thought maybe Gabriella had filled you in. I'll let her give you the details. Be in touch soon." With that Detective Richards and Detective Harold departed.

As soon as the door closed behind them the Professor turned to the team. "What's he talking about, the mystery box?"

KJ took a deep breath. "You probably need to sit down for this, Dr. Brotman."

The Professor took his seat back by the fireplace and leaned forward waiting.

KJ began to unfold the team's plan to keep the project secret. "Detective Richards kept pushing for information that could lead to who or why someone would try to kill you. We couldn't tell him about the project, so we had to come up with something to take him in a different direction. I suggested we use the alien information from Gabi's father as a decoy, since apparently it was top secret and dangerous information at the time he wrote it."

KJ paused and then realized, "But you didn't know what was in the box shipped to Gabriella, did you? You have no idea what we're talking about."

Gabriella jumped in and took over the conversation before the Professor could reply. "It was my father's research he did over many years regarding extraterrestrial existence. The information was so important that the detective believed it was possible that anyone associated with my father's work could be in danger. Since the box was in the possession of your office for several months, he thought someone might be trying to silence you or use you to send a warning to me. What he found out in his investigation, however, is the reason he calls it the mystery box."

The Professor's eyebrows were narrowing as he leaned even closer towards Gabriella. "What *did* he find out?"

"I showed him the letter from Mr. Donald. There was no return address but with some investigative work, he found out Mr. Donald has been dead for over five years. Now we have no idea who's had the box all this time. Why did they send it to me now?"

"And he's trying to find out that information, I assume." The Professor's voice revealed definite concern as he listened to the explanations.

"Detective Richards said he would keep working on the case until he's exhausted every possible lead. What started out to be an innocent decoy away from the project to give us time to finish, has now turned into a mystery of its own, but least he doesn't know anything about the Omega Watchers Project." Gabriella paused to see how the Professor would respond. He said nothing.

He turned toward the fireplace and stared into the burning fire, as if waiting for wisdom and guidance. After several minutes he nodded at the fire as if he knew now how to proceed.

He turned to Gabi. "Have you finished your father's journal?" He knew she had not and watched her intently as she hesitated.

"Almost. I only lack a few chapters. I had planned to do that yesterday, but..." There was no way she could explain, so she admitted to him, "I didn't finish."

He could see the mixture of hurt and anger in her eyes and let it drop for the time being. He also felt the tension among the group that had never been there before. He was fully aware it had been an extremely trying week for all of them and now it was time to come back together in one accord and finish the project.

"Let's get to work, team. Everyone get their notes and give me an update on where we're at in the translation."

Sandee was trying to get the opportunity to speak privately to him. He had to know about Gabi. "I think you should rest a little after the long drive. You don't want to push it too much. Remember what the doctor said?"

"I've had all week to rest. I'm ready to work." Sandee made a playful, pouting face and the Professor laughed under his breath. "Ok, if you insist, but the rest of you get your notes out and be ready. Much to do, my young friends! Much to do."

"I'll bring you a cup of hot tea. It will help you rest." Sandee got up and went to the kitchen.

"She's like a mother hen," he said with a wink and a smile, as he proceded towards the main level bedroom in the back of the lodge. "I won't be long. I'm ready to get at it."

Gabriella felt alone again as she watched him go down the wooden walled hallway. He paused once halfway down the hall and looked back at her. "Finish the journal, Gabi." His words were not open to argument. Shortly afterwards, Sandee followed him with his tea.

The lead of the team had shifted back to KJ again. "Let's get our notes ready and review everything. I'm both excited and nervous. This could make or break the project. Oh, man, we forgot to ask him about the scroll. Surely he brought it!"

Gabriella got up and started up the stairs. "You don't need me. I'm going to read the rest of my father's journal." She did not indicate in any way that Caleb should join her. He felt totally useless and it could not have hurt more if an actual knife had been stabbed in to his stomach. He watched her go up the stairs and out of sight.

"Oh, God, show me what to do." He said out loud.

"He will, brother. He will." KJ laid his hand on Caleb's shoulder and he found comfort in KJ's words.

Faith's heart broke for Caleb. She could see the pain in his eyes. She had always known he was in love with Gabriella. Now Gabriella had finally realized her love for him and they were being torn apart.

Her voice was soft with compassion. "I think you need some alone time, Caleb. We can handle this. Find a place to talk to God like He was your best friend. Pour your heart out and He'll listen. Prayer changes things."

He picked up the Book of Psalms that Aaron had loaned him and went outside to find solace. He sat in one of the oversized rocking chairs holding the book next to his heart. "What do I do? Show me how to reach her." All the emotions pent up inside begin to flow. He did talk to God. It was so easy. An unexplainable peace began to settled in his mind and his heart.

He opened the book and read from Psalms 91.

Chapter 47

Gabriella closed the bedroom door behind her. She expected the tears to again flow, but none came. Her heart was growing hard as she felt betrayed by her friends and the man she loved. Loneliness was something she was accustomed to, but this reached a whole new level. Bitterness was gradually claiming her soul.

"If I forsake my inner powers, I will be denying my father's years of research," she said to herself. "If only I could get the team to look at the facts his research presents. I believe we could all work together towards truth, but they are narrowminded and not willing to see any other possibility except for their biblical interpretations."

She walked to the window and looked out towards Mt. Hermon. She felt strangely drawn to that beautiful, majestic mountain. Her thoughts went to the night journeys when she and Arcturus would ascend to the apex of the mystical mountain. Even though she was awake, she felt her soul being pulled to the stargate, towards the peace and serenity she found in her astral travels. She was certain from that portal she could visit anywhere in the universe, find any truth she needed, communicate with her parents and understand eternal mysteries only known in the spirit world. If only she could make the team understand there is a spiritual realm just waiting to be tapped into and powers beyond human imagination! If only.

She went to the bed where Caleb placed her father's black box. She unlocked it and pulled the lid up. With shaking hands she picked up the journal, held it to her heart and spoke into the empty air. "I need wisdom to reveal the truth. How can I make them understand?"

She sat in the padded, wooden rocking chair by the window and opened the journal. She was determined to finish reading his entries.

She opened to the marked page where she had left off. She turned to the next entry and realized there were many years of silence. The journal entry was a personal letter to her.

April 13, 2000
My dear Gabriella,

It has been over a decade since I made my last journal entry. Not because I have ignored my search for truth, but for fear of writing my findings in this journal lest it fall into the wrong hands. I even thought several times of destroying it but knew I had to have a written record for you, when the time was right, to understand my journey for truth.

It has been so lonely without your mother but you have been the sunshine that has brightened every day of my life. As you have grown, you have become so much like her. You have her smile, her same blue eyes and beautiful blonde hair. When you laugh I hear the echoes of her voice. Without a doubt, you are strong-willed and self-confident as she was.

I have done everything in my power to protect you from the ones that wanted to silence me and did silence your mother. My work has continued in secret and been preserved under a pseudo name. Most of the late nights of work, while you were sleeping, and the business travel, were not connected to my teaching positions as you supposed, but to my research. I shared the information with no one, until two years ago. I knew the time had come. If I was to make a difference with the knowledge I had obtained I could no longer keep it to myself.

I had read about a scientist in a news article that I believed could assist me with the final steps to the ultimate truth. After some research I knew contacting him was my best course of action. It was a huge step for me, but it is proving to be the wisest decision I have ever made.

Gabriella was interrupted by sounds coming from the bedroom beneath her. It was the Professor's room and she could hear Sandee's voice. It kept getting louder and louder, but it was too muffled to understand most of the words.

There was a brief silence and then she could hear the Professor. "We can't wait any longer." He sounded very upset.

The voices went back and forth for several minutes and then there was silence. She had never known the two of them to argue about anything. She sat quietly with her head against the back of the rocking chair listening for any other sounds. The stillness became a sedative. She felt herself drifting into a slumber.

The slumber quickly became a deep sleep. She, again, was standing at the river and Arcturus' hand was reaching towards her. "I told you I can't come to you, but you can come to me. I have the mysteries of the universe to reveal to you, if you will only come and complete the convergence. You determine your destiny, Gabriella."

"Arcturus, how can I make my friends understand the truth? They need to understand! I need help!"

"You have to choose to cross over. You have free will. Choose today whom you will serve. Will it be the deception of the people that surround you or the inner powers you possess? Cross over and enter into your godhood. Use your powers for the good of mankind, to prepare the way for the Ascended Master."

She tried to take a step into the water, but her foot would not move. She could hear Caleb in the distance. She looked all around her and could not see him, but his voice that began with a faint whisper was getting louder and louder. His words were saturating the atmosphere around her: "You can go to the God Most High to hide. You can go to God All-Powerful for protection. I say to the LORD, You are my place of safety, my fortress. My God, I trust in you. God will save you from hidden dangers."

"NO!" Arcturus cried out. "Don't listen to him. He will destroy your powers!"

She turned quickly towards Arcturus. His voice was demanding. "Come to me! Cross the waters, NOW! Listen to my voice. Not his!"

Caleb's voice rang louder than Arcturus'. "You can go to the God Most High for protection. He will cover you like a bird spreading its wings over its babies. You can trust Him to surround and protect you like a shield. You will have nothing to fear."

Arcturus was frantically motioning for her to cross the waters. The sound of his voice was being overshadowed by the voice of Caleb growing consistently louder. Faintly, she could hear Arcturus demanding, "You have to come now. Cross now! Choose now! Now, I say!"

She could feel the same sinister force she felt in the lava cave. It was pulling her towards Arcturus. The sensations were no longer pleasant and peaceful. Arcturus no longer appeared beautiful. His face was distorted and his eyes were turning red. Evil seemed to ooze from his very being.

She wanted to be in Caleb's arms of safety, but she could not see him. Everything around her was clouded in a dark mist that was closing in and sucking the life from her. She could not breathe and fell to the ground unable to move. She was sinking deeper and deeper and deeper into darkness.

Caleb's voice was fading in the distance. "The Lord says, if someone trusts Me, I will save them. I will protect My followers who call to Me for help. When My followers call to Me, I will answer them. I will be with them when they are in trouble."

She tried to cry out for help, but no words would come. She was being pulled through a long, dark tunnel and blackness engulfed her. She fell into unconsciousness. She heard nothing. Felt nothing. Saw nothing.

Chapter 48

Caleb sat on the porch and prayed the words of Psalms 91, asking God to protect Gabriella. He felt peace flooding through him mixed with extreme concern for her. It was a different feeling, one he was not familiar with at all, but his entire life was different now. Everything felt different.

"She's in Your hands, Father." Caleb surrendered Gabriella to God and went back in to join the rest of the team.

Faith looked up first when he rejoined them around the table. "You okay?"

Caleb could hear Sandee in the kitchen preparing dinner. The Professor was coming down the hall to rejoin them. His footsteps echoed on the dark cedar floors as he made his way to the great room. Everything seemed fairly normal on the outside, but Caleb kept sensing in his spirit that something was very wrong.

"I can't explain it, Faith. It's weird. While I was praying I felt like I was in a war for Gabi. Like she was being torn back and forth and I was fighting a major battle against some unseen evil force. I just kept reading Psalms 91. That was the only way I knew to fight for her."

KJ was intently listening. "That *is* the way to fight for her, and any other spiritual battle you face. The Word of God is our two edged sword and the powers of darkness can't stand against it. The Spirit is revealing deeper truth to you, Caleb. All you gotta do is seek and He's there waiting to guide you."

"I just can't shake this feeling that something's really wrong. I know her mood swings have been off the scale, but this feels different."

The Professor settled into his recliner listening to their conversation. "I understand from Sandee we have major problems with Gabi. Things haven't gone as planned."

They all looked straight at him. Aaron asked puzzled. "What do you mean? What plan?"

"Time is of the essence. We've got to finish the project and then the whole picture will be crystal clear. From the beginning my goal has been to protect all of you. I was protecting you when you didn't even know you needed it...especially Gabi. As we entered the last phase of the Omega Watcher Project, I told you of the possible dangers involved and you had the choice if you wanted to pull out."

Faith looked confused. "We've always been in danger? I never felt it. We were just doing our job. Why would we be? Why, especially Gabi?"

"It's what you were looking for that put you in danger." He explained. "We couldn't let anyone know the purpose of your explorations. That's why everything has been under the radar, so to speak. Not that I didn't trust you, but the less you knew the safer you were."

The Professor hesitated as if trying to decide how much to tell them. "Let me put it this way, finishing the project will fully explain everything."

"Then let's get at it!" KJ went to the table opened his computer and was ready to roll.

Faith looked towards the dark wooden staircase. "Should I get Gabi?"

"Let's let her finish what she needs to do. Big changes are about to take place when she finishes the journal."

The team looked at each other and wondered why he was talking in mysteries. This was not like him at all. Being a man of science he was straight-forward and precise in everything he said. Still, it was obvious he would say no more about her for the time being.

"Now catch me up on where we are at in the translations." The Professor pulled himself out of the recliner and joined them at the massive wood table, waiting for their report.

KJ was ready. He explained the process of reverse morphing to be able to translate the ancient language. He showed him how they translated the Ge'ez back to Dahlaki then back to Tabadawi and then forward again to Ge'ez.

"The writings from the cave were in Tabadawi. The challenge has been every letter in the Hebrew language is a picture, a word, and a number.

Aaron was brilliant in bringing this together and I think we have it. At least we sure hope so. It's ready for your final translation."

Aaron was rightfully beaming with pride. "Professor, it's all in your hands now."

The Professor leaned forward in his chair, anxious to see the charts. "I've heard of Tabadawi but it's been lost for millenniums. Linguistic scientists consider it to be the mother of all languages. Where did you find all this information? We've been searching for years." They could tell from his expression they had struck the mother lode.

KJ could not hold back any longer. "That's the miraculous part. Just recently some ancient Egyptian writings were discovered. It was Tabadawi. I believe we will be the first to actually have both the ancient writing and a translation. Coincidence or divine intervention?"

"You know the word 'coincidence' is not in the Hebrew language." The Professor smiled and winked. He knew he had made that abundantly clear many years prior.

The Professor asked for his magnifying glass, which Sandee promptly produced. He moved it over each symbol, carefully inspecting every detail. The team heard him muttering, "After all these years could it be? Could it really be?"

Aaron walked over and gently gave him a loving pat on the shoulders. "Yes, it could, and I believe it is. This is the final Ge'ez translation of what was found in the cave and on the clay tablet."

The Professor sat straight up. He shifted his position so light would shine from the window onto the papers. "Give me a pencil, please."

As he read, he was writing above each Ge'ez word the translation. The team did not make a sound. He said nothing as he worked translating word for word. The only sounds came from the kitchen where Sandee continued dinner preparations, unaware that the project was nearing completion.

The Professor looked up briefly. "Someone bring me my briefcase." Caleb jumped up and quickly grabbed it from the table.

The Professor took a book from the briefcase and shuffled through the pages. He knew exactly what he needed. He compared his notes to the book he had in hand. He kept going back and forth until finally he laid the book down and looked up. The team held their breath in anticipation.

"Shouldn't Gabi be here for this?" Caleb asked.

The Professor nodded his head. "We'll wait while you go get her, Caleb."

The team was trying to read the Professor's face while they waited for Gabriella to join them. A heavy silence hung in the air as an extreme apprehension was becoming obvious in the Professor's countenance.

Caleb ran up the massive wood steps, his long legs taking them two at a time. The thumping sound of each step echoed with an ominous vibration throughout the great room. They heard him knock on the door and call her name. There was a moment of silence. He knocked again but louder.

"Gabi, we need you downstairs." Caleb waited for an answer from behind the closed door, but none came. "Gabi!" He turned the doorknob and pushed the door slightly. "I'm coming in, okay?" Still no answer. He opened the door and had a full view of the room that was as silent as the grave. She was nowhere to be seen. "Where could she have gone?" He whispered as he turned to leave. Then he caught a glimpse of her long, blonde hair on the rug. Her body was hidden by the bed.

"Gabi!" His screaming was heard though the doorway, down the stairs and echoed so loud Sandee even heard it in the kitchen. She came running out in a panic and the team all jumped up simultaneously to run to Gabriella.

KJ led them in a rush up the stairs. Sandee's voice was heard above the deafening sound of pounding feet on the wooden stairs. "Oh, my God! NO! Please God, no!"

When they entered the room they found Caleb sitting in the floor, holding Gabi's limp body in his arms. "Call for help! *Now!*"

Sandee ran down the stairs to the phone.

Caleb held Gabi against his chest and rocked back and forth. Tears were running down his cheeks and dropping on her face. "Wake up, Gabi! Please wake up. God, help her, please help her!"

Faith's face was filled with fear. "Is she...breathing?"

"Barely," Caleb whispered. "Pray!"

They gathered around Caleb and Gabriella and began to cry out to Yeshua. The Professor's voice was heard above all the rest. "You gave me a miracle, Heavenly Father, now give her one. Let her know the truth."

As they continued to pray there was a battle waging in the spirit realm for the soul of Gabriella.

Caleb held her, waiting for help to come. Her breathing was shallow and she was unresponsive. He continued to pray, unashamed for anyone to hear his uncontrollable cries for her to come back to him.

The Professor sat down in the rocking chair next to the window where Gabriella had been sitting. He entered into intercessory prayer asking for angelic protection. "Heavenly Father, we pray for her spiritual and physical awakening."

Faith was sitting on the side of the bed crying uncontrollably, while KJ and Aaron paced the floor praying.

They were all waiting for Sandee to come back with help, hoping against hope it would not be too late.

The sound of multiple footsteps could be heard running up the stairway. Sandee entered the door and the person behind her brought everyone to a dead silence...everyone but the Professor.

The man that accompanied her wore the black clothing and hat of a Hasidic Jew. His long gray-black beard covered most of his face. The black rim, tinted glasses camouflaged his eyes. He perfectly fit the description of the Prophet they had heard so much about!

The stranger rushed to Gabriella and took her in his arms, as Caleb reluctantly released her. The team looked at each other in total confusion, waiting for an explanation that was not forthcoming.

With a heavy accent and tears flowing from his eyes, the strange man began to pray in a language that none of them understood. He was praying in the language of the Heavenly Father.

Chapter 49

"Sandee, did you call a doctor?" Faith pleaded with tears still flowing. "Who is this?"

"A doctor's on the way." Sandee had barely said the words when a car door was heard slamming outside. The sound of footsteps echoed from downstairs and got louder hurrying up the stairway. In rushed Dr. Nicholson, a man the team all knew well. He was a personal friend of the Professor and had been in their company numerous times when they were on retreat.

"I'm glad the security code didn't change," he muttered as he moved towards Gabriella. "Lay her on the bed, please."

Sandee and Faith moved to make room for Caleb to take her from the stranger. Caleb briefly held her close then stretched Gabriella's limp body on the bed. The strange man stayed by her side.

Quickly and without words, Dr. Nicholson checked her blood pressure and pulse. He lifted her eyelids and checked both eyes. He continued to examine her while sounds of prayers could be heard coming from everyone in the room.

Finally he put his instruments away and sat down on the side of the bed. "All the vitals are normal. Her breathing is shallow but nothing overly concerning. There's a bump on her head that probably happened when she fell. She may have a slight concussion but her eyes aren't dilated, so I'm not concerned about any internal bleeding or pressure to the brain. She appears to be perfectly normal, just in a deep sleep. It could be a temporary state of unconsciousness caused by the blow to the head. Do you want to move her to a hospital?"

"What do you think? Should we, Doc?" The Professor asked, fully realizing they needed to stay secluded.

"My professional opinion based on all her vital signs is she just passed out and then hit her head. Has she been under any stress?"

The look on the faces of everyone in the room answered his question.

Sandee explained to the doctor about Gabriella receiving the black box and the ensuing emotional battle.

"Since she's been reading her dad's journal she has totally changed." Faith interjected. "The more she read the more she pulled away from us."

Dr. Nicholson was puzzled. "You think this has something to do with her condition?"

"Are you familiar with astral comas or what's sometimes called astral sleep, Doc?" The Professor asked.

The doctor leaned forward and cautiously replied. "I've heard of it, but it isn't a medical term."

The Professor nodded in agreement. "I know it isn't medical, but it *is* a very real spiritual phenomenon. In my many years of exploring ancient and modern day truths concerning the spirit realm, I've often read about various cases. I've never personally encountered it before, until now. She apparently has been slipping in and out of this spiritual world for over a week now."

"How do you know? What are the signs?" The doctor was captivated by what he was hearing.

"She's been confiding in Caleb, hoping he would join this journey with her. She thought she was finding an inner godhood and supernatural powers. That's what the deceiving spirit was telling her."

"She talked to a...spirit?" The doctor leaned a little closer to the Professor, as if being closer would help him better understand.

"That's what she said." The Professor went on to explain to the doctor all that Caleb had shared with Sandee. "There's probably much more that she hasn't told."

Dr. Nicholson leaned back staring at the window, lost in his thoughts. "I've seen several cases of comas and unconscious experiences in my practice I couldn't explain. Patients would wake up and tell hair-raising stories of what they'd experienced while unconscious. Everything from trips to hell, being in heaven, talking to the dead...the list of strange happenings goes on and on. Most of my patients didn't remember anything, not even what happened to cause their condition; however, there were some that remembered very specific details. They described leaving their body and being able to see and hear everything around them. They just weren't able to communicate with the living. These things can't be explained in scientific terms."

"Exactly!" The Professor needed the doctor to realize Gabriella was experiencing much more than a temporary state of unconsciousness. "When you are dealing with the paranormal world, you are treading on dangerous ground. Her soul could go either way. The choice will be hers."

The stranger addressed them for the first time with his thick accent. "NO! We won't lose her! We will fight with the Word of Yahweh!" With great passion he began to quote scriptures from the Psalms. "Though I walk through the valley of the shadow of death I will fear no evil for You are with me. Your rod and Your staff comfort me."

Caleb closed his eyes and listened to the words he had read himself when he first found spiritual truth. He agreed with the stranger. "No, we will not lose her!"

The doctor was obviously out of his comfort zone of knowledge. "I'm going to do some research on this. I honestly have no idea how to advise you except from a medical standpoint. She'll need someone to be with her at all times until she wakes up." Dr. Nicholson stood up and began to pack his instruments away.

The stranger took the place of the doctor and sat beside Gabriella on the bed. He took her small, soft hand in his own and held it tightly. With his heavy accent he assured the doctor, "I will not leave her side." Then he continued to pray in the Spirit.

"Me, neither," said Caleb. He pulled the rocking chair next to the bed and planted himself by her side. He looked directly at the stranger with a look of determination, letting him know he had every right to be there as his eyes questioned who this man was.

"Call me if you need me. Otherwise, I'll check on her tomorrow." The doctor snapped his bag shut and started towards the door. The Professor followed him downstairs where they continued the conversation on astral comas. The doctor knew the Professor was a man of both supernatural and spiritual understanding. He could not ignore the Professor's diagnosis.

Upstairs, Sandee was struggling with what to tell the team about the stranger. She stood beside him and put her hand on the stranger's shoulder. After a deep breath the introduction came.

"It's time you meet Eli. He's a dear friend. He's been taking care of the property and living in the guesthouse behind the lodge. He's a believer in Yeshua and a prayer warrior. He will be praying with us for Gabi."

It was the truth...just not the whole truth.

Chapter 50

Gabriella was sinking deeper into astral sleep. She felt her body drifting through a long, black tunnel. Her eyes tried to focus but there was no light, not even a glimmer. There were no sounds to be heard. She tried to cry out but could release no sound. She closed her eyes and allowed her soul to travel. She felt total peace. When she reopened her eyes a light had appeared at the end of the tunnel. She exited into a strange illumination. A heavy mist, filled with effervescent lights, engulfed her.

"Where am I? Somebody help me!" She turned in a complete circle and was surrounded by the glistening fog, completely blocking her view in all directions.

Arcturus' voice could be heard in the distance. "I'm here. You're entering untime, Gabriella, where there are no limits to time, space or the secrets of the universe."

"Am I dead?" Her first thought was of Caleb and a longing to again be in the safety of his arms. She listened for his voice that had grown louder and louder, before the blackness captured her. There was only silence.

"There is no death, only the metamorphosis from the physical earth to the astral planes."

"Is that where I am? I have left my earth life?" She peered through the glittering mist trying to see beyond the cloud holding her captive.

Arcturus' voice was soothing. "Only your soul has departed. Your human body remains on the earth plane but unconnected to your higher consciousness."

She suddenly remembered the last glimpse of Arcturus she had before she passed through the tunnel. She shuddered, recalling the evil that vibrated from him. Fear began to grip her. She did not want to see that horrible image again.

"How do I get back? I want to go back!"

"You're crossing over, Gabriella. You are becoming one with the universe. You know you have been chosen. It's time to complete the convergence. What you could not do in your human body, you will now be able to do from the spirit realm. You were surrounded by unbelievers who were destroying your vibrational frequencies. You had to be separated. You now have access to the universal Akashic knowledge. You will be a spirit guide to truth for others on the earth plane. We must prepare for the coming of the Ascended Master. It is time for the transformation into the age of peace and harmony for all mankind. All negative forces will be removed. It is the evolution of the universal consciousness. Anyone that will not conform will be removed from the earth and taken to our planet for self evaluation and concurrence with the higher consciousness."

The fog began to fade. This time there was no peaceful, flowing river surrounded with flowers whose colors vibrated into a musical symphony. There were no tranquil misty rainbows crisscrossing majestic mountaintops. There was only a dark ominous gulf that stood between them.

Arcturus beckoned for her to come to him. "It's time to cross over." His smile was beguiling as he kept motioning for her. She wanted world peace and all the things the earth transformation would offer. She desperately wanted Caleb and her friends to find the truth of universal knowledge.

She was drawn towards him. "How do I come to you, Arcturus? How do I get across the gulf?" She tried to take a step closer to the edge, but she could not move. Why was she frozen in this celestial place? A figure was moving from behind Arcturus coming closer and closer to him.

As the form grew clearer Gabriella gasped, "Momma!" Her mother was dressed in a translucent white gown. Light was vibrating around her and through her. Her long, golden hair flowed in gentle breezes as she motioned for Gabriella to come to her.

"Momma, I'm coming!" She longed to be in her mother's arms. Her mother moved to the edge of the gulf that divided them and continued to motion to her.

"Gabriella, all you have to do is make the choice to join me. Just say it and we can be together forever." The voice was soothing and Gabriella longed in her soul to be with her mother again.

An unseen force began to pull Gabriella backwards. Her eyes were drawn to her right. She turned to see the most beautiful sight she had ever beheld. The tunnel of light that transported her ended facing a massive white gate, with giant pearls crowning the top, glistening against a translucent, golden street that passed through the gates. A feeling of purity emanated and pulsated towards her. A spirit of holiness surrounded her and she was overcome with the impurity of her existence. There was a huge lock that shone as pure gold holding the doors closed. She knew she could not pass through.

A thunderous sound was heard behind her, creating a force and pulling her backwards away from both the beautiful gate and the great gulf. It was the sound of many voices crying out in unison. The voices blended together in a beautiful harmony that created a magnetic force drawing her towards them.

She heard clearly a very familiar voice above all the others. *"For unto You I cry out. For You, O Lord, You are good and forgiving, abounding in steadfast love to all who call on You. Your mercy to me is great; You have taken my soul up from the deep places of the underworld."*

Gabriella was trying to turn towards the voices which were growing increasingly louder. She looked towards Arcturus and her mother as she was pulled backwards away from the gulf separating them.

"NO! Don't turn, Gabriella! Come to us!" The evil within Arcturus was completely exposed by the warring sounds that were invading like an army from behind her. The louder they grew, the more hideously evil his appearance became.

She was caught between two forces. One was pulling her backward and then the other forward. She heard that familiar voice behind her again that rang louder than all of the others. "Bring her back to us. Reveal to her the truth of the world of darkness, and the evil one that would deceive her. Save her from destruction!"

Her desire was to be with her beautiful, loving mother. She pushed forward with the force pulling her towards the edge of the gulf. She was slipping across the edge when in unison the voices behind her cried, "Save her, Yeshua Jesus!"

Suddenly, the image of her mother changed. Gabriella saw the lying spirit, appearing as her mother, begin to distort. The sparkling white gown changed into a ragged, black garment with chains hanging from it.

Her glowing face became dark and distorted. The long, golden hair was replaced with a black hood.

Truth was revealed to Gabriella. She now understood. This was a familiar spirit! "You're not my mother! I will not come. *I choose not to come*!" The blended voices behind her became louder and louder, pulling her away from the gulf.

At that very moment the distorted figure of what she had thought was her mother wailed at Arcturus. "Abaddon, we are losing her!"

Gabriella discerned the force saving her from the powers of darkness were prayers. It was the prayers coming from the people that loved her. The words created sharp swords that began to rain down between her and the gulf, creating a barrier that could not be crossed. The two figures on the other side were screaming, trying to block the sound of the prayers. The wall of swords was moving across the gulf pushing the evil beings farther and farther into the darkness. The one she had called Arcturus shouted, "I am Abbadon and I am released upon the earth! The Fallen Watchers have returned! You released me, Gabriella, and you are mine! This is not the end! Not yet!"

What had appeared to Gabriella as a comforting spirit guide and the eternal soul of her precious, loving mother, were now exposed. The demonic spirits had appeared as messengers of the light to draw her into a great deception.

The prayers had created a spiritual force that surrounded and protected her. The powerful force was pulling her back into the tunnel of light and back towards her human body.

Peace flowed through her as she gravitated backwards towards the sound of the praying voices. Numerous souls passed her, traveling through the tunnel towards the brilliant light that would end at the majestic pearl gate emanating with holiness.

She saw embryos of babies in huge numbers passing her. People of all ages had radiant looks of joy as they journeyed through, focusing only upon the translucent light at the end. Purity emanated from the souls and made Gabriella fully aware that she was spiritually unclean.

The force of the prayers continued to pull her until she exited the tunnel and her body, soul and spirit were once again reunited.

She could hear voices becoming clearer, but she could not respond. The prayers that brought her back from the brink of the abyss were the prayers coming from her lodge bedroom. She could now discern the voices of Caleb, Faith, Aaron, KJ, Sandee and the Professor. Yet, there was one more voice praying even louder than all the others in a heavy Israeli accent and in a language she did not understand. The voice was full of love and was soothing to her soul.

She tried to move, to make some gesture to let them know she was still alive. Her body would not move. She could make no sounds. Then there was only silence as she was captured by a supernatural sleep.

Abaddon, who disguised himself as the beautiful Arcturus, no longer had access to her soul and mind. She was now suspended between the natural and spiritual worlds in a state of unconsciousness...between time and untime.

Chapter 51

Gabriella was now suspended between time and untime. The prayers of her loved ones had protected her during the intense spiritual battle that had been raging. The powers of darkness had lost their control, however, a state of unconsciousness held her.

For two days Caleb and Eli had not left Gabriella's side. They had long hours to talk while they kept watch over her. Eli shared words of wisdom with Caleb, helping him understand the chain of prophetic events that were taking place. Caleb shared with Eli how much he loved Gabriella and their journey throughout the years, especially the last few weeks. Eli listened, with an obvious expression of agony, as he heard the details of the spiritual battle for her soul.

Gabriella lay peacefully with no body movement whatsoever. Caleb prayed and watched for signs she was returning to them. None came.

"Where was Gabriella in her search for truth when this happened?" Eli asked.

Caleb answered bluntly. "About as far away from the real truth as you can get. She didn't believe one word of it."

Eli's eyes filled with tears. "She's got to wake up. She's got to have the opportunity to confess Yeshua as Lord, before it's too late."

Caleb watched him intently. "It's amazing to me you're so concerned for someone you don't even know."

Eli attentively watched Gabriella, hoping for some sign of movement as he continued the conversation. "The Professor has told me all about the team since you came to the University of Haifa. I know her much better than you realize. I know about the Omega Watchers Project, too."

Caleb was surprised. "Really? The Professor is so secretive about his work."

"I also know they are working, as we speak, on completing the project. That is what Gabriella would want. Time is running out, you know."

Caleb looked Eli directly in the eyes. "The Professor keeps saying that, too. How can you be so sure?"

"The signs are all around us, Caleb. Prophecies of the end of days are being fulfilled at an exponential rate. Something major is getting ready to happen in Israel, and Israel is the time clock for the rest of the world."

"And what's supposed to happen next?"

Eli turned back to face Caleb. "According to the prophecy of Psalms 83 there will soon be a regional war against Israel. As a result of this war, the prophet Isaiah wrote the oldest city in the world, Damascus, Syria will be completely destroyed."

He watched the expression on Caleb's face. "I know this is difficult to believe, Caleb, but this war will start soon. Shortly after this war will be a much larger war. Ezekiel 38 calls it the war of Gog and Magog, and it will include many powerful countries. These two wars will change the entire world, resulting in chaos and mass confusion. According to The Book of Revelation, it will be a time of horrible events like no other that has ever been on the earth. When you combine the writings of the ancient prophets, they create a roadmap showing the direction the world will take, right up until the end."

"But, how soon?" Caleb was struggling to understand. It was all new to him and so confusing.

Eli spoke with a solemn voice. "It could literally be any time. These wars will be signs that Yeshua is coming to take those that believe in Him out before the day of His wrath."

"Coming?"

"Yes, Caleb, to take to heaven all that believe. After the judgment of this wicked world is complete against all the evil, we will return with Him to set up His Messianic Kingdom that will rule the earth. There will be no more evil." Eli smiled at the thought.

Caleb thought back over the pages and pages of the journal. "That sounds a lot like what Gabi's father said the ETs would do. Cleanse the earth, bring peace and harmony and there would be a Master leader ruling the earth. Gabriella thought she was chosen to help them in this great transformation."

"I know." Eli's face flooded with pain. "She was greatly deceived by the journal. If only she had finished reading it." With a quivering voice he whispered the words, "Wake up, Gabi, you've got to know the truth."

"What happens to her if she doesn't accept it, Eli? We can't force her. God knows how many times the team tried to share truth with her and it only made her angry and more determined not to believe."

"I don't even want to think about it." Eli could hardly speak the words as the tears filled his eyes. "She's got to wake up. She's got to confess her sins and accept the atonement of the blood of Yeshua before it's too late."

"And if she doesn't?" Caleb held his breath waiting for Eli's reply.

"She'll be left behind." Eli dropped his head into his hands and sobbed uncontrollably.

Caleb walked over to Eli and put his hand on his shoulder. He felt an unexplainable kindred spirit with this man. Eli reached up and covered Caleb's hand with his. "You're a good man. Gabriella couldn't have fallen in love with anyone better."

"She hates me now. She thinks I deserted her." Caleb said as he sat down on the side of Gabriella's bed and kissed her cheek. He took her hand, whispering through his tears, "Wake up, Gabi. Please wake up."

She lay as still as death.

Caleb and Eli heard the sound of footsteps echoing on the wooden stairway and rushing down the hall to Gabriella's room. Her door flung open.

"We've done it! We've finished the translation!" The Professor's face was gleaming as he heralded the news.

Eli jumped up and slapped the Professor on the back. "I knew it! I never gave up hope!"

Caleb jumped up and was smiling in spite of the agony in his heart. "We're finished? It's over? But, where's the scroll? Don't you need that, too?"

"It's a long story, but bottom line is Eli had it safely in his possession." The Professor answered.

"I want to hear this long story," Caleb insisted. "This doesn't make any sense to me. I thought no one else knew about the project."

The Professor looked at Eli. "Is it time?"

Eli nodded his head in affirmation.

The team was coming through the door carrying chairs to gather around Gabriella. The Professor sat down in the rocking chair next to her bed. "We decided I would reveal the prophetic timelines for the first time here, gathered around Gabriella. All of you have been a vital part and together we'll know the message that's being revealed for the end of days. I only wish Gabriella was awake to know, too."

Caleb sat back down on the side of the bed next to Gabriella and reached over and laid his hand over hers. He would be amazed at what was about to be unveiled.

"Before I read the translation there is something of utmost importance I must tell you. I want to introduce you to the man that has financed this entire project and also who owns this beautiful lodge that we've enjoyed over the years."

The team all looked with excitement towards the door to see who would enter. No one came through and there was no sound of anyone else in the lodge.

They turned their eyes back to the Professor as he got up from his chair and walked over to Eli. He laid his hand on Eli's shoulder. "Team, this man has gone by the name of Eli for twelve years now. For reasons that will soon be obvious to you, it was necessary for him to change his identity and live a totally secluded life."

A smile was on Sandee's face as she came and stood by the Professor. Apparently she knew, too, what the team did not. Her voice was filled with excitement as she spoke. "It's been torture to me to keep this secret. So many times I wanted to tell you, especially this past week."

Eli took off his hat and glasses, and slowly removed the fake beard. He reached down in his shirt and pulled out a child's key that hung on a chain around his neck. He held the key in the palm of his hand as stood before the team. Caleb looked closely at him. Something was very familiar. He had seen pictures of this man. He moved closer and he could not believe what he was seeing.

"Are you?" Caleb held his breath. "It couldn't be!"

The Professor cleared his voice. "Team, this is Edward Gabe Russell, Gabriella's father."

Faith sank to her knees. "Oh, my God! Oh, my God!"

"WHAT?" Aaron and KJ exclaimed at the same time.

Caleb sat in shock. "How in the world?" Anger was rising up inside of him like nothing he had ever experienced.

Caleb's voice that was never raised was now almost screaming. "Why would you keep this from Gabi all these years and let her suffer like she has? Why didn't you tell her all the alien stuff was a bunch of bull! You could've stopped this before it happened!" Caleb tried to get a hold on his emotions, but he felt he was going to explode knowing all of her suffering was unnecessary.

The Professor held up his hand and Caleb knew full well what that meant. "Enough!" The Professor waited for the team to get emotional control before he continued.

"I know this is a shock but there are so many things you don't understand, my young friends. If Gabi had known he was still alive, I can almost guarantee you she wouldn't be. Everyone, even his own daughter, had to believe he was dead. It was the only way Gabe could live and his work could continue."

Faith's voice was filled with perplexity. "I just can't believe it. I can't!"

"Poor Gabi," Aaron's voice joined the chorus of unbelief. "If she had only known."

Sandee went over and hugged the team members one by one. "Of course we wanted her to know, but we couldn't have continued the project. Plus, all of you would have been in danger."

Gabe went to the other side of the bed and sat down beside Gabriella. He took the chain from around his neck, which held the child's key, and carefully raised Gabriella's head, placing the chain around her neck and laying the key next to her heart. "Gabi, you gave me this key when you were just a child and I've worn it next to me heart all these years, just as I promised I would. Now it will come from my heart to yours." Tears ran down Gabe's face as the transfer was made.

"Now you do this!" Caleb's said with eyes glaring.

"I started to tell her as soon as you returned from Saudi Arabia, Caleb. We knew then the project was almost finished and I was anxious to tell her the truth. I called her apartment two nights in a row just to hear her voice, but I knew I couldn't reveal myself that way. The shock would have been too much for her. I decided to appear as the Prophet first to be able to warn her of the dangerous traps ahead. I was going to explain everything as soon as it was safe. I just pray it's not too late." The last sentence was barely a whisper.

"How did you pull this off?" Caleb asked in a voice still edged with anger. "Gabi was absolutely sure you were dead."

"It took two years of planning," the Professor explained. "Only one other person knew Gabe had taken a new identity and was still alive. Gabe became a Jewish man named Eli who is the groundskeeper and maintenance man here at the lodge."

Gabe nodded his head in agreement. "The guesthouse is where Gabi was conceived. Her mother and I leased it the year we were exploring here in 1982. It's the one place I could hold to the memories of my dead wife and feel close to Gabi."

KJ had tried to stay silent since he had not been with them through the years after Gabriella had lost her father, but he could stay silent no more. "Who else knew?"

The Professor filled in the blanks for them. "We had everything already set up with a fake identity...birth certificate, passport, credit cards, bank account, and a home address in Israel...everything that would be needed for Gabe to start his new life under a new name. We had been waiting for the right opportunity. We knew we had to fake a funeral and make it appear to be Gabe's. The only other person that knew he was still alive was Bob Donald, his landlord who also owned the local funeral home."

The Professor looked at Gabe. "Do you want to tell them the rest of the story?"

Gabe looked down at Gabriella, desperately wishing she could hear the explanation as to why he had to do what he did. "Bob had become a good friend to me and understood the importance of my work and the potential danger. He was keeping my research in his possession for protection and helping me to create a new identity. He was getting concerned that someone was following him, watching him. Being concerned for the safety of his family, we knew we had to do something soon."

Gabe got up and stood by Gabi's bedside facing the team. "We were waiting for a body to come to the morgue that could not be identified. Bob called late one night right after the 9/11 attacks in America. He told me a John Doe had come in with no identification and no way to find out who he was. With all the confusion after the attacks and so many people unaccounted for, we knew the timing was perfect. The next day I had an unexpected heart attack, so everyone was told, and John Doe became Edward Gabe Russell. With a closed casket funeral, which I had previously requested, no one had reason to question. Bob made sure the local paper did a front page story of my unexpected demise."

He took a breath and admitted. "I knew that would make it even more painful for Gabi but there was nothing else we could do. If she was going to be safe, I had no other recourse. A death certificate was issued in my name and immediately I left the country under a new identity. Bob had already shipped the black box to the Professor, even before John Doe came in. We didn't want to raise any red flags if someone was watching his movements around the time of the funeral. The box was safely stored, awaiting the day it could be in Gabi's possession. We had no idea how long that would be. I never went back to America, and as planned in advance, didn't contact Bob again. I was sorry to hear about his passing. I believe he literally saved my life and Gabriella's." Gabe was overcome with emotion.

Sandee continued the explanation of the series of events. "We were waiting for the right opportunity to give the box to Gabi so she could read and understand her father's journey to truth. When Aaron emailed the pictures from the cave in Saudi Arabia, we knew we were reaching the project breakthrough and it was time Gabriella knew everything."

Caleb wanted every mystery answered. "Gabe, what about your letter when you wrote you were going to contact someone to help you with the truth you'd discovered? Who was that?"

"That would be me." The Professor admitted.

KJ jumped out of his seat. "This is the man you wrote my mother about, isn't it? Who would've guessed it?" KJ just shook his head in amazement and dropped back into his seat.

"Exactly," the Professor admitted.

"But is he the 'Prophet' that supposedly visited you? I'm so confused." Faith was still in a maze of unbelief.

"It's absolutely true I was visited by a man or an angel, I don't know which, that I call the Prophet. He did give me the clay tablets, just as I told you. That is a mystery that has no explanation." The Professor declared emphatically. "That's what gave us the idea for Gabe to take that disguise. With the clothes, the beard, the Hasidic look, and heavy accent, he mingled right in with the Orthodox Jews of Israel and no one suspected a thing."

Sandee offered another piece to the mystery puzzle. "The Professor and Gabe had it planned that Gabriella would be offered a scholarship to Haifa University and a scholarship much too good to turn down which was funded by her father."

"Yes," Gabe admitted. "I needed her close to me. I had to be able to at least see her on occasion. It broke my heart to not be able to let her know that often I was within sight. I would frequently sit in the park pretending to read, but instead would watch her as she had her morning coffee or a stroll by the sea. Many times, Caleb, I would see you two together and it was obvious to me you two were in love. I also realized, Gabi wouldn't admit it to herself."

Caleb kept shaking his head in disbelief. "If only she had known."

Gabe went around the bed to where Caleb stood and put his arm around his shoulder. "Believe me, I tried to think of a way, but every idea still put her in the middle of danger. I just couldn't take that chance. I held on to the fact that when the project was finished, then we would reunite. I have longed for this day." Gabe looked down at Gabriella before continuing. "Now I can't explain anything to her."

Sandee once again continued for Gabe, knowing he was overwhelmed with grief. "The Professor and I were Gabe's constant liaisons making sure Gabi was all right and reporting to him."

Gabe regained control and looked at the young team. "Caleb, Aaron, Faith, you were unexpected blessings and I am so thankful she had you as friends. You've been her family and you've made a great team."

The room was silent as each team member took a moment to mentally and emotionally adjust to the revelation of Gabriella's father.

Finally Aaron broke the silence. "So, Gabe, you rented the guesthouse and have lived here all these years?"

Sandee and the Professor laughed out loud. Sandee answered with a smile, "He owns the entire grounds. It's been the perfect place for him to find seclusion. Now you understand why we've had so many retreats here, but Gabe always made sure he was out of sight when we came. He knew if he was close, Gabi would recognize him."

The team looked at him in obvious shock and with the same question on their faces.

Gabe answered their confused looks. "I told Gabi in the journal I made some sizeable investments in the stock market. I didn't tell her what they were. In the late 80's the up and coming electronic stocks were selling low. I bought a huge amount of stock with the life insurance proceeds from my wife. I knew I would have to make sure Gabi was taken care of financially if something happened to me. The stocks exploded and I became a very wealthy man. Yahweh knew what I would need for the days ahead to provide behind the scenes for both Gabi and the project."

"You've been the financial force behind all of this?" Aaron asked bluntly and ashamedly. "Just you?"

Gabe nodded his head. "The research was just too sensitive and dangerous to let anyone else in. We couldn't take a chance of my identity being revealed. The Professor and I had great reservations about getting you kids involved, even in the exploration, but we had to have brilliant young minds to do the legwork for us. I knew Gabi could do it and that's the reason she was put in the lead. The rest of you proved your abilities in flying colors."

"This is mind boggling." Faith confessed still in confusion. "If you could only know all the hours Gabi talked about you, Gabe, and how much she missed you. She was absolutely lost without you."

Faith could see the pain in his face as he just nodded his head. "I kept telling myself I had saved her life and we would be together again. Now we're together and I can't explain any of it to her."

"Are you the so called Prophet that visited her?" Caleb was still trying to piece the remaining shocking pieces together. "You appeared as the Prophet and gave her the scroll?"

Gabe's expression changed dramatically to one of confusion. "That's the strange part, Caleb. I was the one that visited her at the café. I thought if I warned her about time and untime she would realize there was danger in the content of the journal and be cautious. I had no idea it would consume her. All of this is my fault! The very thing I was trying to keep her from, I have caused."

Gabe struggled with his next words. "But I am not the one that gave her the scroll."

"What are you saying?" Caleb asked.

He looked straight at Caleb and did not hesitate. "The Professor and I agree she had a visitation from the same old man the Professor calls 'the Prophet'. The writing on the clay tablets and the scroll were the same. There could be no other explanation."

"And what would that mean?" Caleb waited breathlessly for an explanation.

Gabe shook his head in total confusion. "We wish we knew. The day Gabi was given the scroll by the Prophet, the Professor called me as soon as he left the apartment. We made plans to meet in a secluded place in the mountains. He showed me the scroll and we were trying to make sense of another visitation from the Prophet, especially being right after the cave writings were found. After our meeting, I was behind him coming down the mountain and saw the car speed up. I watched for the brake lights and there were none. Just a little further and he would have gone over a cliff. I truly believe that was the plan."

Gabe walked over to the window and looked out for a moment, knowing they were wondering why he would leave the Professor alone after an accident. "There were no other cars anywhere around so I stopped. I managed to get the back door open and crawled over the seat to check his pulse. He was still breathing. There was nothing I could do so I grabbed his briefcase to make sure it was in safe hands. His cell phone had landed in the back seat, so I used it to call for help. I didn't want mine traced. I knew I couldn't be seen or questioned so I quickly left. I pulled over farther down the mountain and waited until an ambulance and the police were on their way up. The rest you know."

The Professor spoke what they all suspected. "I believe it's more than coincidence someone tried to take my life the very same day the Prophet returned."

Chapter 52

The young team was overwhelmed with the revelations of Gabriella's father, the accident and the Prophet. It would take time for their minds to assimilate all the information. The project had taken shocking twists and turns, requiring even further emotional adjustments.

Caleb remained by Gabriella's side, taking in every detail of her beautiful face and imagining the joy she would experience if she knew her father was still alive. Her crystal blue eyes were concealed by eyelids that were without even the slightest twitch. "Wake up, Gabi," he whispered. "Please, wake up."

Caleb turned to face Gabriella's father. "Gabe, I think we all need to know exactly what you discovered that you had to totally drop off the radar. It had to be really prodigious for you to let Gabi suffer all these years the way she has."

Gabe stood by the window facing the team, ready to finally reveal his life journey. He took one long look at Gabriella, desperately wishing she could understand the complexities that brought him to this place.

"You are all aware of my extraterrestrial research and how the Professor helped me to understand the intergalactic visitations were actually demonic spirits, appearing as aliens to deceive the world into believing a lie."

The team nodded affirming they were with him so far. "You are also somewhat aware of the so called 'alien implants' that were discovered."

"Gabi had told us about reading this in your journal," KJ commented. "Could these in any way be part of a genetic type of Armageddon?"

Gabe's face grew grave as he continued. "Good thinking, KJ, and that's part of what I discovered and why they tried to silence me. I started reading about nanotechnology in the early 80's but had no idea how it would connect to my alien research."

"I'm familiar with the word," KJ replied, "but have to admit, being a computer geek and not a scientist, I really don't understand the process."

"Let me try to explain in terms you can understand. Nanotechnology is the manipulation of matter on an atomic, molecular, and supramolecular scale. For decades it's been a very broad study, including many fields of science, but the one that literally can change the world is semiconductor physics or 'device physics'. My research on the implants took me too close to the truth of what was being developed."

The team was all sitting on the edge of their seats as Gabe continued to expose the plan for world control. "Let me first explain, the implants seem to have roots in the Roswell Incident. As I wrote in my journal, an explosion of technology came with the reverse engineering of the Roswell craft. It spurred our own government's technological prowess to new heights. I know that sounds absurd, but hear me out."

The Professor briefly injected a comment. "Listen closely, team. It all ties together with our research on the return of the Watchers, aka the fallen angels. Gabe, explain in detail what you uncovered."

Gabe continued. "I discovered that an implant was being developed from information gleaned from the Roswell crash, a device that could be injected under the skin."

"Permit me to start with the history of the implants from 1947 to now. Electronic ID technology has been around for some time thanks to the reverse engineering done at Roswell, also known as Area 51. It began very low-tech by using magnetic strips with a digital code number on it much like a credit card. They were used for inventory ID and theft control. These were passive devices. In other words, they could only be read with a magnetic strip reader and the data on the strip could not be changed, but it could be erased. The next generation of ID devices, which are still commonly used today, was the silicon ROM chip that could contain much more data and were much smaller, about the size of a grain of rice. They were named RFID's or Radio Frequency Identification devices. They too are passive in nature and are read with an RFID scanner, but had expanded applications. They are used not only for inventory control but extensively as injectable pet and livestock ID devices. They have also been successfully tested on humans. The chips contained the persons ID data plus their medical records."

Gabe looked at the team to make sure they understood before he continued. "Although chip RFID devices were a vast improvement over the magnetic strips, the engineers at Roswell were trying to reverse engineer the alien "active" technology to a point where the implants could actually alter DNA, could track the recipient, and the data function could be altered by external means. So far, they have been able to replicate the active devices to a point where they can contain large amounts of data; i.e. health records, personal data, life history, and also track the recipient anywhere on the planet using satellites. The data can be read and/or modified by satellite or a hand held scanner. The implant is activated by extremely high frequency RF energy transmitted by a satellite (or scanner) whereby its RF energy is absorbed by the chip and becomes the power source to operate the chip. The chip will then become "active" and able to transmit and receive data back and forth to the satellite or scanner.

To my knowledge the ability to electronically modify DNA is beyond human capabilities and remains the secret of the supernatural beings, however, it is my opinion that the Satanic Anti-Christ will add his DNA component to these active devices and proclaim that these implants will cure diseases, eliminate death, and increase knowledge thereby creating a utopia for all of the recipients."

Gabe waited to see if there were questions or comments. It was obvious to him they were captivated by the information so he continued.

"We believe this is a major part of 'the great deception', as the implants will actually give the Anti-Christ total control over the recipients' everyday life and wellbeing. In actuality, Yeshua will bring in the true Messianic Kingdom. The evil one, the Anti-Christ, will offer a counterfeit of the world that is to come under the true Messiah. A world where all the 'promises' of this evil man will be a reality."

"What happens to all the people that are injected with this device?" Caleb asked.

With a sad voice, Gabe replied, "The people who take the implant will never experience the Lords Kingdom, as they will be unredeemable. In other words, those who choose to take the implant are immediately dooming themselves to eternal judgment when they accept the DNA of Satan himself."

Faith's voice quivered as she spoke. "That sounds like what the Book of Revelation calls the mark of the beast. No one will be able to buy or sell anything unless they have this implant. Right, Gabe?" Faith asked.

"Correct. No food, no medical supplies, nothing. This is the avenue by which one man can control the world. This is the great deception! It will look like a wonderful thing and it is ready to be implemented when the Anti-Christ takes his prophetic position. Professor, do you want to explain that part?"

The Professor got up from the rocking chair and took Gabe's place by the window. Gabe sat down next to Gabriella's bed and held her hand.

The Professor cleared his throat in his usual manner of letting them know the importance of his next words. "These implant devices are capable of all the things Gabe has explained. Revelation 13 tells us that the people of earth will 'wonder after the beast', which is another name for the Anti-Christ, who will deceive the nations. This man will be a world leader capable of performing miracles. The masses of people will want to follow him because of the powers he will possess."

The Professor turned to look out the window towards Mt. Hermon. For a moment he was lost in deep concentration, then he turned back to face the team. "He will offer the world the same thing the fallen angels offered."

Faith gasped! "How could that be, Professor? Are you talking about the Watchers? Like it was in the days of Noah?"

"I am talking about the days of Noah and the return of the fallen Watchers, but in a very different way. Ultimately, it will in effect be the same."

The Professor's face was filled with an expression the team could not completely read. It was different from anything they had seen before. "The Anti-Christ will offer the same lies to the entire world that were told to Eve by Satan in the Garden of Eden. Remember he told Eve that she would live forever and that she would have all knowledge and understanding just as God did?"

The team, being familiar with the story of Adam and Eve, nodded their heads but had no idea where the Professor was going.

The Professor motioned for Sandee to come stand beside him. She joined him at the window and he took her hand giving an analogy. "What if I told Sandee that by having a quick injection under the skin of her hand that her DNA would be altered so she would never be sick again, she would forever look young, have the energy of a teenager, be able to have all necessities of life and would enter an eternal age of peace and harmony on the earth. What do you think her response would be?"

KJ didn't hesitate. "Well, naturally, everybody would want it."

"Of course they would," the Professor agreed. "The only people that will understand the great deception and refuse the implant are those that were taught from the Bible and understand the ancient writings of God's prophets, warning this dreadful day would come. It will be those that knew about salvation but refused to accept it. When they enter into the great tribulation they will know the truth and refuse the implant, but the consequences will be great." The Professor shook his head in sorrow at the thought.

Gabe laid Gabriella's hand back on the bed and picked back up where the Professor left off. "When this Man of Sin, the Anti-Christ, appears and beguiles the world into receiving this miraculous implant he will be outraged by those that refuse. Those who reject his implant will be hunted down and many killed. BUT! If they cry out to Yeshua and not take the mark of the beast they can still be eternally saved. Some will survive until the end of the end of the tribulation period but many will be killed. It will be a horrible time, like nothing this earth has ever experienced."

Gabriella's father looked at her as she lay lifeless. He finished with the most important part. "Those that have their DNA altered by the implants will for a short time enjoy the benefits promised. It will seem like a utopia. They will not realize they have been implanted with a satanic device that mixes Satan's DNA with the human DNA. By receiving this 'mark of the beast', they have brought eternal damnation on their soul."

"Sadly," the Professor added, "the greatest part of the world population will take the implant, not knowing they have forfeited their opportunity to be saved. It will be just as the fallen angels and their offspring, the nephilim. They were unredeemable, being part human and part angel. Those who choose to take the implant are immediately dooming themselves to eternity in hell. When their DNA becomes mixed with Satan's there is no hope for redemption."

The Professor summed up their project. "This is the entire crux of why we began The Omega Watchers. How could our society be 'as it was in the days of Noah'? Now we know."

Gabe leaned towards Gabriella with tears streaming down his face. "We need Gabi to wake up so I can explain all of this to her and she can escape those things that are about to come upon the earth."

Caleb dropped his head in his hands and fought back the tears, struggling for words. "Why wouldn't she listen? The Professor, Sandee, Aaron, and Faith all through the years told us about Yeshua. Finally I realized the truth, but Gabi was just too stubborn. Now it may be too late. The thought of Gabi being left behind without any of us...well, I just can't stand it!"

Sandee went to Caleb and gave him a motherly hug. "We're not giving up hope, Caleb. Maybe there's still time."

Gabe replied emphatically. "No, we are not giving up! I pray she has the opportunity to confess with her mouth that she believes in the atoning blood of Yeshua Jesus and He is the Son of the Living God who died for her sins. She must if she will be ready to go when the trumpet sounds and the children of Yahweh are taken to be with Him."

The Professor knew Gabe was overwhelmed and finished their explanation. "You can see, team, why this project has been so secret. When Gabe discovered the implants were being developed and their intended purpose, naturally his life was in danger. Gabriella would have been a prime target, too. His only choice was to appear to be dead and let the information seemingly die with him."

The Professor took his seat and picked up his notes. "As you know, team, our project purpose has been to prove the coming great deception. Additionally, to glean from the ancient writings the timelines in which they would occur, with the hope many, both Jew and Gentile, would accept Yeshua as their savior and not be left behind to endure the time of the great tribulation." He took a deep breath and cleared his throat. "After many agonizing years of research and exploration, it's time the translations are revealed."

The Professor was about to begin when he was interrupted by the sounds of the door slamming downstairs and footsteps running up the stairway. Officer Harris came through the door with fear written all over his face. "I just got a call from my mother. Damascus has just been destroyed by a nuclear bomb. The entire city is gone and the nations are saying Israel did it. All the sirens in Israel are going off and people are instructed to immediately go to their bunkers. The news is reporting there will be an imminent retaliation...soon!" The officer took a deep breath waiting for their response.

"Oh, my God!" Sandee whispered. "It's begun!"

Gabe took immediate control. "I knew this day would come and that's one reason I built this place in the mountains where there would be less danger. I've got my own bunker ready."

Faith was about to lose control. "What do we do? Where do we go? What about Gabi?"

The Professor held up his hand. Everyone immediately hushed, waiting for his direction. "Sandee, get Dr. Nicholson on the phone. I'm sure he's already heard what's happened. The rest of you grab whatever you brought with you and head downstairs. Quick!"

Sandee rushed out of the room to follow his instructions and the Professor followed her downstairs to make preparations. The team went to their rooms to hurriedly get their belongings.

Gabe grabbed Gabriella's roll bag and quickly packed her personal items. He knew they were running out of time. As he packed, he would glance over at the bed and continually pray she would awaken. Pangs of agony pierced through his stomach, realizing she had put her entire adult life into this project, all because of him and now she lay lifeless and there was nothing he could do to help her.

He zipped her bag and placed it by the door. He sat down by Gabi and took her hand. "My little princess, I am so, so sorry. I did the only thing I knew to do to protect you. I've prayed all these years that you would find the peace of Yahweh that I found, and I trust Him that it's not too late." He brushed her hair back from her face and kissed her cheek. "You've always been the best part of me."

Within minutes Caleb was back in the room ready to carry Gabriella downstairs. Gabe followed behind with her luggage. They all gathered in the great room and heard the end of the phone conversation between the Professor and the doctor. Caleb laid Gabriella on the couch waiting for further instructions.

"Yes, that's right. You're coming now? We'll be ready." The Professor's voice was in total control of his emotions. "The doctor is aware of the imminent attack and he and his wife will be joining us in the bunker. We have no idea how long we will be confined so the doctor will be prepared to put Gabriella on life support, if needed."

Caleb gasped as he heard the words. The Professor placed a comforting hand on his shoulder. "There's no way of knowing how long this will last and we have to be prepared for the worst."

A booming sound came from over the lodge. "What's that?" KJ exclaimed heading for the front door. He slung the door opened and ran out where he could see the sky. "Look!" He exclaimed as he pointed towards the sky.

The rest followed him out. Fighter jets were coming from the direction of Syria over the mountains and headed towards Israel.

The Professor watched the jets and then looked at the team. "The Psalms 83 War has begun. The beginning of the end is near."

Chapter 53

The Professor heard his own words ringing in his ears. "The Psalms 83 War has begun."

He had studied this prophecy for years and knew the fulfillment was approaching but to actually see it begin, with his own eyes, was very surreal.

Officer Harris had no idea what the group was talking about. "What do you mean, Professor? What makes this war any different from the wars we've already had?"

"No time to explain now, Officer Harris, there's much to do. We'll talk later." It was obvious the Professor was concerned with getting everyone to safety.

"Just call me Chris," the officer replied. "I'm going to try to contact Detective Richards for instructions." Chris stayed outside to make his call while the Professor hurried inside to begin preparations.

"Follow me," Gabe instructed. He led them back into the house and through the kitchen to a pantry entry. He opened the door and entered a large room where food and supplies had been stored for the team's stay at the lodge. He quickly walked to the back wall of the pantry. He pushed against a board at the top and a four-foot section of the rear wall pivoted 60 degrees exposing a stairway. He reached inside, switched on the lights and motioned for them to follow. "Caleb, bring Gabi down first. Team, bring your personal items and follow us down."

Caleb held Gabriella safely in his strong arms while he descended the flight of wooden stairs to the bottom. Her long blonde hair bounced against him as step by step they continued downward. The team silently followed, carrying their personal belongings. The only sound was the echo of footsteps.

When they reached the bottom and stepped onto the tile floor they were stunned. "This is a bunker?" Aaron spoke for the entire team as they gazed in every direction.

They had entered an underground, lavish home. Except for the lack of windows, it had everything you could possibly want or need. The massive main area was designed to be a gathering room with a huge kitchen on the right side and a large, wooden dining table directly beside it. Comfortable couches in shades of light blue faced a media center displaying a big screen TV and all the electronic devices one could hope for. Yellow walls were on each side of the media center lined with shelves displaying a large assortment of video games, movies, and a huge collection of books. The shades of blue would be soothing to the mind and soul, while the yellow colors would offer an illusion of sunlight.

Three bedrooms lined the left side of the living room and three more were in the back of the bunker. Each bedroom was painted a light green and had two large beds with comfortable side chairs all in earth tone colors, supplying the perfect atmosphere for rest.

Two large bathrooms were strategically placed between the series of bedrooms. There was a door to the right of the kitchen close to the stairway, which opened to a massive storage area stocked with an assortment of supplies and non-perishable foods that would last for years.

"We're equipped here for everything we'll need," Gabe commented as he turned on the TV for news updates. There was consternation in his voice as he spoke. "I've prepared for every scenario I could imagine."

Caleb stood holding Gabriella in his strong arms and was in wonder of his surroundings. "A person could hide out here and never be found."

"That was the plan, Caleb. The bunker water supply comes from an underground artesian water stream. There are windmills at the highest point on my property to continue to feed electricity in the event we lose power. For additional electrical back-up there are solar generators on the roof top."

Gabe opened a cabinet and took out a radio. "This is an AN/PRC 148 handheld, multiband, tactical software-defined two way radio that is standard issue to many military forces around the world, including the

Israeli Military and NATO forces. We may need this to know what's going on outside this bunker."

"Caleb, follow me and the rest of you choose any bedroom you want," Gabe instructed.

He led Caleb into a bedroom and pulled back the comforter for him to lay Gabriella down. Caleb kissed her cheek as he released her, speaking with a voice filled with torment. "My princess has become Sleeping Beauty and her Prince Charming can do nothing to help her." He pulled the comforter up over her and kissed her one more time, inwardly praying his kiss would awaken her as in the fairy tale. Still there was no movement.

Gabe was deeply touched by the obvious love Caleb had for his daughter. He knew, however, they could not linger. There was much to do and little time. "We need to make sure everyone's personal items are brought down and all the food that's in the kitchen and the pantry. You young men take care of that and Faith can sit with Gabi."

"You got it." Caleb started back up the stairs taking the steps two by two with KJ and Aaron following right behind. Faith pulled a chair next to Gabriella and with her bible in hand began to read Psalms 91, praying for protection.

There was a flurry of activity from upstairs to the bunker. Going back and forth, the young men brought the supplies. The Professor brought down his briefcase with the project research safely stored inside and was getting settled in his bedroom. Sandee was stocking the cabinets with items being brought down to the bunker.

Chris carried down the black box filled with Gabe's research and set it on the kitchen table. Then he turned and addressed the group. "Could I have a minute to address everyone, please?" The room grew still as he gave the message from Haifa.

"I just talked with Detective Richards. Haifa has been hit pretty hard. So has Tel Aviv and Jerusalem. He doesn't know the extent of the damage yet. Travel is currently impossible. He said we are to stay put and wait for instructions. He expects cell service will be interrupted soon. He advises to make any personal calls now, while we still can."

"It's just as I expected it would be," Gabe replied. "I knew Syria and their coalition of nations would bomb the major cities first to hit the most populated areas. We must keep in mind, stray rockets can hit anywhere at anytime. Unfortunately, our location places us in exceptional danger from the Katyusha short-range rockets used by Lebanon. They just fire them randomly with no strategic planning and no one knows where they'll hit. We should be safe, though, from the fighter jet attacks."

The sounds of footsteps could be heard through the open door above. Chris covered his mouth indicating for everyone to be silent. The officer moved towards the stairway, ready to draw his gun. He started up the steps when a voice was heard calling to them.

"Professor! We're here!" The familiar voice of the doctor brought instant relief to the strained atmosphere.

Chris called back up the stairs. "We're coming up."

The young men again ascended the stairs to assist Dr. Nicholson and his wife. Aaron and KJ joined them to help unload the doctor's van filled with medical supplies and personal items.

As they were ready to carry the last of the boxes into the lodge another flight of Syrian jets flew over them and within seconds they heard the explosion of bombs in the distance.

"I wonder where they've hit this time. It sounds really close." Aaron stated with pain in his voice. "We may not have homes to go back to, even if we have the chance." He put the box he was holding down and walked away from the group to try to call his family. The others followed suit.

KJ went to the far side of the lodge for a private moment to call his mother in Kentucky. There was no answer. He took a deep breath and left a message on voice mail. "Mom, I know you've probably heard. Isaiah 17 has just been fulfilled. Damascus has been destroyed and war has been declared. I wanted to let you know we're safe with Dr. Brotman in a bunker in the mountains. We've plenty of supplies to ride it out, but we all know what this means." KJ hesitated trying to get control of his emotions before he left the final message. "If I don't see you again on this side, I'll see you in heaven. I love you, Mom." He disconnected the phone wondering if he would ever hear her voice again.

As they made their way back towards the entry they saw Israel's F-18 fighter jets heading east. They stood still as the earth rumbled from the deafening sounds of the formation passing over the Golan Heights. There were no words to describe the trepidation as they were actually living the fulfillment of the ancient prophecies.

Gabe called from the open front door. "Hurry, guys!"

The last trip was made down to the bunker. The soundproof door closed behind them, concealing their location and locking them into safety.

No one knew how long they would be in this underground seclusion. When they finally emerge, what will they find?

Chapter 54

With the thump of the door closing and locking above them, each person in the bunker was lost in their private thoughts. They all found a place to sit and attempt to prepare mentally for the days ahead. Faith and Aaron had been able to reach their family, which were currently safe in their home bunkers. Everyone knew the days ahead would change Israel forever.

Caleb's family in Germany had been trying to reach him prior to his call home. News had spread around the world a Mid-East war had begun and the blame was being laid at the feet of Israel. Caleb had lived in Israel long enough to know they did not want to initiate wars and any military action taken was necessary for the country's survival, however, the western media always made it sound as if Israel was the culprit standing in the way of peace.

After several minutes of silence, the Professor cleared his voice to speak. "We have no idea if we will be here a few hours, days or an extended length of time. There are many variables at this juncture. For now we are together and we are safe. Get settled in. Then we'll meet back here in an hour. It appears as though we will be celebrating Rosh Hashanah underground this year."

Sandee came to the Professor and laid her hand on his shoulder. "You need to rest for awhile, Professor."

Dr. Nicholson confirmed her advice. "It's imperative you rest, Professor. We're going to need your guidance in the days ahead. I have some information regarding our conversation on astral sleep, but it can wait until later."

Dr. Brotman got up from his chair and moved slower than the team had ever seen. For the first time they admitted he was aging and recent events had taken a toll. "Okay, if you insist, Sandee. We'll talk in a bit, Doc."

Sandee walked with him to his room and then on to hers. She looked back over her shoulder before closing her door. "I'll be back shortly to start dinner." Her voice reflected the emotions of all the others, the uncertainty of what to expect.

The TV was left on, giving continued reports of the attacks as the group unpacked their few belongings. Within minutes the young team was back on the couches watching the updates and anxious to know details of the world above them. It seemed to be getting worse with each passing hour.

They saw 'breaking news' flash across the screen and the Channel 2 news reporter, with a very grim face, gave the dreaded words. "Egypt, Jordan and Saudi Arabia have now declared their support of Lebanon and Syria. Iranian and Russian ships are entering the Mediterranean Sea, headed toward our coast. Israel is literally surrounded on every side."

"Where's the United States in this?" Caleb said angrily. "I thought they were a friend to Israel."

Aaron chuckled sarcastically. "That ended several years ago. Any 'friendship' has just been lip service since President Bush left office. The only thing the US wants is for us to give up land for peace and then America will take the credit for pulling off the deal...a deal that would bring total destruction to Israel."

Just as Aaron spoke, there was more breaking news. It was obvious the newscaster was struggling to keep his composure. "Reports have just come in that there have been simultaneous terrorist attacks in the United States. New York, Atlanta, Chicago, Dallas, and San Francisco are among the cities that have been hit. Large venues such as Disneyland, shopping malls and sports arenas have also been attacked. The sleeper terrorist cells, that have been waiting years for their signal, have awakened. There are unsubstantiated reports that nuclear bombs have been used but no information is available on the extent of devastation. There are also reports a huge earthquake has hit the New Madrid fault line that runs along the Mississippi River and divides the US. There is speculation it was triggered by a nuclear explosion in Memphis, Tennessee, which sits directly on the fault line. The U.S. President will be making a statement soon and we will broadcast it live, if we can maintain reception."

The entire group looked at KJ.

"I knew this was coming." KJ was trying to control the overwhelming emotions surging through him. "The Prophet Joel wrote that God will judge the nation that divides the land of Israel. Aaron is right. Our government has pushed and pushed for Israel to be divided for the sake of peace, so they say. When God brings judgment on a nation it's normally through attacks by enemy nations and natural disasters. We got both at the same time. The glory of America is no more, and never will be again."

KJ ran his hand across his bald head and took off his glasses as tears filled his eyes. "I have friends in many of those cities. I may never know if they survived, but more than that, the New Madrid fault line runs right through Kentucky. I wonder if that's why my Mom didn't answer her phone. Communication may be knocked out." With a quivering voice he forced the words, "or worse."

Faith's dark eyes filled with sorrow for KJ as she watched him get up and go to his bedroom and quietly close the door. Everyone in the room was dealing with emotional anxieties beyond explanation.

The Professor, hearing the conversations came out of his bedroom. He took the TV control and muted the sound. He stood in front of the group and announced in no uncertain terms, "We will not allow fear to overtake us. We knew these things were coming. The important thing is to know where we stand spiritually. The time is almost here and all suffering will finally be over for those that are ready to go with Yeshua. We are going to pray together for both wisdom and peace in the days ahead."

KJ, Gabe and Sandee came from their bedrooms and joined them for prayer. Gabe left the bedroom door open for a full view of Gabriella lying on her bed. Everyone in the room bowed their heads as the Professor interceded to the Heavenly Father.

Officer Harris still had no idea what they were talking about, but he did sense the atmosphere change when they prayed. A feeling of tranquility entered the room as they said in unison, "Father, your will be done. Amen."

The Professor asked Caleb to get his briefcase. "We have been interrupted each time I've intended to read the prophecies translated from the tablet given to me by the Prophet, the writing on the cave wall and the ancient manuscript given to Gabriella. I believe those were divine interruptions and it is in this place and at this time these prophecies are to be known. The world stage has been set for the fulfillment of these ancient writings."

The Professor sat down in front of the group and opened his briefcase pulling out his notes. "It is almost sundown and the Feast of Trumpets will begin. I believe it is by divine appointment Yahweh has chosen this time to reveal His plan."

The Professor looked at Dr. Nicholson, his wife Ruth and Officer Harris. "I will give you an explanation of the events that have led us to this place. Since we are going to be together in this bunker for an unknown length of time, we must all be in one accord and understanding."

The team relived the project journey with Dr. Brotman as he shared the details step by step from the beginning to this moment when The Omega Watchers had reached fruition.

"Before you read the translation, Professor, I would like for Caleb to bring Gabriella to the couch. We want her with us. This is what she worked so hard for." The sound of a breaking heart could be heard in Gabe's voice.

Caleb crossed the floor without a word, went into her room and gathered her in his arms. Her body was limp and her head fell against his shoulder as he carried her to be with the others. He laid her on the couch next to Gabe and sat in the floor beside her where he could hold her hand during the reading. Gabe laid her head in his lap stroking her soft, curly hair.

"It breaks my heart that I will be reading the translations without Gabriella mentally with us, but the time has come. Through the words of the ancient prophets we know what is about to come upon the earth." The Professor picked up his notes...the long wait was now ending.

The group sat silently in anticipation as the Professor took a deep breath and then laid the notes back down in his lap. "There is something I must share before I read this. Through all the years of research, I had hoped to secure proof to have time to warn people, before it was too late. I regret to inform you I don't believe that is going to be possible. We are quickly approaching our day of deliverance from the tribulation to come."

Once again the Professor picked up the notes that would reveal the secrets hidden through time. "I see in these translations a message for those that will be left behind. You will understand as I read and just as I anticipated, the translations from the Prophet's clay tablet given to me and the scroll given to Gabriella fit together as one message."

In a solemn voice the team had never before heard, the Professor read:

'In the day of the great judgment, a day of terror and affliction as never seen by man, the fallen Watchers will be released from the chambers of the abyss. My two witnesses will return to proclaim truth against them. I will give power unto my two witnesses, and they shall prophesy a thousand two hundred and threescore days, and when they shall have finished their testimony, the beast that ascends out of the bottomless pit shall make war against them, and shall overcome them, and kill them. Their dead bodies shall lie in the street of the great city for three days. They that dwell upon the earth shall rejoice for they will hate the voice of the prophets. After three days my Spirit will enter their dead bodies and they will rise and ascend to heaven. The world will watch and be amazed. I will then send a great earthquake and I will shake the earth as it has never been shaken. The people will tremble in fear and the beast with his mark will arise and work wonders to deceive the nations. When you see Israel surrounded by her enemies and the man of false peace signs a covenant with my chosen ones, the day of the great tribulation has begun.'

The Professor halted for a moment and looked directly at Caleb, Aaron and Faith. "I will now read to you what was translated from the lava cave wall."

"Here lies a gateway to the Grigori (Watchers), who turned aside from the Lord, 200 myriads. And who went down as prisoners in the bottomless pit, imprisoned in great darkness until the time of the great tribulation when they will be released to align with their prince Satanail before their eternal judgment."

The Professor looked up as he completed the translation. You could hear a pin drop as the room was filled with silence. The Professor allowed the magnitude of the prophecy to settle before he spoke.

"According to this prophecy the appearance of two prophets in the streets of Jerusalem, will be the timeframe for the beginning of the seven year great tribulation. This will be the same time the seven-year peace treaty will be signed in Israel. Approximately the same time, all the chambers of the abyss will open, releasing the imprisoned fallen angels. They will be led by the beast, the Anti-Messiah, which is Satan incarnate. There are no words to describe the horrors that will follow."

The Professor laid the notes back in his lap and waited for a response. A deafening silence permeated the room.

Chapter 55

If there had been any doubt whatsoever that the end was near it was completely erased with the reading of the prophecies.

"What do we do now?" Faith asked.

Gabe stood up and turned towards Gabriella's bedroom. "I know what I'm going to do. I have another journal to write. Caleb, would you bring Gabriella back to her bed, please?"

"What's he doing?" Aaron looked confused as he watched Gabe leave.

The Professor gave his observation. "Knowing Gabe, he will write more letters to Gabriella, just as he did when he knew he was going to disappear the first time, giving her instructions on what has happened and what she must do to survive, just in case..."

"I won't even think of it!" Caleb retorted as he returned from Gabriella's bedroom. "She will wake up. She has to wake up!"

The Professor allowed Caleb to vent his emotions before he spoke. "We all pray for that, Caleb, but there's nothing more we can do. She had chance after chance and wouldn't listen."

Caleb nodded his head, knowing he almost followed her into the paranormal world. "Why did she have to be so stubborn? Now it may be too late." The words hung on his lips with a bitter taste.

Turning to face the doctor the Professor asked, "You had something important to tell me about astral comas?"

"Yes," the doctor replied leaning forward. "I've done some research and there have been many documented cases of people who have visited the spiritual world and when returning would end in a comatose state. The individual that has entered the coma normally has done so for a reason they feel is beneficial to them. It becomes a safe place where they no longer have to deal with the pain and realities of this life. These comas can last for days or even years. If they do return they often tell the same story of having made the choice to stay in a plane of rest. Since Gabriella felt she had been deserted by everyone who loves her, she may have subconsciously chosen not to return."

Caleb immediately felt the stab of guilt. "She thought I had completely deserted and betrayed her. She told me so. She was so angry, having allowed herself to feel love again and then believed I immediately betrayed that love." Agony had spread across his face at the thought he may have caused her state of unconsciousness.

Faith also was feeling guilty. "She's my best friend. We were like sisters and she thought I had turned against her. She thought the rest of the team had, too." Aaron and KJ nodded with looks of anguish.

"We will all have to carry this guilt," the Professor admitted. "Sandee and I both knew Gabe was alive and couldn't tell her. That alone could have made the difference in the choices she made." Sandee agreed, with tears in her eyes.

Gabe came in from Gabriella's bedroom having overheard the conversation. "None of you are to feel guilty. This is all completely my doing. I am the one that led her into the paranormal world through my journal and research. I was completely wrong in thinking it would ultimately lead her to the truth. I lay all the blame at my own feet and no one else's."

Dr. Nicholson held up his hand to interrupt their admissions of failure. "Blaming yourself or anyone else is not going to help. According to my research what will help is to keep trying to communicate with her. Tell her how much you love her. Let her subconscious mind hear your voices and words of affection. It could break through to the realm in which she now exists."

"How long will it take, Dr. Nicholson? Do you have any idea?" Caleb had moved towards her bedroom ready to begin.

"No one knows. Sadly, some never wake up and choose to just pass over to the other side."

Gabe remembered a family story passed from generation to generation. "My Cherokee grandmother told me about her shaman grandmother who would go into a trance and lay lifeless. When she would wake up she would have mystical knowledge, imparted to her by a great spirit. It was much like what Edgar Cayce described when the spirits would speak to him. We all know now those are demonic, often familiar spirits, appearing as spirits of enlightenment. The last time my grandmother went into a trance, she never came back. Her body lay until it withered up and died. I am so afraid to ask this, but if familiar spirits are passed from generation to generation could that same spirit have taken Gabriella, Doctor Nicholson?"

The room was silent as they waited for an answer. The doctor finally ventured an educated guess. "This is all pretty new to me, Gabe, but it seems that is very possible. Based on what I read, if she opened her soul to the spirit world she could have been led past the point of return."

"But our prayers are stronger!" KJ would not accept it. "I know we touched the heart of Jehovah God when we prayed, and I believe we saved her from the very brink of hell. She will return. We have to believe!"

"There's nothing medically that can be done, except life support to keep her hydrated and nourished. That's not necessary just yet. She's young and strong and her body can endure for a few days."

Caleb immediately went to her side and Gabe joined him. They would take turns talking to Gabriella, reminiscing of the good times and affirming their love. While Caleb would talk to her, Gabe would write non-stop in his journal. While Gabe would talk to her, Caleb would write letters declaring his everlasting love.

Gabe opened his Bible and began to write from the Book of Revelation. "Caleb, I'm going to go chapter by chapter and leave instructions for her so she will understand what is happening and what she must do and must not do. If she is left behind she can still be saved and we can be together again in the Messianic Kingdom. She must understand the deception that is coming so she doesn't fall into the trap of the Anti-Christ and take his mark."

Gabe wrote through the night and through the next two days non-stop. He would read his journaling to Caleb so he also understood the things that were about to take place on the earth and what Gabriella might be facing.

When Gabe finished the writing he wrote a personal letter to his little princess, pleading with her to read every word of the journal and understand the coming events. He stacked the papers and laid them neatly beside her bed, with his letter on the top so she would see them as soon as she awakened.

Tears were flowing from both Gabe's and Caleb's eyes. They knew there was a real possibility if and when she finally awakened, the rapture may have taken place and everyone she loved would be gone.

Chapter 56

As Gabe wrote his instructions for Gabriella, day turned into night and night turned into another day and the war drums only grew louder. The TV was constantly left on with Israeli news continuing to flow and growing increasingly worse. For two days the entombed group watched the news waiting for the IDF clearance allowing them to return to daylight.

The entire time Caleb and Gabe stayed in Gabriella's room, taking turns sitting by her bedside writing and reaffirming to her their love. They kept the door opened to hear the continued news updates.

Caleb overheard KJ talking to Officer Harris explaining the prophetic events taking place. It was obvious Chris was having a very difficult time accepting the reality of all the happenings having been foretold from ancient times. Caleb knew what he had to do and went into the gathering room, sitting down opposite the officer.

"I know where your head's at, Chris. I've been there. It just didn't make sense to me to believe in a power I couldn't see and I thought I had to reason it all out in my mind. Gabi and I both were searching for the truth of the gods but we thought we had to have tangible proof. When the Professor was in the hospital and the team prayed for him, I felt a Presence enter the room and I knew it was beyond anything on this earth. I finally realized I had to accept it by faith and not by sight. It changed my life, man, and it's available to you, too. All you have to do is believe with your heart and confess with your mouth that Yeshua Jesus is the Son of God, died for your sins, and arose from the dead. It's just that simple."

Tears were welling up in Chris's eyes. It was obvious the Spirit of the Lord was speaking to him. "I don't know, Caleb. You realize Jews don't believe Yeshua was the Messiah. I've never been a religious Jew but how can I go against what the Rabbis teach?"

Aaron answered his question. "Chris, I'm a Jew and I believe. The Professor, Sandee, Faith, Dr. Nicholson and his wife are Jews, too. We know that Yeshua is the Messiah and He's coming very soon for those that believe in Him. KJ just told you what's going to happen after we're out of here. You still have time to accept Him as your Messiah."

The Professor entered the conversation. "It has been two days now since the Feast of Trumpets began. It will soon be sundown. If it's at all possible the priests will be blowing 'the last trump' to signal the end of this holy convocation. Prophetically, this holy day is a rehearsal for the coming of the Bridegroom for his bride. It is known as the season of "no man knows the day nor the hour". Could it be with all the events surrounding us, we are about to hear the last trumpet sound when the dead shall rise and those that are alive and remaining will meet him in the air?"

Chris was overwhelmed by everything he was hearing and was not willing to make this spiritual step immediately. He got up and walked toward his room. "I've got to give this some thought." He closed the door behind him.

"I'm proud of you, Caleb." The Professor spoke with words of obvious approval. "All we can do is share the truth. Each person must decide for themselves. Without a doubt, we *will* all face Yahweh one day. For those that rejected Him, there will be eternal death. For us, Caleb, will be eternal life."

The Professor gave Caleb a fatherly hug. "Now go be with Gabi. Talk to her. We will continue to pray."

Caleb forced a smile and returned to her bedside. Gabe was on one side and Caleb on the other. They took turns reminiscing of the past and reliving the wonderful times they had together with Gabriella. As they declared their love, her soul was slowly returning to the natural world.

Gabriella could hear in a far distance, Caleb's voice and she was trying to reach to him but her body would not move. As he continued to talk, she felt her soul drawing nearer and nearer to him.

"Gabi, I'm here beside you. We all are praying you will come back to us. I'm so sorry you doubted my love. There's never been anyone for me but you. I knew it from the day I first laid eyes on you. Come back to me, Gabi Girl, please come back to me."

She tried to squeeze his hand but not a muscle would move. She could hear her father's voice. "My little princess, I need you to wake up. I need you to understand why I had to do it. I was protecting you and that was the only reason I left you."

Her thoughts were so jumbled, nothing made sense. She kept asking herself, "What do I need to know? Why am I hearing both Caleb's voice and my father's at the same time? Am I hearing voices both from time and untime?"

"Gabe," Caleb asked in a deeply questioning voice. "You know Gabi has to have proof for everything she believes. Will your journal give enough information to truly make her believe?"

"Believe what?" She wanted to scream out, but the words would not come. "How is Caleb talking to my father?"

Gabe's eyes turned from Gabriella to focus fully on Caleb's desire to understand. "The proof is all around us now, Caleb. The prophecies of the last days are exploding into reality. The Book of Revelation will be all the proof she needs and I've left her the path for survival."

"I hope so," Caleb replied with uncertainty. "I can honestly say I don't really understand this disappearing thing either but I don't doubt it."

"I'll quote some of the Bible verses that explain what's getting ready to take place. Yeshua told us in the Book of Revelation 3:10: '*Because you have kept my command and patiently endured, I also will keep you from the hour of temptation, which shall come upon all the world, to try them that dwell upon the earth*.' This is referring to the seven years of tribulation we have been talking about, the judgment that will come on the earth. Yahweh promises he will keep those that believed in Him from the horrible time.

Caleb's eyes were questioning. "But how do you know He will take us out and not just keep us safe here?"

Gabriella was now mentally awake hearing every word of their conversation. Even if she could not physically respond, the words were being branded into her mind.

Gabe smiled as he continued. "That's a question many people have asked. There are numerous writings of the prophets that explain we will be 'caught up', 'raptured', 'changed in the twinkling of an eye', and the list goes on. I have written all of these down for Gabriella with a full explanation of what has happened and what she must do if she is left behind."

The smile on Gabe's face quickly faded as the thought fully registered in his mind. Yet he forced himself to continue for Caleb's understanding.

Gabriella's mind was silently screaming out: "Left behind? What are you talking about? Don't leave me! Please don't leave me!"

Gabe continued the explanation. "This is the scripture that I quote to myself over and over when I think about what is coming on the earth. It is from John 14:3. '*And if I go and prepare a place for you, I will come again, and receive you unto Myself; that where I am, you may be also.*' It's a beautiful promise, don't you think, Caleb?"

Caleb could only nod his head. "But I want Gabi to go with us." He was overcome with the battling emotions saturating him, knowing he could experience an immediate translation to an eternal place of peace and safety, while Gabriella would be left alone to face the darkest days that would ever be on the face of the earth.

Rationale was telling Gabriella that Caleb and her father were not in the spirit world, but actually in the room talking face to face. Then she felt Caleb take her in his arms. "Gabi, please wake up. There's still time."

Caleb's tears ran slowly down his face, fell upon Gabi's cheeks, and cascaded down her still face. "Caleb," she desperately tried to cry out. Please, don't leave me!"

She again heard her father's voice. "I was wrong, Gabi. I was wrong about everything. What seemed to be truth was all a lie and I got caught up in the great deception. If you can hear me, Gabi, you must remember one thing...do NOT take the implant of the one that will soon rule the world. Use the truth discovered in your project to reveal the true identity of the evil one who will claim to be the Messiah. Perhaps you were 'chosen' for such a time as this."

Her mind was focusing on every word her father said but her body still would not move.

Gabe's voice was heavy with sorrow and Gabriella could feel the sting of tears in her eyes as Caleb continued to hold her in his familiar arms. At that moment a single tear escaped her eyes and mingled with Caleb's tears that still rested upon her face.

Caleb exclaimed, "She's crying, Gabe. Look!"

Gabe rushed to her side and exclaimed, "Gabi, you're still with us. I knew you were. Wake up, princess. Please!"

Caleb held her close, waiting for any sign of movement, but her body was as still as death.

"She hears us, Gabe. I know she does!"

"Call the others, Caleb!" Gabe instructed him. "Hearing all the familiar voices of the people she loves may bring her back to us.

Caleb ran to the bedroom door. "Come here, everyone. Gabi is waking up. Everyone talk to her. Pray for her! Let her hear your voices and feel your love."

They gathered around her, all talking at the same time. Gabriella could distinguish each voice and realized how wrong she had been about everything. In the midst of the chatter there was an unfamiliar voice in the background breaking through and all the familiar voices were suddenly silenced.

"MORE BREAKING NEWS!" The voice of the news reporter was loud and Gabi could hear obvious fear in his words. "Reports are coming in that Russia, Iran, Turkey, Libya, Sudan and Eastern Europe are forming a coalition for a second wave of attacks against Israel. There are additional reports that many smaller nations are joining with them, also. Israel, in her effort to survive annihilation, is being blamed for the death of millions of people as we have protected ourselves from the attacks of our surrounding nations. The whole world has now decided we cannot exist." His voice went silent for a moment as the reporter was struggling to speak. "We are going live to the streets of Jerusalem now, as the sun is going down ending Yom Teruah, the Feast of Trumpets. Shofars are blowing all across the City of David sounding the spiritual alarm! God help us."

The Professor quoted from the prophecy of Joel 2:1, "Blow the shofar in Zion, sound the alarm! The Day of the LORD has come!"

At that moment, the earth began to shake and the TV screen went black. Gabriella could hear the sounds of books falling from shelves, pictures from the walls and there were noises she could not explain. For several minutes her bed shook, as if warning her to get up. The shaking gradually subsided and the room was filled with a sinister, eerie silence. No voices!

Officer Harris came running from his bedroom. He called out and no one answered. He saw Gabriella lying on her bed, but Caleb and Gabe were no longer with her. He checked the other bedrooms, the storage area and even checked to see if the door to the bunker had been opened. Nothing!

"Where is everyone?" He exclaimed as fear saturated him.

He paced back and forth, trying his best to not panic. "There's got to be an explanation," he kept repeating over and over. "Could the Professor have been right? Did I wait one minute too long?"

The TV blinked several times, went fuzzy and then came back on, resuming broadcasting. The news reporter was making no effort to contain his apparent fears. He was silent for a few minutes as he listened to the microphone in his ear giving him updates from international news. The camera panned the chaotic scenes around the streets of Jeruslem. Men and women were rushing to the temple mount in panic crying out to Yahweh.

The camera again focused on the face of the reporter. "Reports are coming in from all over the world. There has been a barrage of simultaneous disasters. Airplanes are falling from the sky. Cars with no drivers are plunging into each other. People all over the globe are in a state of panic! There is no explanation! Millions upon millions of people have just vanished."

The reporter took a deep breath before continuing. It seemed he could not believe the words he was speaking. "Reports, trying to explain the disappearance of these people, range from an alien invasion, to karma balance, to a Christian evacuation and even a temporary lapse in gravitational pull at certain points on the earth. World leaders are calling an emergency session. Disasters have covered the entire planet."

His voice was silence once again and then his eyes widened in amazement. "The UN has called an emergency session to deal with this international crisis. It's being reported the Pope will be joining the UN meeting to introduce a mysterious leader. Supposedly, this presently unidentified man has the answers to the current events and how to bring peace to our pandemonium world!"

As Gabriella heard the words of the reporter, her eyes suddenly opened both physically and spiritually.

THE END...had just begun.

CPSIA information can be obtained
at www.ICGtesting.com
Printed in the USA
LVHW022118270219
608942LV00019B/1204